MEAN Web Development

Second Edition

Develop your real-time MEAN application efficiently
using a combination of MongoDB, Express, Angular,
and Node

Amos Q. Haviv

BIRMINGHAM - MUMBAI

MEAN Web Development
Second Edition

First published: September 2014

Second Edition: November 2016

Production reference: 1241116

Published by Packt Publishing Ltd.
Livery Place
35 Livery Street
Birmingham B3 2PB, UK.

ISBN 978-1-78588-630-0

www.packtpub.com

Credits

Author
  Amos Q. Haviv

Reviewer
  Liran Tal

Acquisition Editor
  Larissa Pinto

Content Development Editor
  Priyanka Mehta

Technical Editors
  Bhavin Savalia

  Dhiraj Chandanshive

Copy Editor
  Stuti Srivastava

Project Coordinator
  Izzat Contractor

Proofreader
  Safis Editing

Indexer
  Tejal Daruwale Soni

Production Coordinator
  Melwyn Dsa

Cover Work
  Melwyn Dsa

About the Author

Amos Q. Haviv is a software developer, technical consultant, and the creator of MEAN.IO and MEAN.JS. He has been a full-stack developer for almost a decade and worked for multiple start-ups and enterprise companies. For the past 6 years, Amos has been working with full-stack JavaScript solutions, including Node.js and MongoDB, as well as frontend frameworks such as Angular and React. In 2013, he created the first popular boilerplate for MEAN applications, MEAN.IO, and currently continues the development of MEAN solutions at `http://meanjs.org`. He also gives lectures on advanced web technologies at meetups and conferences, and he guides development teams at various companies.

I would like to thank my family and friends for their encouragement and support. I would also like to thank the contributors and developers who make the open source community the powerful and creative force that it is. You taught me more than I could have ever imagined.

About the Reviewer

Liran Tal is a top contributor to the open source MEAN.io, and a core team member of the MEAN.js full stack JavaScript framework. He has also authored several Node.js npm packages as well as actively contributed to many open source projects on GitHub. Being an avid supporter and contributor to the open source movement, in 2007, he redefined network RADIUS management by establishing daloRADIUS, a world-recognized and industry-leading open source project (http://www.daloradius.com).

Liran is currently leading the R&D Engineering team for Hewlett Packard Enterprise content marketplace, built on a microservices architecture for a combined technology stack of Java, NodeJS, AngularJS, MongoDB, and MySQL. He loves mentoring and empowering team members, drives for better code methodology, and seeks out innovative solutions to support business strategies.

He enjoys spending time with his beloved wife, Tal, and his son, Ori. Among other things, his hobbies include playing the guitar, hacking all things Linux, and continuously experimenting and contributing to open source projects.

You can connect with him at http://www.linkedin.com/in/talliran or e-mail him at liran@enginx.com.

www.PacktPub.com

eBooks, discount offers, and more

Did you know that Packt offers eBook versions of every book published, with PDF and ePub files available? You can upgrade to the eBook version at www.PacktPub.com and as a print book customer, you are entitled to a discount on the eBook copy. Get in touch with us at customercare@packtpub.com for more details.

At www.PacktPub.com, you can also read a collection of free technical articles, sign up for a range of free newsletters and receive exclusive discounts and offers on Packt books and eBooks.

https://www.packtpub.com/mapt

Get the most in-demand software skills with Mapt. Mapt gives you full access to all Packt books and video courses, as well as industry-leading tools to help you plan your personal development and advance your career.

Why subscribe?

- Fully searchable across every book published by Packt
- Copy and paste, print, and bookmark content
- On demand and accessible via a web browser

This book is dedicated to the makers, whoever you are, wherever you are, whatever you do, I want to thank you for taking us forward.

Table of Contents

Preface

Back in the spring of 1995, web browsers were very different from present day browsers. It had been 4 years since the release of the WorldWideWeb (the first Internet browser written by Tim Berners-Lee, later renamed Nexus), 2 years since the initial release of Mosaic, and Internet Explorer 1.0 was a few months away from release. The World Wide Web began to show signs of popularity, and though some of the big companies showed interest in the field, the main disruptor back then was a small company named Netscape.

Netscape's already popular browser, Netscape Navigator, was in the works for its second version, when the client engineering team and co-founder Marc Anderseen decided that Navigator 2.0 should embed a programming language. The task was assigned to a software engineer named Branden Eich, who completed it in ten days between May 6 and May 15, 1995, naming the language Mocha, then LiveScript, and eventually JavaScript.

Netscape Navigator 2.0 was released in September 1995 and transformed the way we perceived the web browser. By August 1996, Internet Explorer 3.0 introduced its own implementation of JavaScript, and in November of that year, Netscape had announced that they had submitted JavaScript to ECMA for standardization. In June 1997, the ECMA-262 specification was published, making JavaScript the de facto standard programming language for the Web.

For years, JavaScript was denigrated by many as the programming language for amateurs. JavaScript's architecture, fragmented implementation, and original "amateur" audience made professional programmers dismiss it. But then AJAX was introduced, and when Google released their Gmail and Google Maps applications in the mid-2000s, it suddenly became clear that AJAX technology could transform websites into web applications. This inspired the new generation of web developers to take JavaScript development to the next level.

What began with the first generation of utility libraries, such as jQuery and Prototype, soon got boosted by Google's next great contribution, the Chrome browser and its V8 JavaScript engine, released at the end of 2008. The V8 engine, with its JIT compiling capabilities, greatly enhanced JavaScript performance. This led to a new era in JavaScript development. 2009 was JavaScript's annus mirabilis; suddenly, platforms such as Node.js enabled developers to run JavaScript on the server, databases such as MongoDB popularized and simplified the use of JSON storage, and frameworks such as Angular and React are simplifying the creation of complex frontend applications. More than 20 years after its original debut, JavaScript is now everywhere. What used to be an "amateur" programming language, capable of executing small scripts, is now one of the most popular programming languages in the world. The rise of open source collaboration tools, along with the devoted involvement of talented engineers, created one of the richest communities in the world, and the seeds planted by many contributors are now flourishing in a burst of sheer creativity.

The practical implications are enormous. What was once a fragmented team of developers, each an expert in their own domain, can now become a homogeneous team capable of developing leaner, more agile software together using a single language across all layers.

There are many full-stack JavaScript frameworks out there, some built by great teams, some that address important issues, but none of them are as open and modular as the MEAN stack. The idea is simple, we'll take MongoDB as the database, Express as the web framework, Angular as the frontend framework, and Node.js as the platform, and combine them in a modular approach that will ensure the flexibility needed in modern software development. MEAN's approach relies on the communities around each of the open source modules keeping it updated and stable, ensuring that if one of the modules becomes useless, we can just seamlessly replace it with a better-suited one.

I would like to welcome you to the JavaScript revolution and assure you I will do my best to help you become a full-stack JavaScript developer.

In this book, we'll help you set up your environment and explain how to connect the different MEAN components together using the best modules. You'll be introduced to the best practices of maintaining your code clear and simple and be shown how to avoid common pitfalls. We'll walk through building your authentication layer and adding your first entity. You'll learn how to leverage JavaScript non-blocking architecture in building real-time communication between your server and client applications. Finally, we'll show you how to cover your code with the proper tests, and we'll show you what tools to use to automate your development process.

What this book covers

Chapter 1, Introduction to MEAN, introduces you to the MEAN stack and shows you how to install the different prerequisites on each OS.

Chapter 2, Getting Started with Node.js, explains explain the basics of Node.js and how it is used in web application development.

Chapter 3, Building an Express Web Application, explains how to create and structure an Express application by implementing the MVC pattern.

Chapter 4, Introduction to MongoDB, explains the basics of MongoDB and how it can be used to store your applications' data.

Chapter 5, Introduction to Mongoose, shows how to use a Mongoose to connect an Express application with a MongoDB database.

Chapter 6, Managing User Authentication Using Passport, explains how to manage your users' authentication and offer them diverse login options.

Chapter 7, Introduction to Angular, explains how to implement an Angular application in conjunction with your Express application.

Chapter 8, Creating a MEAN CRUD Module, explains how to write and use your MEAN application's entities.

Chapter 9, Adding Real-time Functionality Using Socket.io, shows you how to create and use real-time communication between your client and server.

Chapter 10, Testing MEAN Applications, explains how to automatically test the different parts of your MEAN application.

Chapter 11, Automating and Debugging MEAN Applications, explains how to develop your MEAN application more efficiently.

What you need for this book

This book is suitable for beginner and intermediate web developers with basic knowledge of HTML, CSS, and modern JavaScript development.

Who this book is for

This book is aimed at web developers interested in learning how to build modern web applications using MongoDB, Express, Angular, and Node.js.

Conventions

In this book, you will find a number of text styles that distinguish between different kinds of information. Here are some examples of these styles and an explanation of their meaning.

Code words in text, database table names, folder names, filenames, file extensions, pathnames, dummy URLs, user input, and Twitter handles are shown as follows: "To test your static middleware, add an image named `logo.png` to the `public/img` folder."

A block of code is set as follows:

```
const message = 'Hello World';

exports.sayHello = function() {
  console.log(message);
}
```

When we wish to draw your attention to a particular part of a code block, the relevant lines or items are set in bold:

```
const express = require('express');
const app = express();

app.listen(3000);

console.log('Server running at http://localhost:3000/');
```

Any command-line input or output is written as follows:

```
$ npm start
```

New terms and **important words** are shown in bold. Words that you see on the screen, for example, in menus or dialog boxes, appear in the text like this: "Once you click on the **Next** button, the installation should begin."

 Warnings or important notes appear in a box like this.

 Tips and tricks appear like this.

Reader feedback

Feedback from our readers is always welcome. Let us know what you think about this book—what you liked or disliked. Reader feedback is important for us as it helps us develop titles that you will really get the most out of.

To send us general feedback, simply e-mail feedback@packtpub.com, and mention the book's title in the subject of your message.

If there is a topic that you have expertise in and you are interested in either writing or contributing to a book, see our author guide at www.packtpub.com/authors.

Customer support

Now that you are the proud owner of a Packt book, we have a number of things to help you to get the most from your purchase.

Downloading the example code

You can download the example code files for this book from your account at http://www.packtpub.com. If you purchased this book elsewhere, you can visit http://www.packtpub.com/support and register to have the files e-mailed directly to you.

You can download the code files by following these steps:

1. Log in or register to our website using your e-mail address and password.
2. Hover the mouse pointer on the **SUPPORT** tab at the top.
3. Click on **Code Downloads & Errata**.
4. Enter the name of the book in the **Search** box.
5. Select the book for which you're looking to download the code files.
6. Choose from the drop-down menu where you purchased this book from.
7. Click on **Code Download**.

Once the file is downloaded, please make sure that you unzip or extract the folder using the latest version of:

- WinRAR / 7-Zip for Windows
- Zipeg / iZip / UnRarX for Mac
- 7-Zip / PeaZip for Linux

The code bundle for the book is also hosted on GitHub at `https://github.com/PacktPublishing/MEAN-Web-Development`. We also have other code bundles from our rich catalog of books and videos available at `https://github.com/PacktPublishing/`. Check them out!

Errata

Although we have taken every care to ensure the accuracy of our content, mistakes do happen. If you find a mistake in one of our books—maybe a mistake in the text or the code—we would be grateful if you could report this to us. By doing so, you can save other readers from frustration and help us improve subsequent versions of this book. If you find any errata, please report them by visiting `http://www.packtpub.com/submit-errata`, selecting your book, clicking on the **Errata Submission Form** link, and entering the details of your errata. Once your errata are verified, your submission will be accepted and the errata will be uploaded to our website or added to any list of existing errata under the Errata section of that title.

To view the previously submitted errata, go to `https://www.packtpub.com/books/content/support` and enter the name of the book in the search field. The required information will appear under the **Errata** section.

Piracy

Piracy of copyrighted material on the Internet is an ongoing problem across all media. At Packt, we take the protection of our copyright and licenses very seriously. If you come across any illegal copies of our works in any form on the Internet, please provide us with the location address or website name immediately so that we can pursue a remedy.

Please contact us at `copyright@packtpub.com` with a link to the suspected pirated material.

We appreciate your help in protecting our authors and our ability to bring you valuable content.

Questions

If you have a problem with any aspect of this book, you can contact us at `questions@packtpub.com`, and we will do our best to address the problem.

1
Introduction to MEAN

The MEAN stack is a powerful, full-stack JavaScript solution that comprises four major building blocks: MongoDB as the database, Express as the web server framework, Angular as the web client framework, and Node.js as the server platform. These building blocks are being developed by different teams, and involve a substantial community of developers and advocates pushing forward the development and documentation of each component. The main strength of the stack lies in its centralization of JavaScript as the main programming language. However, the problem of connecting these tools together can lay the foundation for scaling and architecture issues, which can dramatically affect your development process.

In this book, I will try to present the best practices and known issues of building a MEAN application, but before you begin with actual MEAN development, you will first need to set up your environment. This chapter will cover a bit of a programming overview, but mostly present the proper ways of installing the basic perquisites of a MEAN application. By the end of this chapter, you'll learn how to install and configure MongoDB and Node.js on all the common operating systems and how to use NPM. In this chapter, we will cover the following topics:

- Introduction to the MEAN stack architecture
- Installing and running MongoDB on Windows, Linux, and Mac OS X
- Installing and running Node.js on Windows, Linux, and Mac OS X
- Introduction to npm and how to use it to install Node modules

Three-tier web application development

Most web applications are built in a three-tier architecture that consists of three important layers: data, logic, and presentation. In web applications, the application structure usually breaks down to database, server, and client, while in modern web development, it can also be broken into database, server logic, client logic, and client UI.

A popular paradigm for implementing this model is the **Model-View-Controller** (**MVC**) architectural pattern. In the MVC paradigm, the logic, data, and visualization are separated into three types of object, each handling its own tasks. The **View** handles the visual part, taking care of user interaction. The **Controller** responds to system and user events, commanding the Model and View to change appropriately. The **Model** handles data manipulation, responding to requests for information or changing its state according to the Controller's instructions. A simple visual representation of the MVC architecture is shown in the following diagram:

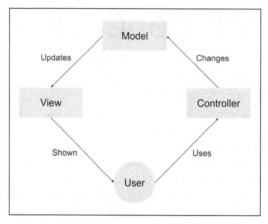

Common MVC architecture communication

In the 25 years of web development, many technology stacks became popular for building three-tier web applications. Among those now ubiquitous stacks, you can find the LAMP stack, the .NET stack, and a rich variety of other frameworks and tools. The main problem with these stacks is that each tier demands a knowledge base that usually exceeds the abilities of a single developer, making teams bigger than they should be, less productive, and exposed to unexpected risks.

The evolution of JavaScript

JavaScript is an interpreted computer programming language that was built for the Web. First implemented by the Netscape Navigator web browser, it became the programming language that web browsers use to execute client-side logic. In the mid 2000s, the shift from websites to web applications, along with the release of faster browsers, gradually created a community of JavaScript developers writing more complex applications. These developers started creating libraries and tools that shortened development cycles, giving birth to a new generation of even more advanced web applications. They, in turn, created a continuous demand for better browsers. This cycle went on for a few years, where the vendors kept improving their browsers and JavaScript developers kept pushing the boundaries.

The real revolution began in 2008, when Google released its Chrome browser, along with its fast JIT-compiling V8 JavaScript engine. Google's V8 engine made JavaScript run so much faster that it completely transformed web application development. More importantly, the release of the engine's source code allowed developers to start reimagining JavaScript outside of the browser. One of the first products of this revolution was Node.js.

After looking into other options for a while, programmer Ryan Dahl found that V8 engine fit his non-blocking I/O experiment called Node.js. The idea was simple: help developers build non-blocking units of code to allow better use of system resources and create more responsive applications. The result was a minimal yet powerful platform, which utilized JavaScript's non-blocking nature outside of the browser. Node's elegant module system enabled developers to freely extend the platform using third-party modules to achieve almost any functionality. The reaction by the online community was a creation of various tools, from modern web frameworks to robotics server platforms. However, server-side JavaScript was only the beginning.

When Dwight Merriman and Eliot Horowitz set out to build their scalable hosting solution back in 2007, they already had a lot of experience with building web applications. However, the platform they built did not succeed as planned, so in 2009, they decided to take it apart and open source its components, including a V8-based database called MongoDB. Derived from the word "humongous", MongoDB was a scalable NoSQL database that used a JSON-like data model with dynamic schemas. MongoDB gained a lot of traction right away by giving developers the flexibility they needed when dealing with complex data, while providing RDBMS features such as advanced queries and easy scaling—features that eventually made MongoDB one of the leading NoSQL solutions. JavaScript broke another boundary. However, the JavaScript revolutionaries haven't forgotten where it all began. In fact, the popularization of modern browsers created a new wave of JavaScript frontend frameworks.

Back in 2009, while building their JSON as a platform service, developers Miško Hevery and Adam Abrons noticed that the common JavaScript libraries weren't enough. The nature of their rich web application raised the need for a more structured framework that would reduce grunt work and maintain an organized code base. Abandoning the original idea, they decided to focus on the development of their frontend framework and open sourced the project, naming it AngularJS. The idea was to bridge the gap between JavaScript and HTML, and help popularize single-page application development.

The result was a rich web framework, which presented frontend web developers with concepts such as two-way data binding, cross-component dependency injection, and MVC-based components. Angular, along with other modern frameworks, revolutionized web development by transforming the once unmaintainable frontend code base into a structured code base that can support more advanced development paradigms such as **Test-driven Development (TDD)**.

The rise of open source collaboration tools, along with the devoted involvement of these talented engineers, created one of the richest communities in the world. More importantly, these major advancements allowed the development of three-tier web applications to be unified under JavaScript as the programming language across all three layers—an idea that is commonly referred to as the full-stack JavaScript. The MEAN stack is just a single example of this idea.

Introduction to ECMAScript 2015

After years of work, the ES6 specification was released on June 2015. It presented the biggest advancements in JavaScript since ES5 and introduced several features into the language that will completely transform the way we JavaScript developers write code. It would be ambitious to describe all the improvements made by ES2015. Instead, let's try to work through the basic features we'll use in the next chapters.

Modules

Modules are now a supported language-level feature. They allow developers to wrap their component in a Module pattern, and export and import modules inside their code. The implementation is very similar to the CommonJS module implementation described in the previous chapters, although ES2015 modules also support asynchronous loading. The basic keywords for working with ES2015 modules are `export` and `import`. Let's look at a simple example. Suppose you have a file named `lib.js` that contains the following code:

```
export function halfOf(x) {
    return x / 2;
}
```

So, in your `main.js` file, you can use the following code:

```
import halfOf from 'lib';
console.log(halfOf(84));
```

However, modules can be much more fun. For instance, let's say our `lib.js` file looks like this:

```
export function halfOf(x) {
    return x / 2;
}
export function multiply(x, y) {
    return x * y;
}
```

In your main file, use the following code:

```
import {halfOf, multiply} from 'lib';
console.log(halfOf(84));
console.log(multiply(21, 2));
```

ES2015 modules also support default `export` values. So, for instance, let's say you have file named `doSomething.js` that contains the following code:

```
export default function () {
    console.log('I did something')
};
```

You'll be able to use it as follows in your `main.js` file:

```
import doSomething from 'doSomething';
doSomething();
```

It is important to remember that the default import should identify their entities using the module name.

Another important thing to remember is that modules export bindings and not values. So for instance, let's say you have a `validator.js` file that looks like this:

```
export let flag = false;
export function touch() {
    flag = true;
}
```

You also have a `main.js` file that looks like this:

```
import { flag, touch } from 'validator';
console.log(flag);
touch();
console.log(flag);
```

The first output would be `false`, and the second would be `true`. Now that we have a basic understanding of modules, let's move to classes.

Classes

The long debate about classes versus prototypes came to a conclusion that classes in ES2015 are basically just a syntactic sugar over the prototype-based inheritance. Classes are easy-to-use patterns that support instance and static members, constructors, and super calls. Here is an example:

```
class Vehicle {
    constructor(wheels) {
        this.wheels = wheels;
    }
    toString() {
        return '(' + this.wheels + ')';
    }
}

class Car extends Vehicle {
    constructor(color) {
        super(4);
        this.color = color;
    }
    toString() {
        return super.toString() + ' colored:  ' + this.color;
    }
}

let car = new Car('blue');
car.toString();

console.log(car instanceof Car);
console.log(car instanceof Vehicle);
```

In this example, the `Car` class extends the `Vehicle` class. Thus, the output is as follows:

```
(4) in blue
true
true
```

Arrow functions

Arrows are functions shorthand by the `=>` syntax. For people familiar with other languages such as C# and Java 8, they might look familiar. However, arrows are also very helpful because they share the same lexical `this` as their scope. They are mainly used in two forms. One is using an expression body:

```
const squares = numbers.map(n => n * n);
```

Another form is using a statement body:

```
numbers.forEach(n => {
   if (n % 2 === 0) evens.push(n);
});
```

An example of using the shared lexical would be:

```
const author = {
  fullName: "Bob Alice",
  books: [],
  printBooks() {
      this.books.forEach(book => console.log(book + ' by ' +
        this.fullName));
  }
};
```

If used as a regular function, `this` would be the `book` object and not the `author`.

Let and Const

`Let` and `Const` are new keywords used for symbol declaration. Let is almost identical to the `var` keyword, so it'll behave the same as global and function variables. However, `let` behaves differently inside a block. For instance, look at the following code:

```
function iterateVar() {
  for(var i = 0; i < 10; i++) {
    console.log(i);
  }

  console.log(i)
}

function iterateLet() {
  for(let i = 0; i < 10; i++) {
    console.log(i);
  }

  console.log(i)
}
```

The first function will print `i` after the loop, but the second one will throw an error, since `i` is defined by `let`.

The const keyword forces single assignment. So, this code will throw an error as well:

```
const me = 1
me = 2
```

Default, Rest, and Spread

Default, Rest, and Spread are three new features related to functions parameters. The default feature allows you to set a default value to the function parameter:

```
function add(x, y = 0) {
    return x + y;
}
add(1)
add(1,2)
```

In this example, the value of y will be set to 0 if a value is not passed or is set to undefined.

The Rest feature allows you to pass an array as trailing arguments as follows:

```
function userFriends(user, ...friends) {
    console.log(user + ' has ' + friends.length + ' friends');
}
userFriends('User', 'Bob', 'Alice');
```

The Spread feature turns an array into a call argument:

```
function userTopFriends(firstFriend, secondFriend, thirdFriends) {
    console.log(firstFriend);
    console.log(secondFriend);
    console.log(thirdFriends);
}

userTopFriends(...['Alice', 'Bob', 'Michelle']);
```

Summary

Going into modern web development, ES2015 will become a viable part of your daily programming sessions. What is shown here is the tip of the iceberg, and it is strongly recommended that you continue to investigate it deeper. However, for the purposes of this book, it will suffice.

Introducing MEAN

MEAN is an abbreviation for MongoDB, Express, Angular, and Node.js. The concept behind it is to use only JavaScript-driven solutions to cover the different parts of your application. The advantages are great and are as follows:

- A single language is used throughout the application
- All the parts of the application can support and often enforce the use of the MVC architecture
- Serialization and deserialization of data structures is no longer needed, because data marshaling is done using JSON objects

However, there are still a few important questions that remain unanswered:

- How do you connect all the components together?
- Node.js has a huge ecosystem of modules, so which modules should you use?
- JavaScript is paradigm agnostic, so how can you maintain the MVC application structure?
- JSON is a schema-less data structure, so how and when should you model your data?
- How do you handle user authentication?
- How should you use the Node.js non-blocking architecture to support real-time interactions?
- How can you test your MEAN application code base?
- Considering the rise of DevOps and CI, what kind of JavaScript development tools can you use to expedite your MEAN application development process?

In this book, I'll try to answer these questions and many more. However, before we go any further, you will first need to install the basic prerequisites.

Installing MongoDB

For MongoDB's stable versions, the official MongoDB website supplies linked binaries that provide the easiest way to install MongoDB on Linux, Mac OS X, and Windows. Notice that you need to download the right architecture version for your operating system. If you use Windows or Linux, ensure that you download either the 32-bit or 64-bit version according to your system architecture. Mac users are safe to download the 64-bit version.

The MongoDB versioning scheme works in such a way that only even version numbers mark stable releases. So, versions 3.0.x and 3.2x are stable, while 2.9.x and 3.1.x are unstable releases and should not be used in production. The latest stable version of MongoDB is 3.2.x.

When you visit the download page at `http://mongodb.org/downloads`, you'll be offered a download of an archive that contains the binaries you need to install MongoDB. After downloading and extracting the archive file, you will need to locate the `mongod` binary, which is usually located in the `bin` folder. The `mongod` process runs the main MongoDB server process, which can be used as a standalone server or a single node of a MongoDB replica set. In our case, we will use MongoDB as a standalone server. The `mongod` process requires a folder to store the database files (the default folder is `/data/db`) and a port to listen to (the default port is `27017`). In the following subsections, we'll go over the setup steps for each operating system. We'll begin with the common Windows installation process.

It is recommended that you learn more about MongoDB by visiting the official documentation at `https://mongodb.org`.

Installing MongoDB on Windows

Once you have downloaded the right version, run the `.msi` file. MongoDB should be installed in the `C:\Program Files\MongoDB\` folder. While running, MongoDB uses a default folder to store its data files. On Windows, the default folder location is `C:\data\db`. So, in the command prompt, go to `C:\` and issue the following command:

```
> md c:\data\db
```

You can tell the mongod service to use an alternative path for the data files, using the `--dbpath` command-line flag.

Once you've finished creating the data folders, you'll get two options while running the main MongoDB service.

Running MongoDB manually

To run MongoDB manually, you will need to run the mongod binary. So, open the command prompt and navigate to the C:\Program Files\MongoDB\Server\3.2\ bin folder. Then, issue the following command:

```
C:\Program Files\MongoDB\Server\3.2\bin> mongod
```

The preceding command will run the main MongoDB service that starts listening to the default 27017 port. If everything goes well, you should see a console output similar to the following screenshot:

```
Command Prompt - mongod
C:\Program Files\MongoDB\Server\3.0\bin>mongod
2015-10-16T18:04:14.738+0200 I CONTROL
2015-10-16T18:04:14.738+0200 W CONTROL   32-bit servers don't have journaling ena
bled by default. Please use --journal if you want durability.
2015-10-16T18:04:14.738+0200 I CONTROL
2015-10-16T18:04:14.738+0200 I CONTROL   Hotfix KB2731284 or later update is not
installed, will zero-out data files
2015-10-16T18:04:14.753+0200 I CONTROL   [initandlisten] MongoDB starting : pid=6
04 port=27017 dbpath=C:\data\db\ 32-bit host=IE9Win7
2015-10-16T18:04:14.753+0200 I CONTROL   [initandlisten]
2015-10-16T18:04:14.753+0200 I CONTROL   [initandlisten] ** NOTE: This is a 32 bi
t MongoDB binary.
2015-10-16T18:04:14.753+0200 I CONTROL   [initandlisten] **       32 bit builds a
re limited to less than 2GB of data (or less with --journal).
2015-10-16T18:04:14.753+0200 I CONTROL   [initandlisten] **       Note that journ
aling defaults to off for 32 bit and is currently off.
2015-10-16T18:04:14.753+0200 I CONTROL   [initandlisten] **       See http://doch
ub.mongodb.org/core/32bit
2015-10-16T18:04:14.753+0200 I CONTROL   [initandlisten]
2015-10-16T18:04:14.753+0200 I CONTROL   [initandlisten] targetMinOS: Windows XP
SP3
2015-10-16T18:04:14.753+0200 I CONTROL   [initandlisten] db version v3.0.7
2015-10-16T18:04:14.753+0200 I CONTROL   [initandlisten] git version: 6ce7cbe8c6b
899552dadd907604559806aa2e9bd
2015-10-16T18:04:14.753+0200 I CONTROL   [initandlisten] build info: windows sys.
getwindowsversion(major=6, minor=1, build=7601, platform=2, service_pack='Servic
e Pack 1') BOOST_LIB_VERSION=1_49
2015-10-16T18:04:14.769+0200 I CONTROL   [initandlisten] allocator: tcmalloc
2015-10-16T18:04:14.769+0200 I CONTROL   [initandlisten] options: {}
2015-10-16T18:04:14.785+0200 I NETWORK   [initandlisten] waiting for connections
on port 27017
```

Running the MongoDB server on Windows

Depending on the Windows security level, a security alert dialog, which notifies you about the blocking of some service features, will be issued. If this occurs, select a private network and click on **Allow Access**.

> You should be aware that the MongoDB service is self-contained, so you can alternatively run it from any folder of your choice.

Running MongoDB as a Windows service

The more popular approach is running MongoDB automatically after every reboot cycle. Before you begin setting up MongoDB as a Windows service, it's considered a good practice to specify a path for the MongoDB log and configuration files. Start by creating a folder for these files by running the following command in your command prompt:

```
> md C:\data\log
```

Then, you'll need to create a configuration file at C:\Program Files\MongoDB\ Server\3.2\mongod.cfg that contains these lines:

```
systemLog:
    destination: file
    path: c:\data\log\mongod.log
storage:
    dbPath: c:\data\db
```

When you have your configuration file in place, open a new command prompt window with administrative privileges by right-clicking on the command prompt icon and clicking on **Run as administrator**. Notice that if an older version of the MongoDB service is already running, you'll first need to remove it using the following commands:

```
> sc stop MongoDB
```

```
> sc delete MongoDB
```

Then, install the MongoDB service by running the following command:

```
> "C:\Program Files\MongoDB\Server\3.2\bin\mongod.exe" --config
  "C:\Program Files\MongoDB\Server\3.2\mongod.cfg" --install
```

Notice that the install process will only succeed if your configuration file is set correctly. After installing your MongoDB service, you can run it by executing the following command in the administrative command prompt window:

```
> net start MongoDB
```

Be aware that the MongoDB configuration file can be modified to accommodate your needs. You can learn more about it by visiting http://docs.mongodb.org/manual/ reference/configuration-options/.

Installing MongoDB on Mac OS X and Linux

In this section, you'll learn the different ways of installing MongoDB on Unix-based operating systems. Let's begin with the simplest way to install MongoDB, which involves downloading MongoDB's precompiled binaries.

Installing MongoDB from binaries

You can download the right version of MongoDB using the download page at `http://www.mongodb.org/downloads`. Alternatively, you can do this via CURL by executing the following command:

```
$ curl -O http://downloads.mongodb.org/osx/mongodb-osx-x86_64-3.2.10.tgz
```

Notice that we have downloaded the Mac OS X 64-bit version, so make sure you alter the command to fit the version suitable for your machine. After the downloading process is over, unpack the file by issuing the following command in your command-line tool:

```
$ tar -zxvf mongodb-osx-x86_64-3.2.10.tgz
```

Now, change the name of the extracted folder to a simpler folder name by running the following command:

```
$ mv mongodb-osx-x86_64-3.2.10 mongodb
```

MongoDB uses a default folder to store its files. On Linux and Mac OS X, the default location is /data/db, so in your command-line tool, run the following command:

```
$ mkdir -p /data/db
```

 You may experience some trouble creating this folder. This is usually a permission issue, so use sudo or super user when running the preceding command.

The preceding command will create the data and db folders, because the -p flag creates parent folders as well. Notice that the default folder is located outside your home folder, so make sure you set the folder permission by running the following command:

```
$ chown -R $USER /data/db
```

Now that you have everything prepared, use your command-line tool and go to the bin folder to run the mongod service as follows:

```
$ cd mongodb/bin
$ mongod
```

This will run the main MongoDB service, which will start listening to the default `27017` port. If everything goes well, you should see a console output similar to the following screenshot:

```
● ● ●                    bin — mongod — 80×24
[Amos@amoss-macbook-pro:~/MEAN/mongodb/bin$ ./mongod                      ]
2015-10-18T18:47:33.493+0200 I JOURNAL  [initandlisten] journal dir=/data/db/jou
rnal
2015-10-18T18:47:33.493+0200 I JOURNAL  [initandlisten] recover : no journal fil
es present, no recovery needed
2015-10-18T18:47:33.510+0200 I JOURNAL  [durability] Durability thread started
2015-10-18T18:47:33.510+0200 I CONTROL  [initandlisten] MongoDB starting : pid=2
5538 port=27017 dbpath=/data/db 64-bit host=amoss-macbook-pro.home
2015-10-18T18:47:33.510+0200 I JOURNAL  [journal writer] Journal writer thread s
tarted
2015-10-18T18:47:33.510+0200 I CONTROL  [initandlisten]
2015-10-18T18:47:33.510+0200 I CONTROL  [initandlisten] ** WARNING: soft rlimits
 too low. Number of files is 256, should be at least 1000
2015-10-18T18:47:33.510+0200 I CONTROL  [initandlisten] db version v3.0.7
2015-10-18T18:47:33.511+0200 I CONTROL  [initandlisten] git version: 6ce7cbe8c6b
899552dadd907604559806aa2e9bd
2015-10-18T18:47:33.511+0200 I CONTROL  [initandlisten] build info: Darwin mci-o
sx108-13.build.10gen.cc 12.3.0 Darwin Kernel Version 12.3.0: Sun Jan  6 22:37:10
 PST 2013; root:xnu-2050.22.13~1/RELEASE_X86_64 x86_64 BOOST_LIB_VERSION=1_49
2015-10-18T18:47:33.511+0200 I CONTROL  [initandlisten] allocator: system
2015-10-18T18:47:33.511+0200 I CONTROL  [initandlisten] options: {}
2015-10-18T18:47:33.530+0200 I NETWORK  [initandlisten] waiting for connections
on port 27017
▌
```

Running the MongoDB server on Mac OS X

Installing MongoDB using a package manager

Sometimes, the easiest way to install MongoDB is using a package manager. The downside is that some package managers are falling behind in terms of supporting the latest version. Luckily, the team behind MongoDB also maintains the official packages for RedHat, Debian, and Ubuntu, as well as a Homebrew package for Mac OS X. Note that you'll have to configure your package manager repository to include the MongoDB servers to download the official packages.

To install MongoDB on Red Hat Enterprise, CentOS, or Fedora using Yum, follow the instructions at `http://docs.mongodb.org/manual/tutorial/install-mongodb-on-red-hat-centos-or-fedora-linux/`.

To install MongoDB on Ubuntu using APT, follow the instructions at `http://docs.mongodb.org/manual/tutorial/install-mongodb-on-ubuntu/`.

To install MongoDB on Debian using APT, follow the instructions at `http://docs.mongodb.org/manual/tutorial/install-mongodb-on-debian/`.

To install MongoDB on Mac OS X using Homebrew, follow the instructions at
`http://docs.mongodb.org/manual/tutorial/install-mongodb-on-os-x/`.

Using the MongoDB shell

The MongoDB archive file includes the MongoDB shell, which allows to you to
interact with your server instance using the command line. To start the shell,
navigate to the MongoDB `bin` folder and run the `mongo` service as follows:

```
$ cd mongodb/bin
```

```
$ mongo
```

If you successfully installed MongoDB, the shell will automatically connect to your
local instance, using the test database. You should see a console output similar to the
following screenshot:

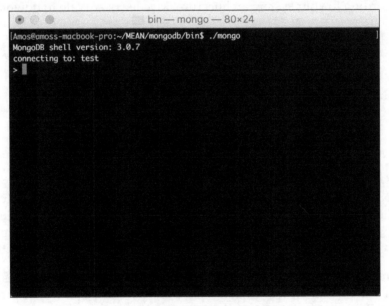

Running the MongoDB shell on Mac OS X

To test your database, run the following command:

```
> db.articles.insert({title: "Hello World"})
```

The preceding command will create a new article collection and insert a JSON object
containing a `title` property. To retrieve the article object, execute the following
command:

```
> db.articles.find()
```

The console will output a text similar to the following message:

```
{ _id: ObjectId("52d02240e4b01d67d71ad577"), title: "Hello World" }
```

Congratulations! This means your MongoDB instance is working properly, and you have successfully managed to interact with it using the MongoDB shell. In the upcoming chapters, you'll learn more about MongoDB and how to use the MongoDB shell.

Installing Node.js

For the stable versions, the official Node.js website supplies linked binaries that provide the easiest way to install Node.js on Linux, Mac OS X, and Windows. Note that you need to download the right architecture version for your operating system. If you use Windows or Linux, make sure to download either the 32-bit or 64-bit version according to your system architecture. Mac users are safe to download the 64-bit version.

> After the merge between the Node.js and io.js projects, the version scheme continued directly from 0.12.x to 4.x. The team now uses the **Long-term Support (LTS)** policy. You can read about it at https://en.wikipedia.org/wiki/Long-term_support. The latest stable version of Node.js is 6.x.

Installing Node.js on Windows

Installing Node.js on a Windows machine is a simple task that can be easily accomplished using the standalone installer. To begin with, navigate to https://nodejs.org/en/download/ and download the right .msi file. Notice there are 32-bit and 64-bit versions, so make sure you download the right one for your system.

After downloading the installer, run it. If you get any security dialog boxes, just click on the **Run** button, and the installation wizard should start. You will be prompted with an installation screen similar to the following screenshot:

Node.js Windows installation wizard

Once you click on the **Next** button, the installation should begin. A few moments later, you'll see a confirmation screen similar to the following screenshot, telling you that Node.js was successfully installed:

Node.js Windows installation confirmation

Installing Node.js on Mac OS X

Installing Node.js on Mac OS X is a simple task that can be easily accomplished using the standalone installer. Start by navigating to the `https://nodejs.org/en/download/` page and download the `.pkg` file. After downloading the installer, run it, and you will be prompted with an installation screen similar to the following screenshot:

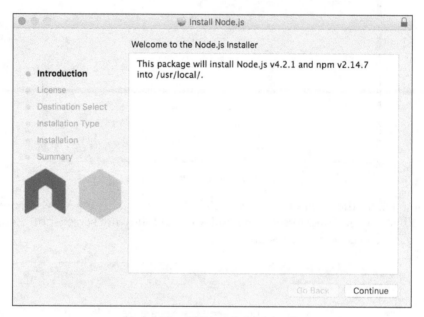

Node.js Mac OS X installation wizard

Click on **Continue**, and the installation process should begin. The installer will ask you to confirm the license agreement and then ask you to select the folder destination. Choose the option most suitable for you before clicking on the **Continue** button again. The installer will then ask you to confirm the installation information and ask you for your user password. A few moments later, you'll see a confirmation screen similar to the following screenshot, telling you that Node.js was successfully installed:

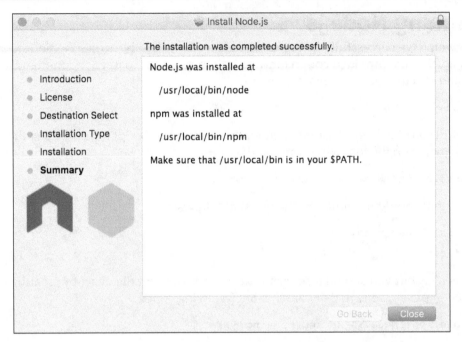

Node.js Mac OS X installation confirmation

Installing Node.js on Linux

To install Node.js on a Linux machine, you'll have to use the tarball file from the official website. The best way of doing so is to download the latest version and then build and install the source code using the `make` command. Start by navigating to the `http://nodejs.org/en/download/` page, and download the suitable `.tar.gz` file. Then, expand the file and install Node.js by issuing the following commands:

```
$ tar -zxf node-v6.9.1.tar.gz
$ cd node-v6.9.1
$ ./configure && make && sudo make install
```

If everything goes well, the commands will install Node.js on your machine. Note that these commands are for the Node.js 6.9.1 version, so remember to replace the version number with the version you downloaded.

 It is recommended that you learn more about Node.js by visiting the official documentation at `https://nodejs.org`.

Running Node.js

After you have successfully installed Node.js, you will be able to start experimenting with it using the provided command-line interface (CLI). Go to your command-line tool and execute the following command:

```
$ node
```

This will start the Node.js CLI, which will wait for a JavaScript input. To test the installation, run the following command:

```
> console.log('Node is up and running!');
```

The output should be similar to the one that follows:

```
Node is up and running!
undefined
```

This is nice, but you should also try to execute a JavaScript file. Start by creating a file named application.js that contains the following code:

```
console.log('Node is up and running!');
```

To run it, you'll have to pass the file name as the first argument to the Node CLI by issuing the following command:

```
$ node application.js
Node is up and running!
```

Congratulations! You have just created your first Node.js application. To stop the CLI, press *CTRL + D* or *CTRL + C*.

Introducing npm

Node.js is a platform, which means its features and APIs are kept to a minimum. To achieve more complex functionality, it uses a module system that allows you to extend the platform. The best way to install, update, and remove Node.js modules is using npm. npm is mainly used as:

- A registry of packages for browsing, downloading, and installing third-party modules
- A CLI tool to manage local and global packages

Conveniently, npm is installed during the Node.js installation process, so let's quickly jump in and learn how to use it.

Using npm

To understand how npm works, we will install the Express web framework module, which you'll use in the upcoming chapters. npm is a robust package manager, which keeps a centralized registry for public modules. To browse the available public packages, visit the official website at `https://www.npmjs.com/`.

Most of the packages in the registry are open source and contributed by the Node.js community developers. When developing an open source module, the package author can decide to publish it to the central registry, allowing other developers to download and use it in their projects. In the package configuration file, the author will choose a name that will later be used as a unique identifier to download that package.

 It is recommended that you learn more about Node.js by visiting the official documentation at `https://docs.npmjs.com`.

The installation process of npm

It is important to remember that npm has two installation modes: local and global. The default local mode is used more often and installs third-party packages in a local `node_modules` folder placed inside your application folder. It has no effect system-wise and is used to install the packages your application needs, without polluting your system with unnecessary global files.

The global mode is used to install the packages you want Node.js to use globally. Usually, these are CLI tools, such as Grunt, that you'll learn about in the upcoming chapters. Most of the time, the package author will specifically instruct you to install the package globally. Therefore, whenever in doubt, use the local mode. The global mode will usually install the packages in the `/usr/local/lib/node_modules` folder for Unix-based systems and the `C:\Users\%USERNAME%\AppData\Roaming\npm\node_modules` folder for Windows-based systems, making it available to any Node.js application running on the system.

Installing a package using npm

Once you find the right package, you'll be able to install it using the `npm install` command, as follows:

```
$ npm install <Package Unique Name>
```

Installing a module globally is similar to its local counterpart, but you'll have to add the -g flag, as follows:

```
$ npm install -g <Package Unique Name>
```

 You may find out that your user doesn't have the right permissions to install packages globally, so you'll have to use the root user or install it using sudo.

For example, to locally install Express, you'll need to navigate to your application folder and issue the following command:

```
$ npm install express
```

The preceding command will install the latest stable version of the Express package in your local node_modules folder. Furthermore, npm supports a wide range of semantic versioning. So, to install a specific version of a package, you can use the npm install command, as follows:

```
$ npm install <Package Unique Name>@<Package Version>
```

For instance, to install the second major version of the Express package, you'll need to issue the following command:

```
$ npm install express@2.x
```

This will install the latest stable version of Express 2. Note that this syntax enables npm to download and install any minor version of Express 2. To learn more about the supported semantic versioning syntax, it is recommended that you visit https://github.com/npm/node-semver.

When a package has dependencies, npm will automatically resolve those dependencies, installing the required packages in a node_modules folder inside the package folder. In the preceding example, the Express dependencies will be installed under node_modules/express/node_modules.

Removing a package using npm

To remove an installed package, you'll have to navigate to your application folder and run the following command:

```
$ npm uninstall < Package Unique Name>
```

npm will then look for the package and try to remove it from the local node_modules folder. To remove a global package, you'll need to use the -g flag, as follows:

```
$ npm uninstall -g < Package Unique Name>
```

Updating a package using npm

To update a package to its latest version, issue the following command:

```
$ npm update < Package Unique Name>
```

npm will download and install the latest version of this package, even if it doesn't exist yet. To update a global package, use the following command:

```
$ npm update -g < Package Unique Name>
```

Managing dependencies using the package.json file

Installing a single package is nice, but pretty soon, your application will need to use several packages. So, you'll need a better way to manage these dependencies. For this purpose, npm allows you to use a configuration file named package.json in the root folder of your application. In your package.json file, you'll be able to define various metadata properties of your application, including properties such as the name, version, and author of your application. This is also where you define your application dependencies.

The package.json file is basically a JSON file that contains the different attributes you'll need to describe your application properties. An application using the latest Express and Grunt packages will have a package.json file as follows:

```
{
  "name" : "MEAN",
  "version" : "0.0.1",
  "dependencies" : {
    "express" : "latest",
    "grunt" : "latest"
  }
}
```

 Your application name and version properties are required, so removing these properties will prevent npm from working properly.

Creating a package.json file

While you can manually create a package.json file, an easier approach would be to use the npm init command. To do so, use your command-line tool and issue the following command:

```
$ npm init
```

npm will ask you a few questions about your application and will automatically create a new `package.json` file for you. A sample process should look similar to the following screenshot:

```
This utility will walk you through creating a package.json file.
It only covers the most common items, and tries to guess sensible defaults.

See `npm help json` for definitive documentation on these fields
and exactly what they do.

Use `npm install <pkg> --save` afterwards to install a package and
save it as a dependency in the package.json file.

Press ^C at any time to quit.
[name: (Amos) mean
[version: (1.0.0) 0.0.1
[description: My First MEAN Application
[entry point: (.mongorc.js) server.js
[test command:
[git repository:
[keywords: MongoDB, Express, AngularJS, Node.js
[author: Amos Haviv
[license: (ISC) MIT
About to write to /Users/Amos/package.json:

{
  "name": "mean",
  "version": "0.0.1",
  "description": "My First MEAN Application",
  "main": "server.js",
  "directories": {
    "test": "test"
  },
  "scripts": {
    "test": "echo \"Error: no test specified\" && exit 1"
  },
  "keywords": [
    "MongoDB",
    "Express",
    "AngularJS",
    "Node.js"
  ],
  "author": "Amos Haviv",
  "license": "MIT"
}

[Is this ok? (yes) yes
Amos@amoss-macbook-pro:~$
```

Using npm init on Mac OS X

After creating your `package.json` file, you'll need to modify it and add a `dependencies` property. Your final `package.json` file should look like the following code snippet:

```
{
  "name": "mean",
  "version": "0.0.1",
  "description": "My First MEAN Application",
  "main": "server.js",
  "directories": {
```

```
      "test": "test"
    },
    "scripts": {
      "test": "echo \"Error: no test specified\" && exit 1"
    },
    "keywords": [
      "MongoDB",
      "Express",
      "Angular",
      "Node.js"
    ],
    "author": "Amos Haviv",
    "license": "MIT",
    "dependencies": {
      "express": "latest",
      "grunt": "latest"
    }
}
```

 In the preceding code example, we used the latest keyword to tell npm to install the latest versions of these packages. However, it is highly recommended that you use specific version numbers or range to prevent your application dependencies from changing during development cycles. This is because new package versions might not be backward compatible with older versions, which will cause major issues in your application.

Installing the package.json dependencies

After creating your package.json file, you'll be able to install your application dependencies by navigating to your application's root folder and using the npm install command, as follows:

$ npm install

npm will automatically detect your package.json file and install all your application dependencies, placing them under a local node_modules folder. An alternative and sometimes better approach to installing your dependencies is to use the following npm update command:

$ npm update

This will install any missing packages and will update all of your existing dependencies to their specified version.

Updating the package.json file

Another robust feature of the `npm install` command is the ability to install a new package and save the package information as a dependency in your `package.json` file. This can be accomplished using the `--save` optional flag when installing a specific package. For example, to install the latest version of Express and save it as a dependency, you can just use the following command:

```
$ npm install express --save
```

npm will install the latest version of Express and will add the Express package as a dependency to your `package.json` file. For clarity, in the upcoming chapters, we prefer to manually edit the `package.json` file. However, this useful feature can come in pretty handy in your daily development cycles.

> It is recommended that you learn more about npm's vast array of configuration options by visiting the official documentation at `https://docs.npmjs.com/files/package.json`.

Summary

In this chapter, you learned how to install MongoDB and how to connect to your local database instance using the MongoDB shell. You also learned how to install Node.js and use the Node.js CLI. You learned about npm and discovered how to use it to download and install Node.js packages. You also learned how to easily manage your application dependencies using the `package.json` file.

In the next chapter, we'll discuss some Node.js basics, and you'll build your first Node.js web application.

Getting Started with Node.js

In the previous chapter, you set up your environment and discovered the basic development principles of Node.js. This chapter will cover the proper way of building your first Node.js web application. You'll go through the basics of JavaScript event-driven nature and how to utilize it to build Node.js applications. You'll also learn about the Node.js module system and how to build your first Node.js web application. You'll then proceed to the Connect module and learn about its powerful middleware approach. By the end of this chapter, you'll know how to use Connect and Node.js to build simple yet powerful web applications. In this chapter, we will cover the following topics:

- Introduction to Node.js
- JavaScript closures and event-driven programming
- Node.js event-driven web development
- CommonJS modules and the Node.js module system
- Introduction to the Connect web framework
- Connect's middleware pattern

Introduction to Node.js

At JSConf EU 2009, a developer named Ryan Dahl went onstage to present his project named Node.js. Starting in 2008, Dahl looked at the current web trends and discovered something odd in the way web applications worked. The introduction of the **Asynchronous JavaScript and XML (AJAX)** technology a few years earlier transformed static websites into dynamic web applications, but the fundamental building block of web development didn't follow this trend.

The problem was that web technologies didn't support two-way communication between the browser and the server. The test case he used was the Flickr upload file feature, where the browser was unable to know when to update the progress bar as the server could not inform it of how much of the file was uploaded.

Dahl's idea was to build a web platform that would gracefully support the push of data from the server to the browser, but it wasn't that simple. When scaling to common web usage, the platform had to support hundreds (and sometimes thousands) of ongoing connections between the server and the browser. Most web platforms used expensive threads to handle requests, which meant keeping a fair amount of idle threads in order to keep the connection alive. So, Dahl used a different approach. He understood that using non-blocking sockets could save a lot in terms of system resources and went as far as proving that this could be done using C. Given that this technique could be implemented in any programming language and the fact that Dahl thought working with non-blocking C code was a tedious task, he decided to look for a better programming language.

When Google announced Chrome and its new V8 JavaScript engine in late 2008, it was obvious that JavaScript could run faster than before—a lot faster. V8's greatest advantage over other JavaScript engines was the compiling of JavaScript code to native machine code before executing it. This and other optimizations made JavaScript a viable programming language capable of executing complex tasks. Dahl noticed this and decided to try a new idea: non-blocking sockets in JavaScript. He took the V8 engine, wrapped it with the already solid C code, and created the first version of Node.js.

After a very warm response from the community, he went on to expand the Node core. The V8 engine wasn't built to run in a server environment, so Node.js had to extend it in a way that made more sense in a server context. For example, browsers don't usually need access to the filesystem, but when running server code, this becomes essential. The result was that Node.js wasn't just a JavaScript execution engine, but a platform capable of running complex JavaScript applications that were simple to code, highly efficient, and easily scalable.

io.js and the Node.js foundation

By the end of 2014, a conflict rose between Joyent, the company that owns the Node.js assets, and a group of core contributors to the project. This group of developers felt that the governance of the project was lacking, so they requested Joyent create a non-profit foundation that will govern the project. In January 2015, the group decided to fork the Node.js project and call it io.js. The new project aimed for faster and more predictable release cycles and was starting to gain some traction.

A few months later, the io.js team, backed by companies and community developers, was invited to Joyent's offices to discuss the future of the project. Together, they agreed on creating a Node foundation led by a Technical Steering Committee, merged the projects under the Node.js brand, and based it on the io.js repository. This led to a big upgrade in Node's release cycles and a more transparent governance of the project.

Node.js ES6 support

Although Node.js already implemented partial ES6 support in older versions, latest versions have been showing better progress in implementing ES6 features. For stability reasons, the Node V8 engine implements ES6 features in three classifications:

- **Shipping**: All features that are considered stable and are turned on by default. This means that they will *not* require any type of runtime flag to be activated.

- **Staged**: All features that are almost stable and are not recommended for production usage. These features can be activated using the `--es_staging` runtime flag or its better-known synonym, the `--harmony` flag.

- **In progress**: All features that are still under work and are not stable. These features can be activated using their respective `--harmony` flags.

While it is outside of this book's scope, it is recommend that you visit the official documentation at `https://nodejs.org/en/docs/es6/` to learn more about ES6 implementation in Node.js.

Node.js LTS support

As the Node.js community grew bigger, companies and larger organizations joined in, leading to a rising demand for stability and predictable version releases. In response to these new needs, the Node.js Foundation decided on a new release cycle. Basically, the team releases a new stable version every year in October. This version will always have an even version number such as v4 or v6. These stable versions are supported by the LTS plan. It includes security and stability updates and can be used in production once they enter the LTS plan in October. Every April, a stable version release is cut from the LTS plan. It means that there are always two active stable versions that overlap for a maximum period of 6 months and that every stable version is covered for 18 months. Odd number versions are considered not stable and are mainly used to present the community with an implementation of the road map. These versions are cut in October so that they can be merged to the new stable version in time.

A simple roadmap for the following few years' release cycle is shown here:

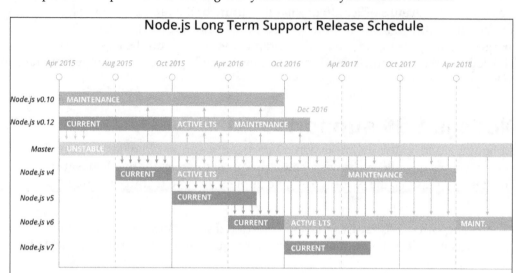

JavaScript event-driven programming

Node.js uses the event-driven nature of JavaScript to support non-blocking operations in the platform, a feature that enables its excellent efficiency. JavaScript is an event-driven language, which means that you register code to specific events, and this code will be executed once the event is emitted. This concept allows you to seamlessly execute asynchronous code without blocking the rest of the program from running.

To understand this better, take a look at the following Java code example:

```
System.out.print("What is your name?");
String name = System.console().readLine();
System.out.print("Your name is: " + name);
```

In this example, the program executes the first and second lines, but any code after the second line will not be executed until the user inputs their name. This is synchronous programming, where I/O operations block the rest of the program from running. However, this is not how JavaScript works.

As it was originally written to support browser operations, JavaScript was designed around browser events. Even though it has vastly evolved since its early days, the idea was to allow the browser to take the HTML user events and delegate them to JavaScript code. Let's have a look at the following HTML example:

```
<span>What is your name?</span>
<input type="text" id="nameInput">
<input type="button" id="showNameButton" value="Show Name">
<script type="text/javascript">
const showNameButton = document.getElementById('showNameButton');

showNameButton.addEventListener('click', (event) => {
    alert(document.getElementById('nameInput').value);
});

// Rest of your code...
</script>
```

In the preceding example, we have a textbox and a button. When the button is pressed, it will alert the value inside the textbox. The main function to watch here is the addEventListener() method. As you can see, it takes two arguments: the name of the event and an anonymous function that will run once the event is emitted. We usually refer to arguments of the latter kind as a *callback* function. Notice that any code after the addEventListener() method will execute accordingly, regardless of what we write in the callback function.

As simple as this example is, it illustrates well how JavaScript uses events to execute a set of commands. Since the browser is single-threaded, using synchronous programming in this example would freeze everything else on the page, which would make every web page extremely unresponsive and impair the web experience in general. Thankfully, this is not how it works. The browser manages a single thread to run the entire JavaScript code using an inner loop, commonly referred to as the event loop. The event loop is a single-threaded loop that the browser runs infinitely. Every time an event is emitted, the browser adds it to an event queue. The loop will then grab the next event from the queue in order to execute the event handlers registered to that event.

After all the event handlers are executed, the loop grabs the next event, executes its handlers, grabs another event, and so on. The event loop cycle is shown in the following diagram:

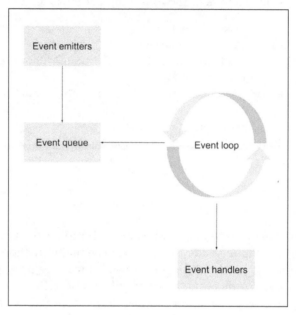

The event loop cycle

While the browser usually deals with user-generated events (such as button clicks), Node.js has to deal with various types of event that are generated from different sources.

Node.js event-driven programming

When developing web server logic, you will probably notice that a lot of your system resources are wasted on blocking code. For instance, let's observe the following PHP database interactions:

```
$output = mysql_query('SELECT * FROM Users');
echo($output);
```

Our server will try querying the database. The database will then perform the SELECT statement and return the result to the PHP code, which will eventually output the data as a response. The preceding code blocks any other operation until it gets the result from the database. This means the process, or more commonly the thread, will stay idle, consuming system resources while it waits for other processes.

To solve this issue, many web platforms have implemented a thread pool system that usually issues a single thread per connection. This kind of multithreading may seem intuitive at first, but has some significant disadvantages. They are as follows:

- Managing threads becomes a complex task
- System resources are wasted on idle threads
- Scaling these kinds of applications cannot be done easily

This is tolerable while developing one-sided web applications, where the browser makes a quick request that ends with a server response. However, what happens when you want to build real-time applications that keep a long-living connection between the browser and the server? To understand the real-life consequences of these design choices, take a look at the following graphs. They present a famous performance comparison between Apache, which is a blocking web server, and NGINX, which uses a non-blocking event loop. The following screenshot shows concurrent request handling in Apache versus NGINX (http://blog.webfaction.com/2008/12/a-little-holiday-present-10000-reqssec-with-nginx-2/):

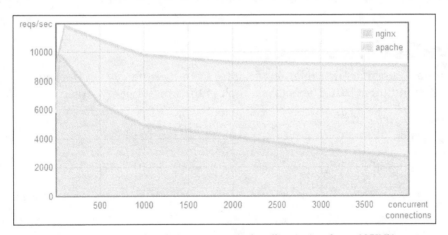

Concurrent connections impact on request handling in Apache vs. NGINX.

In the preceding diagram, you can see how Apache's request-handling ability is degrading much faster than NGINX's ability. An even clearer impact can be seen in the following diagram, where you can see how NGINX's event loop architecture affects memory consumption:

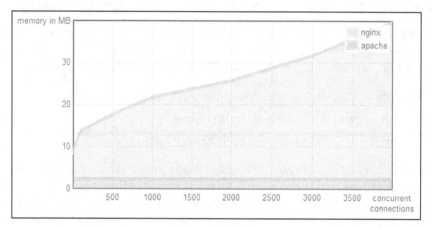

Concurrent connections impact on memory allocation in Apache vs. NGINX.

As you can see from the results, using event-driven architecture will help you dramatically reduce the load on your server while leveraging JavaScript's asynchronous behavior in building your web application. An approach that is easier to implement thanks to a simple design pattern called **Closures**.

JavaScript Closures

Closures are functions that refer to variables from their parent environment. To understand them better, let's take a look at the following example:

```
function parent() {
    const message = 'Hello World';

    function child() {
        alert (message);
    }

    child();
}

parent();
```

In the preceding example, you can see how the child() function has access to a constant defined in the parent() function. However, this is a simple example, so let's look at a more interesting one:

```
function parent() {
   const message = 'Hello World';

    function child() {
    alert (message);
  }

   return child;
}

const childFN = parent();
childFN();
```

This time, the parent() function returned the child() function, and the child() function is called after the parent() function has already been executed. This is counterintuitive to some developers because usually the parent() function's local members should only exist while the function is being executed. This is what closures are all about! A closure is not only the function, but also the environment in which the function was created. In this case, childFN() is a closure object that consists of the child() function and the environment members that existed when the closure was created, including the message constant.

Closures are very important in asynchronous programming because JavaScript functions are first-class objects that can be passed as arguments to other functions. This means that you can create a callback function and pass it as an argument to an event handler. When the event will be emitted, the function will be invoked, and it will be able to manipulate any member that existed when the callback function was created, even if its parent function was already executed. This means that using the closure pattern will help you utilize event-driven programming without the need to pass the scope state to the event handler.

Node modules

JavaScript has turned out to be a powerful language with some unique features that enable efficient yet maintainable programming. Its closure pattern and event-driven behavior have proven to be very helpful in real-life scenarios, but like all programming languages, it isn't perfect. One of its major design flaws is the sharing of a single global namespace.

To understand this problem, we need to go back to JavaScript's browser origins. In the browser, when you load a script into your web page, the engine will inject its code into an address space that is shared by all the other scripts. This means that when you assign a variable in one script, you can accidently overwrite another variable already defined in a previous script. While this could work with a small code base, it can easily cause conflicts in larger applications, as errors will be difficult to trace. It could have been a major threat for Node.js evolution as a platform, but luckily, a solution was found in the CommonJS module standard.

CommonJS modules

CommonJS is a project started in 2009 to standardize the way of working with JavaScript outside the browser. The project has evolved since then to support a variety of JavaScript issues, including the global namespace issue, which was solved through a simple specification of how to write and include isolated JavaScript modules.

The CommonJS standards specify the following key components when working with modules:

- `require()`: A method that is used to load the module into your code.
- `exports`: An object that's contained in each module and allows you to expose pieces of your code when the module is loaded.
- `module`: An object that was originally used to provide metadata information about the module. It also contains the pointer of an `exports` object as a property. However, the popular implementation of the `exports` object as a standalone object literally changed the use case of the `module` object.

In Node's CommonJS module implementation, each module is written in a single JavaScript file and has an isolated scope that holds its own members. The author of the module can expose any functionality through the `exports` object. To understand this better, let's say we created a module file named `hello.js` that contains the following code snippet:

```
const message = 'Hello';

exports.sayHello = function(){
  console.log(message);
}
```

We also created an application file named `server.js`, which contains this code:

```
const hello = require('./hello');
hello.sayHello();
```

In the preceding example, you have the `hello` module, which contains a constant named `message`. The message constant is self-contained within the `hello` module, which only exposes the `sayHello()` method by defining it as a property of the `exports` object. Then, the application file loads the `hello` module using the `require()` method, which allows it to call the `sayHello()` method of the `hello` module.

A different approach to creating modules is exposing a single function using the `module.exports` pointer. To understand this better, let's revise the preceding example. A modified `hello.js` file should look like this:

```
module.exports = function() {
  const message = 'Hello';

  console.log(message);
}
```

Then, the module is loaded in the `server.js` file as follows:

```
const hello = require('./hello');
hello();
```

In the preceding example, the application file uses the `hello` module directly as a function, instead of using the `sayHello()` method as a property of the `hello` module.

The CommonJS module standard allows the endless extension of the Node.js platform, while preventing the pollution of Node's core. Without it, the Node.js platform would become a mess of conflicts. However, not all modules are the same, and while developing a Node application, you will encounter several types of module.

 You can omit the `.js` extension when you need modules. Node will automatically look for a folder with that name, and if it doesn't find one, it will look for an applicable `.js` file.

Node.js core modules

Core modules are modules that were compiled into the Node binary. They come pre-bundled with Node and are explained in great detail in its documentation. The core modules provide most of the basic functionalities of Node, including filesystem access, HTTP and HTTPS interfaces, and much more. To load a core module, you just need to use the `require` method in your JavaScript file.

An example code, using the `fs` core module to read the content of the environment hosts file, would look like the following code snippet:

```
const fs = require('fs');

fs.readFile('/etc/hosts', 'utf8', (err, data) => {
  if (err) {
   return console.log(err);
  }

  console.log(data);
});
```

When you require the `fs` module, Node will find it in the `core modules` folder. You'll then be able to use the `fs.readFile()` method to read the file's content and print it in the command-line output.

 To learn more about Node's core modules, it is recommended you visit the official documentation at `http://nodejs.org/api/`.

Node.js third-party modules

In the previous chapter, you learned how to use npm to install third-party modules. As you probably remember, npm installs these modules in a folder named `node_modules` under the root folder of your application. To use third-party modules, you can just require them as you would normally require a core module. Node will first look for the module in the `core modules` folder and then try to load the module from the `module` folder inside the `node_modules` folder. For instance, to use the `express` module, your code should look like the following code snippet:

```
const express = require('express');
const app = express();
```

Node will then look for the `express` module in the `node_modules` folder and load it into your application file, where you'll be able to use it as a method to generate the `express` application object.

Node.js file modules

In the previous examples, you saw how Node loads modules directly from files. These examples describe a scenario where the files reside in the same folder. However, you can also place your modules inside a folder and load them by providing the folder path. Let's say you moved your `hello` module to a `modules` folder. The application file would have to change, so Node would look for the module in the new relative path:

```
const hello = require('./modules/hello');
```

Note that the path can also be an absolute path, as follows:

```
const hello = require('/home/projects/first-
  example/modules/hello');
```

Node will then look for the `hello` module in that path.

Node.js folder modules

Although this is not common with developers who aren't writing third-party Node modules, Node also supports the loading of folder modules. Requiring folder modules is done in the same way as file modules, as follows:

```
const hello = require('./modules/hello');
```

Now, if a folder named `hello` exists, Node will go through that folder looking for a `package.json` file. If Node finds a `package.json` file, it will try parsing it, looking for the main property, with a `package.json` file that looks like the following code snippet:

```
{
  "name": "hello",
  "version": "1.0.0",
  "main": "./hello-module.js"
}
```

Node will try to load the `./hello/hello-module.js` file. If the `package.json` file doesn't exist or the main property isn't defined, Node will automatically try to load the `./hello/index.js` file.

Node.js modules have been found to be a great solution to write complex JavaScript applications. They have helped developers organize their code better, while npm and its third-party module registry helped them find and install one of the many third-party modules created by the community. Ryan Dahl's dream of building a better web framework ended up as a platform that supports a huge variety of solutions. However, the dream was not abandoned; it was just implemented as a third-party module named `express`.

Developing Node.js web applications

Node.js is a platform that supports various types of application, but the most popular kind is the development of web applications. Node's style of coding depends on the community to extend the platform through third-party modules. These modules are then built upon to create new modules, and so on. Companies and single developers around the globe are participating in this process by creating modules that wrap the basic Node APIs and deliver a better starting point for application development.

There are many modules to support web application development, but none as popular as the Connect module. The Connect module delivers a set of wrappers around the Node.js low-level APIs to enable the development of rich web application frameworks. To understand what Connect is all about, let's begin with a basic example of a basic Node web server. In your working folder, create a file named `server.js` that contains the following code snippet:

```
const http = require('http');

http.createServer(function(req, res) => {
  res.writeHead(200, {
    'Content-Type': 'text/plain'
  });
  res.end('Hello World');
}).listen(3000);

console.log('Server running at http://localhost:3000/');
```

To start your web server, use your command-line tool and navigate to your working folder. Then, run the Node.js CLI tool and run the `server.js` file as follows:

$ node server

Now, open `http://localhost:3000` in your browser and you'll see the **Hello World** response.

So, how does this work? In this example, the `http` module is used to create a small web server listening to the `3000` port. You begin by requiring the `http` module and then use the `createServer()` method to return a new server object. The `listen()` method is then used to listen to the `3000` port. Notice the callback function that is passed as an argument to the `createServer()` method.

The callback function gets called whenever there's an HTTP request sent to the web server. The server object will then pass it the `req` and `res` arguments, which contain the information and functionality needed to send back an HTTP response. The callback function will then follow these two steps:

1. First, it will call the `writeHead()` method of the `res` object. This method is used to set the response HTTP headers. In this example, it will set the content-type header value to `text/plain`. For instance, when responding with HTML, you just need to replace `text/plain` with `html/plain`.

2. Then, it will call the `end()` method of the `res` object. This method is used to finalize the response. The `end()` method takes a single-string argument that it will use as the HTTP response body. Another common way of writing this is to add a `write()` method before the `end()` method and then call the `end()` method as follows:

```
res.write('Hello World');
res.end();
```

This simple application illustrates the Node coding style, where low-level APIs are used to simply achieve certain functionality. While this is a nice example, running a full web application using the low-level APIs will require you to write a lot of supplementary code to support common requirements. Fortunately, a company called Sencha has already created this scaffolding code for you in the form of a Node.js module called Connect.

Meet the Connect module

Connect is a module built to support the interception of requests in a more modular approach. In the first web server example, you learned how to build a simple web server using the `http` module. If you wish to extend this example, you'd have to write code that manages the different HTTP requests sent to your server, handles them properly, and provides the correct response to each request.

Connect creates an API exactly for that purpose. It uses a modular component called *middleware*, which allows you to simply register your application logic to predefined HTTP request scenarios. Connect middlewares are basically callback functions, which get executed when an HTTP request occurs. The middleware can then perform some logic, return a response, or call the next registered middleware.

While you will mostly write custom middleware to support your application needs, Connect also includes some common middleware to support logging, static file serving, and more.

The way a Connect application works is using an object called *dispatcher*. The dispatcher object handles each HTTP request received by the server and then decides the order of middleware execution in a cascading form. To understand Connect better, take a look at the following diagram:

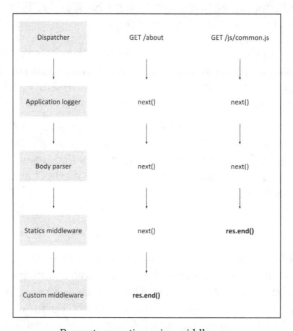

Requests execution using middleware

The preceding diagram illustrates two calls made to the Connect application: the first is handled by a custom middleware and the second is handled by the static files middleware. Connect's dispatcher initiates the process, moving on to the next handler using the next() method, until it gets to a middleware responding with the res.end() method, which will end the request handling.

In the next chapter, you'll create your first Express application, but Express is based on Connect's approach. So, in order to understand how Express works, we'll begin by creating a Connect application.

In your working folder, create a file named server.js that contains the following code snippet:

```
const connect = require('connect');
const app = connect();
```

```
app.listen(3000);

console.log('Server running at http://localhost:3000/');
```

As you can see, your application file is using the connect module to create a new web server. However, Connect isn't a core module, so you'll have to install it using npm. As you already know, there are several ways of installing third-party modules. The easiest one is to install it directly using the npm install command. To do so, use your command-line tool, and navigate to your working folder. Then, execute the following command:

```
$ npm install connect
```

npm will install the connect module inside a node_modules folder, which will enable you to require it in your application file. To run your Connect web server, just use Node's CLI and execute the following command:

```
$ node server
```

Node will run your application, reporting the server status using the console.log() method. You can try reaching your application in the browser by visiting http://localhost:3000. However, you should get a response similar to what is shown in the following screenshot:

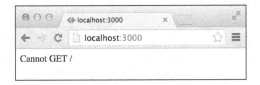

What this response means is that there isn't any middleware registered to handle the GET HTTP request. This means that first, you've successfully managed to install and use the Connect module, and second, it's time for you to write your first Connect middleware.

Connect middleware

Connect middleware is basically a JavaScript function with a unique signature. Each middleware function is defined with the following three arguments:

- req: This is an object that holds the HTTP request information
- res: This is an object that holds the HTTP response information and allows you to set the response properties
- next: This is the next middleware function defined in the ordered set of Connect middleware

When you have a middleware defined, you'll just have to register it with the Connect application using the `app.use()` method. Let's revise the previous example to include your first middleware. Change your `server.js` file to look like the following code snippet:

```
const connect = require('connect');
const app = connect();

function helloWorld(req, res, next) {
  res.setHeader('Content-Type', 'text/plain');
  res.end('Hello World');
};
app.use(helloWorld);

app.listen(3000);
console.log('Server running at http://localhost:3000/');
```

Then, start your Connect server again by issuing the following command in your command-line tool:

```
$ node server
```

Try visiting `http://localhost:3000` again. You will now get a response similar to that in the following screenshot:

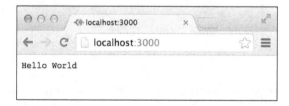

If you see the Connect application's response as that of the previous screenshot, then congratulations! You've just created your first Connect middleware!

Let's recap. First, you added a middleware function named `helloWorld()`, which has three arguments: `req`, `res`, and `next`. Inside your middleware function, you used the `res.setHeader()` method to set the response `Content-Type` header and the `res.end()` method to set the response text. Finally, you used the `app.use()` method to register your middleware with the Connect application.

Understanding the order of Connect middleware

One of Connect's greatest features is the ability to register as many middleware functions as you want. Using the app.use() method, you'll be able to set a series of middleware functions that will be executed in a row to achieve maximum flexibility when writing your application. Connect will then pass the next middleware function to the currently executing middleware function, using the next argument. In each middleware function, you can decide whether to call the next middleware function or stop at the current one. Notice that each middleware function will be executed in a **First-In-First-Out (FIFO)** basis using the next arguments, until there are no more middleware functions to execute or the next middleware function is not called.

To understand this better, we will go back to the previous example and add a logger function that will log all the requests made to the server in the command line. To do so, go back to the server.js file and update it as follows:

```
const connect = require('connect');
const app = connect();

function logger(req, res, next) {
  console.log(req.method, req.url);
  next();
};

function helloWorld(req, res, next) {
  res.setHeader('Content-Type', 'text/plain');
  res.end('Hello World');
};

app.use(logger);
app.use(helloWorld);
app.listen(3000);

console.log('Server running at http://localhost:3000/');
```

In the preceding example, you added another middleware called logger(). The logger() middleware uses the console.log() method to simply log the request information to the console. Notice how the logger() middleware is registered before the helloWorld() middleware. This is important, as it determines the order in which each middleware is executed. Another thing to notice is the next() call in the logger() middleware, which is responsible for calling the helloWorld() middleware. Removing the next() call would stop the execution of middleware functions at the logger() middleware, which means that the request would hang forever as the response is never ended by calling the res.end() method.

To test your changes, start your Connect server again by issuing the following command in your command-line tool:

```
$ node server
```

Then, visit http://localhost:3000 in your browser and notice the console output in your command-line tool.

Mounting Connect middleware

As you may have noticed, the middleware you registered responds to any request, regardless of the request path. This does not comply with modern web application development because responding to different paths is an integral part of all web applications. Fortunately, Connect middleware supports a feature called mounting, which enables you to determine which request path is required for the middleware function to get executed. Mounting is done by adding the path argument to the app.use() method. To understand this better, let's revisit our previous example. Modify your server.js file to look like the following code snippet:

```
const connect = require('connect');
const app = connect();

function logger(req, res, next) {
  console.log(req.method, req.url);

  next();
};

function helloWorld(req, res, next) {
  res.setHeader('Content-Type', 'text/plain');
  res.end('Hello World');
};

function goodbyeWorld(req, res, next) {
  res.setHeader('Content-Type', 'text/plain');
  res.end('Goodbye World');
};

app.use(logger);
app.use('/hello', helloWorld);
app.use('/goodbye', goodbyeWorld);
app.listen(3000);

console.log('Server running at http://localhost:3000/');
```

A few things have been changed in the previous example. First, you mounted the `helloWorld()` middleware to respond only to requests made to the `/hello` path. Then, you added another (a bit morbid) middleware called `goodbyeWorld()` that will respond to requests made to the `/goodbye` path. Notice how, as a logger should do, we left the `logger()` middleware to respond to all the requests made to the server. Another thing you should be aware of is that any requests made to the base path will not be responded to by any middleware because we mounted the `helloWorld()` middleware to a specific path.

Connect is a great module that supports various features of common web applications. Connect middleware is super simple, as it is built with a JavaScript style in mind. It allows the endless extension of your application logic without breaking the nimble philosophy of the Node platform. While Connect is a great improvement over writing your web application infrastructure, it deliberately lacks some basic features you're used to having in other web frameworks. The reason lies in one of the basic principles of the Node community: create your modules lean and let other developers build their modules on top of the module you created. The community is supposed to extend Connect with its own modules and create its own web infrastructures. In fact, one very energetic developer named TJ Holowaychuk did it better than most when he released a Connect-based web framework known as Express.

Summary

In this chapter, you learned how Node.js harnesses JavaScript's event-driven behavior to its benefit. You also learned how Node.js uses the CommonJS module system to extend its core functionality. Moreover, you learned about the basic principles of Node.js web applications and discovered the Connect web module. Finally, you created your first Connect application and learned how to use middleware functions.

In the next chapter, we'll tackle the first piece of the MEAN puzzle, when we discuss the Connect-based web framework called Express.

3
Building an Express Web Application

This chapter will cover the proper way to build your first Express application. You'll begin by installing and configuring the Express module and then learning about Express' main APIs. We'll discuss Express request, response, and application objects and learn how to use them. We'll then cover the Express routing mechanism and learn how to properly use it. We'll also discuss the structure of the application folder and how you can utilize different structures for different project types. By the end of this chapter, you'll learn how to build a complete Express application. In this chapter, we'll cover the following topics:

- Installing Express and creating a new Express application
- Organizing your project's structure
- Configuring your Express application
- Using the Express routing mechanism
- Rendering EJS views
- Serving static files
- Configuring an Express session

Introducing Express

To say that TJ Holowaychuk is a productive developer would be a huge understatement. TJ's involvement in the Node.js community is almost unmatched by any other developer, and with more than 500 open source projects, he's responsible for some of the most popular frameworks in the JavaScript ecosystem.

One of his greatest projects is the Express web framework. The Express framework is a small set of common web application features kept to a minimum in order to maintain the Node.js style. It is built on top of Connect and makes use of its middleware architecture. Its features extend Connect to allow a variety of common web application use cases, such as the inclusion of modular HTML template engines, extending the response object to support various data format outputs, a routing system, and much more.

So far, we have used a single `server.js` file to create our application. However, when using Express, you'll learn more about better project structure, properly configuring your application, and breaking your application logic into different modules. You'll also learn how to use the EJS template engine, manage sessions, and add a routing scheme. By the end of this section, you'll have a working application skeleton that you'll use for the rest of the book. Let's begin the journey of creating your first Express application.

Installing Express

Up until now, we used npm to directly install external modules for our Node application. You could, of course, use this approach and install Express by typing the following command:

```
$ npm install express
```

However, directly installing modules isn't really scalable. Think about it for a bit: you're going to use many Node modules in your application, transfer it between working environments, and probably share it with other developers. So, installing the project modules this way will soon become a dreadful task. Instead, you should start using the `package.json` file, which organizes your project metadata and helps you manage your application dependencies. Begin by creating a new working folder and a new `package.json` file inside it, which contains the following code snippet:

```
{
  "name" : "MEAN",
  "version" : "0.0.3",
  "dependencies" : {
    "express" : "4.14.0"
```

```
    }
  }
```

In the package.json file, note that you included three properties: the name and version of your application and the dependencies property, which defines what modules should be installed before your application can run. To install your application dependencies, use your command-line tool and navigate to your application folder, and then issue the following command:

```
$ npm install
```

npm will then install the Express module because, currently, it is the only dependency defined in your package.json file.

Creating your first Express application

After creating your package.json file and installing your dependencies, you can create your first Express application by adding your already familiar server.js file with the following lines of code:

```
const express = require('express');
const app = express();

app.use('/', (req, res) => {
  res.status(200).send('Hello World');
});

app.listen(3000);
console.log('Server running at http://localhost:3000/');

module.exports = app;
```

You should have already recognized most of the code. The first two lines require the Express module and create a new Express application object. Then, we use the app. use() method to mount a middleware function with a specific path and the app. listen() method to tell the Express application to listen to port 3000. Note how the module.exports object is used to return the app object. This will later help you load and test your Express application.

This new code should also be familiar to you because it resembles the code you used in the previous Connect example. This is because Express wraps the Connect module in several ways. The app.use() method is used to mount a middleware function, which will respond to any HTTP request made to the root path. Inside the middleware function, the res.status() method is then used to set the HTTP response code, and the res.send() method is used to send the response back. The res.send() method is basically an Express wrapper that sets the Content-Type header according to the response object type and then sends a response back using the Connect res.end() method.

> When passing a buffer to the res.send() method, the Content-Type header will be set to application/octet-stream; when passing a string, it will be set to text/html; and when passing an object or an array, it will be set to application/json.

To run your application, simply execute the following command in your command-line tool:

```
$ node server
```

Congratulations! You have just created your first Express application. You can test it by visiting http://localhost:3000 in your browser.

The application, request, and response objects

Express presents three major objects that you'll frequently use. The application object is the instance of an Express application you created in the first example and is usually used to configure your application. The request object is a wrapper of Node's HTTP request object and is used to extract information about the currently handled HTTP request. The response object is a wrapper of Node's HTTP response object and is used to set the response data and headers.

The application object

·The application object contains the following methods to help you configure your application:

- app.set(name, value): This is a method used to set environment variables that Express will use in its configuration.

- app.get(name): This is a method used to get environment variables that Express is using in its configuration.

- `app.engine(ext, callback)`: This is a method used to define a given template engine to render certain file types; for example, you can tell the EJS template engine to use HTML files as templates like this: `app.engine('html', require('ejs').renderFile)`.

- `app.locals`: This is a property used to send application-level variables to all rendered templates.

- `app.use([path], callback)`: This is a method used to create an Express middleware to handle HTTP requests sent to the server. Optionally, you'll be able to mount middleware to respond to certain paths.

- `app.VERB(path, [callback...], callback)`: This is used to define one or more middleware functions to respond to HTTP requests made to a certain path in conjunction with the HTTP verb declared. For instance, when you want to respond to requests that are using the GET verb, you can just assign the middleware using the `app.get()` method. For POST requests, you'll use `app.post()`, and so on.

- `app.route(path).VERB([callback...], callback)`: This is a method used to define one or more middleware functions to respond to HTTP requests made to a certain unified path in conjunction with multiple HTTP verbs. For instance, when you want to respond to requests that are using the GET and POST verbs, you can just assign the appropriate middleware functions using `app.route(path).get(callback).post(callback)`.

- `app.param([name], callback)`: This is a method used to attach a certain functionality to any request made to a path that includes a certain routing parameter. For instance, you can map logic to any request that includes the `userId` parameter using `app.param('userId', callback)`.

There are many more application methods and properties you can use, but using these common basic methods enables developers to extend Express in whichever way they find reasonable.

The request object

The request object also provides a handful of helping methods that contain the information you need about the current HTTP request. The key properties and methods of the request object are as follows:

- `req.query`: This is a property that contains the parsed query-string parameters.

- `req.params`: This is a property that contains the parsed routing parameters.

- `req.body`: This is a property that's used to retrieve the parsed request body. It is included in the `bodyParser()` middleware.

- `req.path` / `req.hostname` / `req.ip`: These are used to retrieve the current request path, hostname, and remote IP.

- `req.cookies`: This is a property used in conjunction with the `cookieParser()` middleware to retrieve the cookies sent by the user agent.

The request object contains many more methods and properties that we'll discuss later in this book, but these methods are what you'll usually use in a common web application.

The response object

The response object is frequently used when developing an Express application because any request sent to the server will be handled and responded to using the response object methods. It has several key methods, which are as follows:

- `res.status(code)`: This is a method used to set the response HTTP status code.

- `res.set(field, [value])`: This is a method used to set the response HTTP header.

- `res.cookie(name, value, [options])`: This is a method used to set a response cookie. The options argument is used to pass an object that defines common cookie configuration, such as the `maxAge` property.

- `res.redirect([status], url)`: This is a method used to redirect the request to a given URL. Note that you can add an HTTP status code to the response. When not passing a status code, it will be defaulted to `302 Found`.

- `res.status([status]).send([body])`: This is a method used for non-streaming responses. It does a lot of background work, such as setting the Content-Type and Content-Length headers and responding with the proper cache headers.

- `res.status([status]).json([body])`: This is identical to the `res.send()` method when sending an object or array. Most of the time, it is used as syntactic sugar, but sometimes you may need to use it to force a JSON response to non-objects, such as `null` or `undefined`.

- `res.render(view, [locals], callback)`: This is a method used to render a view and send an HTML response.

The response object also contains many more methods and properties to handle different response scenarios, which you'll learn about later in this book.

External middleware

The Express core is minimal, yet the team behind it provides various predefined middleware to handle common web development features. These types of middleware vary in size and functionality and extend Express to provide a better framework support. The popular Express middleware are as follows:

- `morgan`: This is an HTTP request logger middleware.

- `body-parser`: This is a body-parsing middleware that is used to parse the request body, and it supports various request types.

- `method-override`: This is a middleware that provides HTTP verb support, such as PUT or DELETE, in places where the client doesn't support it.

- `compression`: This is a compression middleware that is used to compress the response data using GZIP/deflate.

- `express.static`: This is a middleware used to serve static files.

- `cookie-parser`: This is a cookie-parsing middleware that populates the `req.cookies` object.

- `Session`: This is a session middleware used to support persistent sessions.

There are many more types of Express middleware that enable you to shorten your development time along with a larger number of third-party middleware.

 To learn more about the Connect and Express middleware, visit the Connect module's official repository page at `https://github.com/senchalabs/connect#middleware`. If you'd like to browse the third-party middleware collection, visit Connect's wiki page at `https://github.com/senchalabs/connect/wiki`.

Implementing the MVC pattern

The Express framework is pattern-agnostic, which means that it doesn't support any predefined syntax or structure, as some other web frameworks do. Applying the MVC pattern to your Express application means that you can create specific folders where you place your JavaScript files in a certain logical order. All these files are basically CommonJS modules that function as logical units. For instance, models will be CommonJS modules that contain a definition of Mongoose models placed in the `models` folder, views will be HTML or other template files placed in the `views` folder, and controllers will be CommonJS modules with functional methods placed in the `controllers` folder. To illustrate this better, it's time to discuss the different types of application structure.

The application folder structure

We previously discussed better practices when developing a real application, where we recommended the use of the `package.json` file over directly installing your modules. However, this was only the beginning; once you continue developing your application, you'll soon find yourself wondering how you should arrange your project files and break them into logical units of code. JavaScript, in general, and—consequently—the Express framework are agnostic about the structure of your application as you can easily place your entire application in a single JavaScript file. This is because no one expected JavaScript to be a full-stack programming language, but it doesn't mean that you shouldn't dedicate special attention to organizing your project. Since the MEAN stack can be used to build all sorts of applications that vary in size and complexity, it is also possible to handle the project structure in various ways. The decision is often directly related to the estimated complexity of your application. For instance, simple projects may require a leaner folder structure, which has the advantage of being clearer and easier to manage, while complex projects will often require a more complex structure and a better breakdown of logic since it will include many features and a bigger team working on the project. To simplify this discussion, it would be reasonable to divide it into two major approaches: a horizontal structure for smaller projects and a vertical structure for feature-rich applications. Let's begin with a simple horizontal structure.

Horizontal folder structure

A horizontal project structure is based on the division of folders and files by their functional role rather than by the feature they implement, which means that all the application files are placed inside a main application folder that contains an MVC folder structure. This also means that there is a single `controllers` folder that contains all of the application controllers, a single `models` folder that contains all of the application models, and so on. An example of the horizontal application structure would be as follows:

Let's review the folder structure:

- The app folder is where you keep your Express application logic, and it is divided into the following folders that represent a separation of functionality in order to comply with the MVC pattern:

    ○ The controllers folder is where you keep your Express application controllers

    ○ The models folder is where you keep your Express application models

    ○ The routes folder is where you keep your Express application routing middleware

    ○ The views folder is where you keep your Express application views

- The config folder is where you keep your Express application configuration files. In time, you'll add more modules to your application, and each module will be configured in a dedicated JavaScript file, which is placed inside this folder. Currently, it contains several files and folders, which are as follows:

    ○ The env folder is where you'll keep your Express application environment's configuration files

- The `config.js` file is where you'll configure your Express application

- The `express.js` file is where you'll initialize your Express application

- The `public` folder is where you keep your static client-side files, and it is divided into the following folders that represent a separation of functionalities in order to comply with the MVC pattern:

  - The `config` folder is where you keep your Angular application configuration files

  - The `components` folder is where you keep your Angular application components

  - The `css` folder is where you keep your CSS files

  - The `directives` folder is where you keep your Angular application directives

  - The `pipes` folder is where you keep your Angular application pipes

  - The `img` folder is where you keep your image files

  - The `templates` folder is where you keep your Angular application templates

  - The `bootstrap.ts` file is where you initialize your Angular application

- The `package.json` file is the metadata file that helps you organize your application dependencies.

- The `server.js` file is the main file of your Node.js application, and it will load the `express.js` file as a module in order to bootstrap your Express application.

As you can see, the horizontal folder structure is very useful for small projects where the number of features is limited so that files can be conveniently placed inside folders that represent their general roles. Nevertheless, in order to handle large projects, where you'll have many files that handle certain features, it might be too simplistic. In this case, each folder could be overloaded with too many files, and you'd get lost in the chaos. A better approach would be to use a vertical folder structure.

Vertical folder structure

A vertical project structure is based on the division of folders and files by the feature they implement, which means that each feature has its own autonomous folder that contains an MVC folder structure. An example of the vertical application structure would be as follows:

As you can see, each feature has its own application-like folder structure. In this example, we have the `core feature` folder that contains the main application files and the `feature` folder that includes the feature's files. An example feature will be a user management feature that includes authentication and authorization logic. To understand this better, let's review a single feature's folder structure:

- The `server` folder is where you keep your feature's server logic, and it is divided into the following folders that represent a separation of functionality in order to comply with the MVC pattern:
    - The `controllers` folder is where you keep your feature's Express controllers
    - The `models` folder is where you keep your feature's Express models
    - The `routes` folder is where you keep your feature's Express routing middleware
    - The `views` folder is where you keep your feature's Express views
    - The `config` folder is where you keep your feature's server configuration files
    - The `env` folder is where you keep your feature's environment server configuration files
    - The `feature.server.config.js` file is where you configure your features

- The `client` folder is where you keep your feature's client-side files, and it is divided into the following folders that represent a separation of functionality in order to comply with the MVC pattern:
    - The `config` folder is where you keep your feature's Angular configuration files
    - The `components` folder is where you keep your feature's Angular `components`
    - The `css` folder is where you keep your feature's CSS files
    - The `directives` folder is where you keep your feature's Angular directives
    - The `pipes` folder is where you keep your feature's Angular pipes
    - The `img` folder is where you keep your feature's image files
    - The `templates` folder is where you keep your feature's Angular templates
    - The `feature.module.ts` file is where you initialize your feature's Angular module

As you can see, the vertical folder structure is very useful for large projects where the number of features is unlimited and each feature includes a substantial number of files. It will allow large teams to work together and maintain each feature separately, and it can also be useful in sharing features among different applications.

Although these are two distinctive types of most application structures, the reality is that the MEAN stack can be assembled in many different ways. It's even likely for a team to structure their project in a way that combines these two approaches; so essentially, it is up to the project leader to decide which structure to use. In this book, we'll use the horizontal approach for reasons of simplicity, but we'll incorporate the Angular part of our application in a vertical manner to demonstrate the flexibility of the MEAN stack's structure. Keep in mind that everything presented in this book can be easily restructured to accommodate your project's specifications.

File-naming conventions

While developing your application, you'll soon notice that you end up with many files with the same name. The reason is that MEAN applications often have a parallel MVC structure for both the Express and Angular components. To understand this issue, take a look at a common vertical feature's folder structure:

As you can see, enforcing the folder structure helps you understand each file's functionality, but it will also cause several files to have the same name. This is because an application's feature is usually implemented using several JavaScript files, each having a different role. This issue can cause some confusion for the development team, so to solve this, you'll need to use some sort of a naming convention.

The simplest solution would be to add each file's functional role to the filename. So, a feature controller file will be named `feature.controller.js`, a feature model file will be named `feature.model.js`, and so on. However, things get even more complicated when you consider the fact that MEAN applications use JavaScript MVC files for both Express and Angular applications. This means that you'll often have two files with the same name. To solve this issue, it is also recommended that you extend file names with their execution destination. This might seem like overkill at first, but you'll soon discover that it's quite helpful to quickly identify the role and execution destination of your application files.

It is important to remember that this is a best practice convention. You can easily replace the `controller`, `model`, `client`, and `server` keywords with your own keywords.

Implementing the horizontal folder structure

To begin the structuring of your first MEAN project, create a new project folder with the following folders inside it:

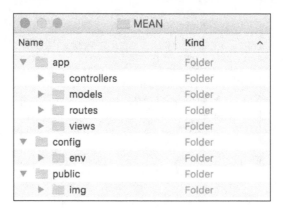

Once you have created all the preceding folders, go back to the application's root folder and create a `package.json` file that contains the following code snippet:

```
{
  "name" : "MEAN",
  "version" : "0.0.3",
  "dependencies" : {
    "express" : "4.14.0"
  }
}
```

Now, in the `app/controllers` folder, create a file named `index.server.controller.js` with the following lines of code:

```
exports.render = function(req, res) {
  res.status(200).send('Hello World');
};
```

Congratulations! You just created your first Express controller. This code probably looks very familiar; that's because it's a copy of the middleware you created in the previous examples. What you do here is use the CommonJS module pattern to define a function named `render()`. Later on, you'll be able to acquire this module and use this function. Once you've created a controller, you'll need to use an Express-routing functionality to utilize the controller.

Handling request routing

Express supports the routing of requests using either the `app.route(path).VERB(callback)` method or the `app.VERB(path, callback)` method, where VERB should be replaced with a lowercase HTTP verb. Take a look at the following example:

```
app.get('/', (req, res) => {
  res.status(200).send('This is a GET request');
});
```

This tells Express to execute the middleware function for any HTTP request using the GET verb and directed to the root path. If you'd like to deal with POST requests, your code should be as follows:

```
app.post('/', (req, res) => {
  res.status(200).send('This is a POST request');
});
```

However, Express also enables you to define a single route and then chain several middleware to handle different HTTP requests. This means that the preceding code example can also be written as follows:

```
app.route('/').get((req, res) => {
  res.status(200).send('This is a GET request');
}).post((req, res) => {
  res.status(200).send('This is a POST request');
});
```

Another cool feature of Express is its ability to chain several middleware in a single routing definition. This means that middleware functions will be called in an order, passing them to the next middleware so that you can determine how to proceed with middleware execution. This is usually used to validate requests before executing the response logic. To understand this better, take a look at the following code:

```
const express = require('express');

function hasName(req, res, next) {
  if (req.param('name')) {
    next();
  } else {
    res.status(200).send('What is your name?');
  }
};

function sayHello(req, res, next) {
  res.status(200).send('Hello ' + req.param('name'));
}

const app = express();
app.get('/', hasName, sayHello);

app.listen(3000);
console.log('Server running at http://localhost:3000/');
```

In the preceding code, there are two middleware functions named hasName() and sayHello(). The hasName() middleware is looking for the name parameter; if it finds a defined name parameter, it will call the next middleware function using the next argument. Otherwise, the hasName() middleware will handle the response by itself. In this case, the next middleware function would be the sayHello() middleware function. This is possible because we've added the middleware function in a row using the app.get() method. It is also worth noting the order of the middleware functions because it determines which middleware function is executed first.

This example demonstrates well how routing middleware can be used to perform different validations when determining what the response should be. You can, of course, leverage this functionality to perform other tasks, such as validating user authentication and resources' authorization. For now, though, let's just continue with our example.

Adding the routing file

The next file you're going to create is your first routing file. In the app/routes folder, create a file named index.server.routes.js with the following code snippet:

```
module.exports = function(app) {
    const index = require('../controllers/index.server.controller');
    app.get('/', index.render);
};
```

Here, you did a few things. First, you used the CommonJS module pattern again. As you may remember, the CommonJS module pattern supports both the exporting of several functions, such as what you did with your controller, and the use of a single module function, such as what you did here. Next, you required your index controller and used its render() method as a middleware to GET requests made to the root path.

 The routing module function accepts a single argument called app, so when you call this function, you'll need to pass it the instance of the Express application.

All that you have left to do is to create the Express application object and bootstrap it using the controller and routing modules you just created. To do this, go to the config folder and create a file named express.js with the following code snippet:

```
const express = require('express');

module.exports = function() {
  const app = express();
  require('../app/routes/index.server.routes.js')(app);
  return app;
};
```

In the preceding code snippet, you required the Express module and then used the CommonJS module pattern to define a module function that initializes the Express application. First, it creates a new instance of an Express application, and then it requires your routing file and calls it as a function, passing it the application instance as an argument. The routing file will use the application instance to create a new routing configuration, and then it will call the controller's render() method. The module function ends by returning the application instance.

The express.js file is where we configure our Express application. This is where we add everything related to the Express configuration.

To finalize your application, you'll need to create a file named server.js in the root folder and copy the following code:

```
const configureExpress = require('./config/express');

const app = configureExpress();
app.listen(3000);
module.exports = app;

console.log('Server running at http://localhost:3000/');
```

That is it! In the main application file, you connected all the loose ends by requiring the Express configuration module and then using it to retrieve your application object instance and listening to port 3000.

To start your application, navigate to your application's root folder using your command-line tool and install your application dependencies using npm, as follows:

$ npm install

Once the installation process is over, all you have to do is start your application using Node's command-line tool:

$ node server

Your Express application should run now! To test it, navigate to http://localhost:3000.

In this example, you learned how to properly build your Express application. It is important that you note the different ways in which you used the CommonJS module pattern to create your files and require them across the application. This pattern will often repeat itself in this book.

Configuring an Express application

Express comes with a pretty simple configuration system that enables you to add certain functionalities to your Express application. Although there are predefined configuration options that you can change to manipulate the way it works, you can also add your own key/value configuration options for any other usage. Another robust feature of Express is its ability to configure your application based on the environment it's running on. For instance, you may want to use the Express logger in your development environment and not in production, while compressing your responses body might seem like a good idea when running in a production environment.

To achieve this, you will need to use the `process.env` property. `process.env` is a global variable that allows you to access predefined environment variables, and the most common one is the `NODE_ENV` environment variable. The `NODE_ENV` environment variable is often used for environment-specific configurations. To understand this better, let's go back to the previous example and add some external middleware. To use this middleware, you will first need to download and install them as your project dependencies.

To do this, edit your `package.json` file to look like the following code snippet:

```
{
  "name": "MEAN",
  "version": "0.0.3",
  "dependencies": {
    "body-parser": "1.15.2",
    "compression": "1.6.0",
    "express": "4.14.0",
    "method-override": "2.3.6",
    "morgan": "1.7.0"
  }
}
```

As we stated previously, the `morgan` module provides a simple logger middleware, the `compression` module provides response compression, the `body-parser` module provides several middleware to handle the request data, and the `method-override` module provides DELETE and PUT HTTP verbs' legacy support. To use these modules, you will need to modify your `config/express.js` file to look like the following code snippet:

```
const express = require('express');
const morgan = require('morgan');
const compress = require('compression');
const bodyParser = require('body-parser');
```

```
const methodOverride = require('method-override');

module.exports = function() {
  const app = express();

  if (process.env.NODE_ENV === 'development') {
    app.use(morgan('dev'));
  } else if (process.env.NODE_ENV === 'production') {
    app.use(compress());
  }

  app.use(bodyParser.urlencoded({
    extended: true
  }));
  app.use(bodyParser.json());
  app.use(methodOverride());

  require('../app/routes/index.server.routes.js')(app);

  return app;
};
```

As you can see, we just used the `process.env.NODE_ENV` variable to determine our environment and configure the Express application accordingly. We simply used the `app.use()` method to load the `morgan()` middleware in a development environment and the `compress()` middleware in a production environment. The `bodyParser.urlencoded()`, `bodyParser.json()`, and `methodOverride()` middleware will always load regardless of the environment.

To finalize your configuration, you'll need to change your `server.js` file to look like the following code snippet:

```
process.env.NODE_ENV = process.env.NODE_ENV || 'development';

const configureExpress = require('./config/express');

const app = configureExpress();
app.listen(3000);
module.exports = app;

console.log('Server running at http://localhost:3000/');
```

Note how the `process.env.NODE_ENV` variable is set to the default `development` value if it doesn't exist. This is because often, the `NODE_ENV` environment variable is not properly set.

It is recommended that you set the NODE_ENV environment variable in your operating system prior to running your application.

In a Windows environment, this can be done by executing the following command in your command prompt:

```
> set NODE_ENV=development
```

While in a Unix-based environment, you should simply use the following export command:

```
$ export NODE_ENV=development
```

To test your changes, navigate to your application's root folder using your command-line tool and install your application dependencies using `npm`, as follows:

```
$ npm install
```

Once the installation process is over, all you have to do is start your application using Node's command-line tool:

```
$ node server
```

Your Express application should now run! To test it, navigate to `http://localhost:3000`, and you'll be able to see the logger in action in your command-line output. However, the `process.env.NODE_ENV` environment variable can be used in an even more sophisticated manner when dealing with more complex configuration options.

Environment configuration files

During your application development, you will often need to configure third-party modules to run differently in various environments. For instance, when you connect to your MongoDB server, you'll probably use different connection strings in your development and production environments. Doing this in the current setting will probably cause your code to be filled with endless `if` statements, which will generally be harder to maintain. To solve this issue, you can manage a set of environment configuration files that hold these properties. You will then be able to use the `process.env.NODE_ENV` environment variable to determine which configuration file to load, thus keeping your code shorter and easier to maintain. Let's begin by creating a configuration file for our default development environment. To do this, create a new file inside your `config/env` folder and call it `development.js`. Inside your new file, paste the following lines of code:

```
module.exports = {
  // Development configuration options
};
```

As you can see, your configuration file is currently just an empty CommonJS module initialization. Don't worry about it; we'll soon add the first configuration option, but first, we'll need to manage the configuration files' loading. To do this, go to your application's `config` folder and create a new file named `config.js`. Inside your new file, paste the following lines of code:

```
module.exports = require('./env/' + process.env.NODE_ENV + '.js');
```

As you can see, this file simply loads the correct configuration file according to the `process.env.NODE_ENV` environment variable. In the upcoming chapters, we'll use this file, which will load the correct environment configuration file for us. To manage other environment configurations, you'll just need to add a dedicated environment configuration file and properly set the `NODE_ENV` environment variable.

Rendering views

A very common feature of web frameworks is the ability to render views. The basic concept is passing your data to a template engine that will render the final view, usually in HTML. In the MVC pattern, your controller uses the model to retrieve the data portion and the view template to render the HTML output, as described in the next diagram. The Express extendable approach allows the usage of many Node.js template engines to achieve this functionality. In this section, we'll use the EJS template engine, but you can later replace it with other template engines. The following diagram shows the MVC pattern in rendering application views:

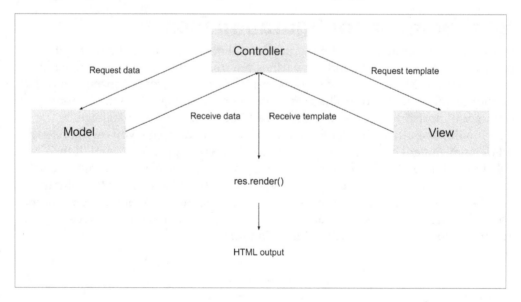

Express has two methods to render views: app.render(), which is used to render the view and then pass the HTML to a callback function, and the more common res.render(), which renders the view locally and sends the HTML as a response. You'll use res.render() more frequently because you usually want to output the HTML as a response. However, if, for instance, you'd like your application to send HTML e-mails, you will probably use app.render(). Before we begin exploring the res.render() method, let's first configure our view system.

Configuring the view system

In order to configure the Express view system, you will need to use the EJS template engine. Let's get back to our example and install the EJS module. You should begin by changing your package.json file to look like the following code snippet:

```
{
    "name": "MEAN",
    "version": "0.0.3",
    "dependencies": {
        "body-parser": "1.15.2",
        "compression": "1.6.0",
        "ejs": "2.5.2",
        "express": "4.14.0",
        "method-override": "2.3.6",
        "morgan": "1.7.0"   }
}
```

Now, install the EJS module by navigating in the command line to your project's root folder and issuing the following command:

```
$ npm update
```

After npm finishes the installation of the EJS module, you'll be able to configure Express to use it as the default template engine. To configure your Express application, go back to the config/express.js file and change it to look like the following lines of code:

```
const express = require('express');
const morgan = require('morgan');
const compress = require('compression');
const bodyParser = require('body-parser');
const methodOverride = require('method-override');

module.exports = function() {
    const app = express();
```

```
    if (process.env.NODE_ENV === 'development') {
      app.use(morgan('dev'));
    } else if (process.env.NODE_ENV === 'production') {
      app.use(compress());
    }

    app.use(bodyParser.urlencoded({
      extended: true
    }));
    app.use(bodyParser.json());
    app.use(methodOverride());

    app.set('views', './app/views');
    app.set('view engine', 'ejs');

    require('../app/routes/index.server.routes.js')(app);

    return app;
  };
```

Note how we use the app.set() method to configure the Express application view folder and template engine. Let's create your first view.

Rendering EJS views

EJS views basically consist of HTML code mixed with EJS tags. EJS templates will reside in the app/views folder and will have the .ejs extension. When you use the res.render() method, the EJS engine will look for the template in the views folder, and if it finds a complying template, it will render the HTML output. To create your first EJS view, go to your app/views folder and create a new file named index.ejs, which contains the following HTML code snippet:

```
<!DOCTYPE html>
<html>
  <head>
    <title><%= title %></title>
  </head>
  <body>
    <h1><%= title %></h1>
  </body>
</html>
```

This code should be mostly familiar to you, except for the `<%= %>` tag. These tags are the way to tell the EJS template engine where to render the template variables—in this case, the `title` variable. All you have left to do is configure your controller to render this template and automatically output it as an HTML response. To do this, go back to your `app/controllers/index.server.controller.js` file and change it to look like the following code snippet:

```
exports.render = function(req, res) {
  res.render('index', {
    title: 'Hello World'
  });
};
```

Note the way the `res.render()` method is used. The first argument is the name of your EJS template without the `.ejs` extension, and the second argument is an object containing your template variables. The `res.render()` method will use the EJS template engine to look for the file in the `views` folder that we set in the `config/express.js` file and will then render the view using the template variables. To test your changes, use your command-line tool and issue the following command:

```
$ node server
```

Well done; you have just created your first EJS view! Test your application by visiting `http://localhost:3000`, where you'll be able to view the rendered HTML.

EJS views are simple to maintain, and they provide an easy way to create your application views. We'll elaborate a bit more on EJS templates later in this book, not as much as you would expect, however, because in MEAN applications, most of the HTML rendering is done on the client side using Angular.

Serving static files

In any web application, there is always a need to serve static files. Fortunately, Express' only built-in middleware is the `express.static()` middleware, which provides this feature. To add static file support to the previous example, just make the following changes in your `config/express.js` file:

```
const express = require('express');
const morgan = require('morgan');
const compress = require('compression');
const bodyParser = require('body-parser');
const methodOverride = require('method-override');

module.exports = function() {
  const app = express();
```

```
    if (process.env.NODE_ENV === 'development') {
      app.use(morgan('dev'));
    } else if (process.env.NODE_ENV === 'production') {
      app.use(compress());
    }

    app.use(bodyParser.urlencoded({
      extended: true
    }));
    app.use(bodyParser.json());
    app.use(methodOverride());

    app.set('views', './app/views');
    app.set('view engine', 'ejs');

    require('../app/routes/index.server.routes.js')(app);

    app.use(express.static('./public'));

    return app;
};
```

The `express.static()` middleware takes one argument to determine the location of the `static` folder. Note how the `express.static()` middleware is placed below the call for the routing file. This order matters because if it were above it, Express would first try to look for HTTP request paths in the `static files` folder. This would make the response a lot slower as it would have to wait for a filesystem I/O operation.

To test your static middleware, add an image named `logo.png` to the `public/img` folder and then make the following changes in your `app/views/index.ejs` file:

```
<!DOCTYPE html>
<html>
  <head>
    <title><%= title %></title>
  </head>
  <body>
    <img src="img/logo.png" alt="Logo">
    <h1><%= title %></h1>
  </body>
</html>
```

Now, run your application using Node's command-line tool:

```
$ node server
```

To test the result, visit `http://localhost:3000` in your browser and watch how Express is serving your image as a static file.

Configuring sessions

Sessions are a common web application pattern that allows you to keep track of the user's behavior when they visit your application. To add this functionality, you will need to install and configure the `express-session` middleware. To do this, start by modifying your `package.json` file as follows:

```
{
    "name": "MEAN",
    "version": "0.0.3",
    "dependencies": {
        "body-parser": "1.15.2",
        "compression": "1.6.0",
        "ejs": "2.5.2",
        "express": "4.14.0",
        "express-session": "1.14.1",
        "method-override": "2.3.6",
        "morgan": "1.7.0"
    }
}
```

Then, install the `express-session` module by navigating to your project's root folder in the command line and issuing the following command:

```
$ npm update
```

Once the installation process is finished, you'll be able to configure your Express application to use the `express-session` module. The `express-session` module will use a cookie-stored, signed identifier to identify the current user. To sign the session identifier, it will use a secret string, which will help prevent malicious session tampering. For security reasons, it is recommended that the cookie secret be different for each environment, which means that this would be an appropriate place to use our environment configuration file. To do this, change the `config/env/development.js` file to look like the following code snippet:

```
module.exports = {
    sessionSecret: 'developmentSessionSecret'
};
```

Since this is just an example, feel free to change the secret string. For other environments, just add the sessionSecret property in their environment configuration files. To use the configuration file and configure your Express application, go back to your config/express.js file and change it to look like the following code snippet:

```
const config = require('./config');
const express = require('express');
const morgan = require('morgan');
const compress = require('compression');
const bodyParser = require('body-parser');
const methodOverride = require('method-override');
const session = require('express-session');

module.exports = function() {
  const app = express();

  if (process.env.NODE_ENV === 'development') {
    app.use(morgan('dev'));
  } else if (process.env.NODE_ENV === 'production') {
    app.use(compress());
  }

  app.use(bodyParser.urlencoded({
    extended: true
  }));
  app.use(bodyParser.json());
  app.use(methodOverride());

  app.use(session({
    saveUninitialized: true,
    resave: true,
    secret: config.sessionSecret
  }));

  app.set('views', './app/views');
  app.set('view engine', 'ejs');

  app.use(express.static('./public'));

  require('../app/routes/index.server.routes.js')(app);

  return app;
};
```

Note how the configuration object is passed to the `express.session()` middleware. In this configuration object, the `secret` property is defined using the configuration file you previously modified. The session middleware adds a session object to all request objects in your application. Using this session object, you can set or get any property that you wish to use in the current session. To test the session, change the `app/controller/index.server.controller.js` file as follows:

```
exports.render = function(req, res) {
  if (req.session.lastVisit) {
    console.log(req.session.lastVisit);
  }

  req.session.lastVisit = new Date();

  res.render('index', {
    title: 'Hello World'
  });
};
```

What you did here was basically record the time of the last user request. The controller checks whether the `lastVisit` property was set in the `session` object, and if so, it outputs the last visit date to the console. It then sets the `lastVisit` property to the current time. To test your changes, use Node's command-line tool to run your application, as follows:

`$ node server`

Now, test your application by visiting `http://localhost:3000` in your browser and watching the command-line output.

Summary

In this chapter, you created your first Express application and learned how to properly configure it. You arranged your files and folders in an organized structure and discovered alternative folder structures. You also created your first Express controller and learned how to call its methods using Express' routing mechanism. You rendered your first EJS view and learned how to serve static files. You also learned how to use `express-session` to track your user's behavior. In the next chapter, you'll learn how to save your application's persistent data using MongoDB.

Introduction to MongoDB

4

MongoDB is an exciting new breed of database. The leader of the NoSQL movement is emerging as one of the most useful database solutions in the world. Designed with web applications in mind, Mongo's high throughput, unique BSON data model, and easily scalable architecture provide web developers with better tools to store their persistent data. The move from relational databases to NoSQL solutions can be an overwhelming task, which can be easily simplified by understanding MongoDB's design goals. In this chapter, we'll cover the following topics:

- Understanding the NoSQL movement and MongoDB design goals
- MongoDB BSON data structure
- MongoDB collections and documents
- MongoDB query language
- Working with the MongoDB shell

Introduction to NoSQL

In the past couple of years, web application development has usually required the usage of relational databases to store persistent data. Most developers are already pretty comfortable with using one of the many SQL solutions. So, the approach of storing a normalized data model using a mature relational database became the standard. Object-relational mappers started to crop up, giving developers proper solutions to marshal their data from the different parts of their application. But as the Web grew larger, more scaling problems were presented to a larger base of developers. To solve this problem, the community created a variety of key-value storage solutions that were designed for better availability, simple querying, and horizontal scaling. This new kind of data store became more and more robust, offering many of the features of the relational databases. During this evolution, different storage design patterns emerged, including key-value storage, column storage, object storage, and the most popular one, document storage.

In a common relational database, your data is stored in different tables, often connected using a primary-to-foreign key relation. Your program will later reconstruct the model using various SQL statements to arrange the data in some kind of hierarchical object representation. Document-oriented databases handle data differently. Instead of using tables, they store hierarchical documents in standard formats, such as JSON and XML.

To understand this better, let's have a look at an example of a typical blog post. To construct this blog post model using a SQL solution, you'll probably have to use at least two tables. The first one would contain post information while the second would contain post comments. A sample table structure can be seen in the following diagram:

Posts table	
ID	...

Comments table		
ID	PostID	...

In your application, you'll use an object-relational mapping library or direct SQL statements to select the blog post record and the post comments records to create your blog post object. However, in a document-based database, the blog post will be stored completely as a single document that can later be queried. For instance, in a database that stores documents in a JSON format, your blog post document would probably look like the following code snippet:

```json
{
    "title": "First Blog Post",
    "comments": [{
        "title": "First Comment"
    }, {
        "title": "Second Comment"
    }]
}
```

This demonstrates the main difference between document-based databases and relational databases. So, while working with relational databases, your data is stored in different tables, with your application assembling objects using table records. Storing your data as holistic documents will allow faster read operations since your application won't have to rebuild the objects with every read. Furthermore, document-oriented databases have other advantages.

While developing your application, you often encounter another problem: model changes. Let's assume you want to add a new property to each blog post. So, you go ahead and change your posts table and then go to your application data layer and add that property to your blog post object. As your application already contains several blog posts, all existing blog post objects will have to change as well, which means that you'll have to cover your code with extra validation procedures. However, document-based databases are often schema-less, which means you can store different objects in a single collection of objects without changing anything in your database. Although this may sound like asking for trouble to some experienced developers, the freedom of schema-less storage has several advantages.

For example, think about an e-commerce application that sells used furniture. In your `products` table, a chair and a closet might have some common features, such as the type of wood, but a customer might also be interested in the number of doors the closet has. Storing the closet and chair objects in the same table means they could be stored in either a table with a large number of empty columns or using the more practical entity-attribute-value pattern, where another table is used to store key-value attributes. However, using schema-less storage will allow you to define different properties for different objects in the same collection, while still enabling you to query this collection using common properties, such as wood type. This means your application, and not the database, will be in charge of enforcing the data structure, which can help you speed up your development process.

While there are many NoSQL solutions that solve various development issues, usually around caching and scale, document-oriented databases are rapidly becoming the leaders of the movement. The document-oriented database's ease of use, along with its standalone persistent storage offering, even threatens to replace the traditional SQL solutions in some use cases. And although there are a few document-oriented databases, none are as popular as MongoDB.

Introducing MongoDB

Back in 2007, Dwight Merriman and Eliot Horowitz formed a company named 10gen to create a better platform to host web applications. The idea was to create a hosting as a service that will allow developers to focus on building their application, rather than handle hardware management and infrastructure scaling. Soon, they discovered the community wasn't keen on giving up so much of the control over their application's infrastructure. As a result, they released the different parts of the platform as open source projects.

One such project was a document-based database solution called MongoDB. Derived from the word humongous, MongoDB was able to support complex data storage, while maintaining the high-performance approach of other NoSQL stores. The community cheerfully adopted this new paradigm, making MongoDB one of the fastest-growing databases in the world. With more than 150 contributors and over 10,000 commits, it also became one of the most popular open source projects.

MongoDB's main goal was to create a new type of database that combined the robustness of a relational database with the fast throughput of distributed key-value data stores. With the scalable platform in mind, it had to support simple horizontal scaling while sustaining the durability of traditional databases. Another key design goal was to support web application development in the form of standard JSON outputs. These two design goals turned out to be MongoDB's greatest advantages over other solutions as these aligned perfectly with other trends in web development, such as the almost ubiquitous use of cloud virtualization hosting or the shift towards horizontal, instead of vertical, scaling.

First dismissed as another NoSQL storage layer over the more viable relational database, MongoDB evolved way beyond the platform where it was born. Its ecosystem grew to support most of the popular programming platforms, with the various community-backed drivers. Along with this, many other tools were formed, including different MongoDB clients, profiling and optimization tools, administration and maintenance utilities, as well as a couple of VC-backed hosting services. Even major companies such as eBay and The New York Times began to use MongoDB data storage in their production environment. To understand why developers prefer MongoDB, it's time we dive into some of its key features.

Key features of MongoDB

MongoDB has some key features that helped it become so popular. As we mentioned before, the goal was to create a new breed between traditional database features and the high performance of NoSQL stores. As a result, most of its key features were created to evolve beyond the limitations of other NoSQL solutions while integrating some of the abilities of relational databases. In this section, you'll learn why MongoDB can become your preferred database when approaching modern web application developments.

The BSON format

One of the greatest features of MongoDB is its JSON-like storage format named BSON. Standing for **Binary JSON**, the BSON format is a binary-encoded serialization of JSON-like documents, and it is designed to be more efficient in size and speed, allowing MongoDB's high read/write throughput.

Like JSON, BSON documents are a simple data structure representation of objects and arrays in a key-value format. A document consists of a list of elements, each with a string typed field name and a typed field value. These documents support all of the JSON specific data types along with other data types, such as the Date type.

Another big advantage of the BSON format is the use of the _id field as the primary key. The _id field value will usually be a unique identifier type, named ObjectId, that is either generated by the application driver or by the mongod service. In the event the driver fails to provide a _id field with a unique ObjectId, the mongod service will add it automatically using:

- A 4-byte value representing the seconds since the Unix epoch
- A 3-byte machine identifier
- A 2-byte process ID
- A 3-byte counter, starting with a random value

So, a BSON representation of the blog post object from the previous example would look like the following code snippet:

```
{
   "_id": ObjectId("52d02240e4b01d67d71ad577"),
   "title": "First Blog Post",
   "comments": [
   ...
   ]
}
```

The BSON format enables MongoDB to internally index and map document properties and even nested documents, allowing it to scan the collection efficiently and, more importantly, to match objects to complex query expressions.

MongoDB ad hoc queries

One of the other MongoDB design goals was to expand the abilities of ordinary key-value stores. The main issue of common key-value stores is their limited query capabilities, which usually means your data is only queryable using the key field, and more complex queries are mostly predefined. To solve this issue, MongoDB drew its inspiration from the relational database dynamic query language.

Supporting ad hoc queries means that the database will respond to dynamically structured queries out of the box, without the need to predefine each query. It is able to do this by indexing BSON documents and using a unique query language. Let's have a look at the following SQL statement example:

```
SELECT * FROM Posts WHERE Title LIKE '%mongo%';
```

This simple statement is asking the database for all the post records with a title containing the word mongo. Replicating this query in MongoDB would look as follows:

```
db.posts.find({ title:/mongo/ });
```

Running this command in the MongoDB shell will return all the posts whose `title` field contains the word mongo. You'll learn more about the MongoDB query language later in this chapter, but for now it is important to remember that it is almost as queryable as your traditional relational database. The MongoDB query language is great, but it raises the question of how efficiently these queries run when the database gets larger. Like relational databases, MongoDB solves this issue using a mechanism called indexing.

MongoDB indexing

Indexes are unique data structures that enable the database engine to efficiently resolve queries. When a query is sent to the database, it will have to scan through the entire collection of documents to find those that match the query statement. This way, the database engine processes a large amount of unnecessary data, resulting in poor performance.

To speed up the scan, the database engine can use a predefined index, which maps document fields and can tell the engine which documents are compatible with this query statement. To understand how indexes work, let's say we want to retrieve all the posts that have more than 10 comments. In this instance, our document is defined as follows:

```
{
  "_id": ObjectId("52d02240e4b01d67d71ad577"),
  "title": "First Blog Post",
  "comments": [
  ...
  ],
  "commentsCount": 12
}
```

So, a MongoDB query that requests documents with more than 10 comments would be as follows:

```
db.posts.find({ commentsCount: { $gt: 10 } });
```

To execute this query, MongoDB would have to go through all the posts and check whether the post has a commentCount property larger than 10. However, if a commentCount index was defined, then MongoDB would only have to check which documents have a commentCount property larger than 10, before retrieving these documents. The following diagram illustrates how a commentCount index would work:

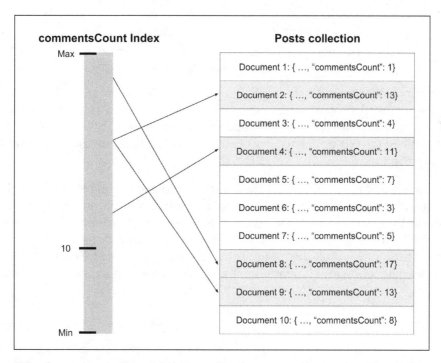

Using the commentsCount index to retrieve documents with more than 10 comments

MongoDB replica set

To provide data redundancy and improved availability, MongoDB uses an architecture called a **replica set**. Replication of databases helps to protect your data to recover from hardware failure and increase read capacity. A replica set is a set of MongoDB services that host the same dataset. One service is used as the primary and the other services that are used are called secondaries. All of the set instances support read operations, but only the primary instance is in charge of write operations. When a write operation occurs, the primary will inform the secondaries about the changes and make sure they've applied them to their datasets' replication. The following diagram illustrates a common replica set:

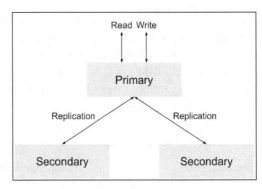

The workflow of a replica set with one primary and two secondaries

Another robust feature of the MongoDB replica set is its automatic failover. When one of the set members can't reach the primary instance for more than 10 seconds, the replica set will automatically elect and promote a secondary instance as the new primary. When the old primary comes back online, it will rejoin the replica set as a secondary instance.

Another feature of the replica set is the ability to add arbiter nodes. Arbiters do not maintain any data; their main purpose is to maintain a quorum in the replica set. This means they participate in the process of electing a new primary but cannot function as a secondary or be elected to be the primary. In short, arbiters help to provide consistency within the replica set with a cheaper resource cost than regular data nodes. The following diagram illustrates a common replica set with an arbiter:

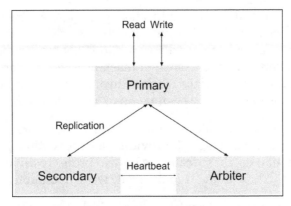

The workflow of a replica set with a primary, a secondary, and an arbiter

Replication is a very robust feature of MongoDB that is derived directly from its platform origin and is one of the main features that makes MongoDB production-ready. However, it is not the only one.

 To learn more about MongoDB replica sets, visit `http://docs.mongodb.org/manual/replication/`.

MongoDB sharding

Scaling is a common problem with a growing web application. The various approaches to solve this issue can be divided into two groups: vertical scaling and horizontal scaling. The differences between the two are illustrated in the following diagram:

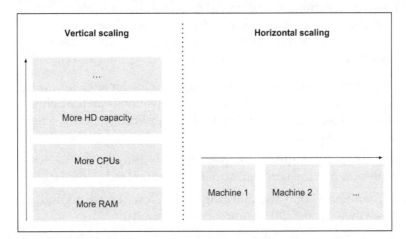

Vertical scaling with a single machine versus horizontal scaling with multiple machines

Vertical scaling is easier and consists of increasing single-machine resources, such as RAM and CPU. However, it has two major drawbacks: first, at some level, increasing a single machine's resources becomes disproportionately more expensive compared to splitting the load between several smaller machines. Second, the popular cloud-hosting providers limit the size of the machine instances you can use. So, scaling your application vertically can only be done up to a certain level.

Horizontal scaling is more complicated and is done using several machines. Each machine will handle a part of the load, providing a better overall performance. The problem with horizontal database scaling is how to properly divide the data between different machines and how to manage the read/write operations between them.

Luckily, MongoDB supports horizontal scaling, which it refers to as sharding. *Sharding is the process of splitting the data between different machines, or shards.* Each shard holds a portion of the data and functions as a separate database. The collection of several shards together is what forms a single logical database. Operations are performed through services called query routers, which ask the configuration servers how to delegate each operation to the right shard.

> To learn more about MongoDB sharding, visit `http://docs.mongodb.org/manual/sharding/`.

MongoDB 3.0

At the beginning of 2015, the MongoDB team introduced the third major version of the MongoDB database. Above all else, this version marks the transition MongoDB is making towards becoming a leading database solution for bigger and more complex production environments. Or, as the team describes it, making MongoDB the "default database" for every organization. In order to do so, the team presented several new features:

- **Storage API**: In this version, the storage engine layer is decoupled from higher-level operations. This means organizations can now choose which storage engines to use according to their application needs, gaining up to 10x better performance.

- **Enhanced query engine introspection**: This allows the DBA to better analyze key queries, making sure performance is optimized.

- **Better authentication and auditing**: This allows larger organization to manage their MongoDB instance more securely.

- **Better logging**: More elaborate logging features allow developers to better track MongoDB's operations.

These features and many others are what make MongoDB so popular. Although there are many good alternatives, MongoDB is becoming more and more ubiquitous among developers and is on its way to become one of the world's leading database solutions. Let's dive a little deeper to find out how you can easily start using MongoDB.

MongoDB shell

If you followed *Chapter 1*, *Introduction to MEAN*, you should have a working instance of MongoDB in your local environment. To interact with MongoDB, you'll use the MongoDB shell, which you encountered in *Chapter 1*, *Introduction to MEAN*. The MongoDB shell is a command-line tool that enables the execution of different operations using a JavaScript syntax query language.

In order to explore the different parts of MongoDB, let's start the MongoDB shell by running the mongo executable, as follows:

```
$ mongo
```

If MongoDB has been properly installed, you should see an output similar to what is shown in the following screenshot:

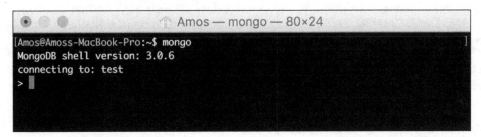

Notice how the shell is telling you the current shell version, and that it has connected to the default test database.

MongoDB databases

Each MongoDB server instance can store several databases. Unless specifically defined, the MongoDB shell will automatically connect to the default test database. Let's switch to another database called mean by executing the following command:

```
> use mean
```

You'll see a command-line output telling you that the shell switched to the `mean` database. Notice that you didn't need to create the database before using it because in MongoDB, databases and collections are lazily created when you insert your first document. This behavior is consistent with MongoDB's dynamic approach to data. Another way to use a specific database is to run the shell executable with the database name as an argument, as follows:

```
$ mongo mean
```

The shell will then automatically connect to the `mean` database. If you want to list all the other databases in the current MongoDB server, just execute the following command:

```
> show dbs
```

This will show you a list of currently available databases that have at least one document stored.

MongoDB collections

A MongoDB collection is a list of MongoDB documents and is the equivalent of a relational database table. A collection is created when its first document is being inserted. Unlike a table, a collection doesn't enforce any type of schema and can host different structured documents.

To perform operations on a MongoDB collection, you'll need to use the collection methods. Let's create a posts collection and insert the first post. In order to do this, execute the following command in the MongoDB shell:

```
> db.posts.insert({"title":"First Post", "user": "bob"})
```

After executing the preceding command, it will automatically create the `posts` collection and insert the first document. To retrieve the collection documents, execute the following command in the MongoDB shell:

```
> db.posts.find()
```

You should see a command-line output similar to what is shown in the following screenshot:

This means that you have successfully created the posts collection and inserted your first document.

To show all available collections, issue the following command in the MongoDB shell:

```
> show collections
```

The MongoDB shell will output the list of available collections, which in your case are the posts collection and another collection called system.indexes, which holds the list of your database indexes.

If you'd like to delete the posts collection, you will need to execute the drop() command as follows:

```
> db.posts.drop()
```

The shell will inform you that the collection was dropped, by responding with a true output.

MongoDB CRUD operations

Create-Read-Update-Delete (CRUD) operations, are the basic interactions you perform with a database. To execute CRUD operations over your database entities, MongoDB provides various collection methods.

Creating a new document

You're already familiar with the basic method of creating a new document using the insert() method, as you previously did in earlier examples. Besides the insert() method, there are two more methods called update() and save() to create new objects.

Creating a document using insert()

The most common way to create a new document is to use the insert() method. The insert() method takes a single argument that represents the new document. To insert a new post, just issue the following command in the MongoDB shell:

```
> db.posts.insert({"title":"Second Post", "user": "alice"})
```

Creating a document using update()

The update() method is usually used to update an existing document. You can also use the upsert flag to create a new document, if no document matches the query criteria:

```
> db.posts.update({
    "user": "alice"
}, {
    "title": "Second Post",
    "user": "alice"
}, {
    upsert: true
})
```

In the preceding example, MongoDB will look for a post created by alice and try to update it. Considering the fact that the posts collection doesn't have a post created by alice and the fact you have used the upsert flag, MongoDB will not find an appropriate document to update and will create a new document instead.

Creating a document using save()

Another way of creating a new document is by calling the save() method, passing it a document that either doesn't have an _id field or has an _id field that doesn't exist in the collection:

```
> db.posts.save({"title":"Second Post", "user": "alice"})
```

This will have the same effect as the update() method and will create a new document instead of updating an existing one.

Reading documents

The find() method is used to retrieve a list of documents from a MongoDB collection. Using the find() method, you can either request all the documents in a collection or use a query to retrieve specific documents.

Finding all the collection documents

To retrieve all the documents in the posts collection, you should either pass an empty query to the find() method or not pass any arguments at all. The following query will retrieve all the documents in the posts collection:

```
> db.posts.find()
```

Furthermore, performing the same operation can also be done using the following query:

```
> db.posts.find({})
```

These two queries are basically the same and will return all the documents in the posts collection.

Using an equality statement

To retrieve a specific document, you can use an equality condition query that will grab all the documents which comply with that condition. For instance, to retrieve all the posts created by alice, you will need to issue the following command in the shell:

```
> db.posts.find({ "user": "alice" })
```

This will retrieve all the documents that have the user property equal to alice.

Using query operators

Using an equality statement may not be enough. To build more complex queries, MongoDB supports a variety of query operators. Using query operators, you can look for different sorts of conditions. For example, to retrieve all the posts that were created by either alice or bob, you can use the following $in operator:

```
> db.posts.find({ "user": { $in: ["alice", "bob"] } })
```

 There are plenty of other query operators you can learn about by visiting http://docs.mongodb.org/manual/reference/operator/query/#query-selectors.

Building AND/OR queries

When you build a query, you may need to use more than one condition. Like in SQL, you can use AND/OR operators to build multiple condition query statements. To perform an AND query, you simply add the properties you'd like to check to the query object. For instance, take a look at the following query:

```
> db.posts.find({ "user": "alice", "commentsCount": { $gt: 10 }  })
```

It is similar to the `find()` query you've previously used, but adds another condition that verifies the document's `commentCount` property and will only grab documents that were created by `alice` and have more than `10` comments. An `OR` query is a bit more complex because it involves the `$or` operator. To understand it better, take a look at another version of the previous example:

```
> db.posts.find( { $or: [{ "user": "alice" }, { "user": "bob" }] })
```

Like the query operators example, this query will also grab all the posts created by either `bob` or `alice`.

Updating existing documents

Using MongoDB, you have the option of updating documents using either the `update()` or `save()` methods.

Updating documents using update()

The `update()` method takes three arguments to update existing documents. The first argument is the selection criteria that indicate which documents to update, the second argument is the `update` statement, and the last argument is the `options` object. For instance, in the following example, the first argument is telling MongoDB to look for all the documents created by `alice`, the second argument tells it to update the `title` field, and the third is forcing it to execute the `update` operation on all the documents it finds:

```
> db.posts.update({
    "user": "alice"
}, {
    $set: {
      "title": "Second Post"
    }
}, {
    multi: true
})
```

Notice how the `multi` property has been added to the `options` object. The `update()` method's default behavior is to update a single document, so by setting the `multi` property, you tell the `update()` method to update all the documents that comply with the selection criteria.

Updating documents using save()

Another way of updating an existing document is by calling the `save()` method, passing it a document that contains an `_id` field. For instance, the following command will update an existing document with an `_id` field that is equal to `ObjectId("50691737d386d8fadbd6b01d")`:

```
> db.posts.save({
  "_id": ObjectId("50691737d386d8fadbd6b01d"),
  "title": "Second Post",
  "user": "alice"
})
```

It's important to remember that if the `save()` method is unable to find an appropriate object, it will create a new one instead.

Deleting documents

To remove documents, you will need to use the `remove()` method. The `remove()` method can accept up to two arguments. The first one is the deletion criteria, and the second is a Boolean argument that indicates whether or not to remove multiple documents.

Deleting all documents

To remove all the documents from a collection, you will need to call the `remove()` method with no deletion criteria at all. For example, to remove all the `posts` documents, you'll need to execute the following command:

```
> db.posts.remove({})
```

Notice that the `remove()` method is different from the `drop()` method, as it will not delete the collection or its indexes. To rebuild your collection with different indexes, it is preferred that you use the `drop()` method.

Deleting multiple documents

To remove multiple documents that match a criteria from a collection, you will need to call the `remove()` method with a deletion criteria. For example, to remove all the posts made by `alice`, you'll need to execute the following command:

```
> db.posts.remove({ "user": "alice" })
```

Note that this will remove all the documents created by `alice`, so be careful when using the `remove()` method.

Deleting a single document

To remove a single document that matches a criteria from a collection, you will need to call the `remove()` method with a deletion criteria and a Boolean stating that you only want to delete a single document. For example, to remove the first post made by `alice`, you'll need to execute the following command:

```
> db.posts.remove({ "user": "alice" }, true)
```

This will remove the first document that was created by `alice` and leave other documents even if they match the deletion criteria.

Summary

In this chapter, you learned about NoSQL databases and how they can be useful for modern web development. You also learned about the emerging leader of the NoSQL movement, MongoDB. You took a deeper dive into understanding the various features that make MongoDB such a powerful solution, and learned about its basic terminology. Finally, you caught a glimpse of MongoDB's powerful query language and how to perform all four CRUD operations. In the next chapter, we'll discuss how to connect Node.js and MongoDB together using the popular Mongoose module.

5
Introduction to Mongoose

Mongoose is a robust Node.js ODM module that adds MongoDB support to your Express application. It uses schemas to model your entities, offers predefined validation along with custom validations, allows you to define virtual attributes, and uses middleware hooks to intercept operations. The Mongoose design goal is to bridge the gap between the MongoDB schemaless approach and the requirements of real-world application development. In this chapter, you'll go through the following basic features of Mongoose:

- Mongoose schemas and models
- Schema indexes, modifiers, and virtual attributes
- Using the model's methods and performing CRUD operations
- Verifying your data using predefined and custom validators
- Using middleware to intercept the model's methods

Introducing Mongoose

Mongoose is a Node.js module that provides developers with the ability to model objects and save them as MongoDB documents. While MongoDB is a schemaless database, Mongoose offers you the opportunity to enjoy both strict and loose schema approaches when dealing with Mongoose models. As with any other Node.js module, before you can start using it in your application, you will first need to install it. The examples in this chapter will continue directly from those in the previous chapters; so, for this chapter, copy the final example from *Chapter 3, Building an Express Web Application*, and let's start from there.

Installing Mongoose

Once you've installed and verified that your MongoDB local instance is running, you'll be able to connect it using the Mongoose module. First, you will need to install Mongoose in your `node_modules` folder, so change your `package.json` file to look like what is shown in the following code snippet:

```json
{
  "name": "MEAN",
  "version": "0.0.5",
  "dependencies": {
    "body-parser": "1.15.2",
    "compression": "1.6.0",
    "ejs": "2.5.2",
    "express": "4.14.0",
    "express-session": "1.14.1",
    "method-override": "2.3.6",
    "mongoose": "4.6.5",
    "morgan": "1.7.0"
  }
}
```

To install your application dependencies, go to your application folder and issue the following command in your command-line tool:

```
$ npm install
```

This will install the latest version of Mongoose in your `node_modules` folder. After the installation process has successfully finished, the next step will be to connect to your MongoDB instance.

Connecting to MongoDB

To connect to MongoDB, you will need to use the MongoDB connection URI. The MongoDB connection URI is a string URL that tells the MongoDB drivers how to connect to the database instance. The MongoDB URI is usually constructed as follows:

```
mongodb://username:password@hostname:port/database
```

Since you're connecting to a local instance, you can skip the username and password and use the following URI:

```
mongodb://localhost/mean-book
```

The simplest thing to do is to define this connection URI directly in your `config/express.js` configuration file and use the `mongoose` module to connect to the database, as follows:

```
const uri = 'mongodb://localhost/mean-book';
const db = require('mongoose').connect(uri);
```

However, since you're building a real application, saving the URI directly in the `config/express.js` file is a bad practice. The proper way to store application variables is to use your environment configuration file. Go to your `config/env/development.js` file and change it to look like what is shown in the following code snippet:

```
module.exports = {
  db: 'mongodb://localhost/mean-book',
  sessionSecret: 'developmentSessionSecret'
};
```

Now in your `config` folder, create a new file named `mongoose.js`, which contains the following code snippet:

```
const config = require('./config');
const mongoose = require('mongoose');

module.exports = function() {
  const db = mongoose.connect(config.db);

  return db;
};
```

Note how you required the `mongoose` module and connected to the MongoDB instance using the `db` property of your configuration object. To initialize your Mongoose configuration, go back to your `server.js` file and change it to look like what is shown in the following code snippet:

```
process.env.NODE_ENV = process.env.NODE_ENV || 'development';

const configureMongoose = require('./config/mongoose');
const configureExpress = require('./config/express');

const db = configureMongoose();
const app = configureExpress();
app.listen(3000);

module.exports = app;
console.log('Server running at http://localhost:3000/');
```

That's it; you have installed Mongoose, updated your configuration file, and connected to your MongoDB instance. To start your application, use your command-line tool and navigate to your application folder to execute the following command:

```
$ node server
```

Your application should be running and be connected to the MongoDB local instance.

> If you experience any problems or get the `Error: failed to connect to [localhost:27017]` output, make sure that your MongoDB instance is running properly.

Understanding Mongoose schemas

Connecting to your MongoDB instance was the first step, but the real magic of the Mongoose module is its ability to define a document schema. As you already know, MongoDB uses collections to store multiple documents, which aren't required to have the same structure as one another. However, when dealing with objects, it is sometimes necessary for documents to be similar. Mongoose uses a schema object to define the document list of properties, each with its own type and constraints in order to enforce the document structure. After specifying a schema, you will go on to define a Model constructor, which you'll use to create instances of MongoDB documents. In this section, you'll learn how to define a user schema and model and how to use a model instance to create, retrieve, and update user documents.

Creating the user schema and model

To create your first schema, go to the `app/models` folder and create a new file named `user.server.model.js`. In this file, paste the following lines of code:

```javascript
const mongoose = require('mongoose');
const Schema = mongoose.Schema;
const UserSchema = new Schema({
  firstName: String,
  lastName: String,
  email: String,
  username: String,
  password: String
});
mongoose.model('User', UserSchema);
```

In the preceding code snippet, you did two things: first, you defined your `UserSchema` object using the `Schema` constructor, and then you used the schema instance to define your User model. Note that for simplicity reasons, we save the password as clear text; however, in real world applications, the user password should be properly encrypted. Next, you'll learn how to use the User model to perform CRUD operations in your application's logic layer.

Registering the User model

Before you can start using the User model, you will need to include the `user.server.model.js` file in your Mongoose configuration file in order to register the User model. To do this, change your `config/mongoose.js` file to look like what is shown in the following code snippet:

```
const config = require('./config');
const mongoose = require('mongoose');

module.exports = function() {
  const db = mongoose.connect(config.db);

  require('../app/models/user.server.model');

  return db;
};
```

Make sure that your Mongoose configuration file is loaded before any other configuration is performed in the `server.js` file. This is important since any module that is loaded after this module will be able to use the User model without loading it by itself.

Creating new users using save()

You can start using the User model right away, but to keep things organized, it is better that you create a `Users` controller that will handle all user-related operations. In the `app/controllers` folder, create a new file named `users.server.controller.js` and paste the following lines of code:

```
const User = require('mongoose').model('User');

exports.create = function(req, res, next) {
  const user = new User(req.body);

  user.save((err) => {
    if (err) {
```

```
            return next(err);
        } else {
            res.status(200).json(user);
        }
    });
};
```

Let's go over this code. First, you used the `mongoose` module to call the `model` method, which will return the `User` model you defined previously. Next, you create a controller method named `create()`, which you will later use to create new users. Using the new keyword, the `create()` method creates a new model instance, which is populated using the request body. Finally, you call the model instance's `save()` method, which either saves the user and outputs the `user` object or fails it, passing the error to the next middleware.

To test your new controller, let's add a set of user-related routes that call the controller's methods. Begin by creating a file named `users.server.routes.js` inside the `app/routes` folder. In this newly created file, paste the following lines of code:

```
const users =
    require('../../app/controllers/users.server.controller');

module.exports = function(app) {
    app.route('/users').post(users.create);
};
```

Since your Express application will serve mainly as a RESTful API for the AngularJS application, it is a best practice to build your routes according to the REST principles. In this case, the proper way to create a new user is to use an HTTP POST request to the base `users` route you defined here. Change your `config/express.js` file to look like what is shown in the following code snippet:

```
const config = require('./config');
const express = require('express');
const morgan = require('morgan');
const compress = require('compression');
const bodyParser = require('body-parser');
const methodOverride = require('method-override');
const session = require('express-session');

module.exports = function() {
    const app = express();

    if (process.env.NODE_ENV === 'development') {
```

```
      app.use(morgan('dev'));
    } else if (process.env.NODE_ENV === 'production') {
      app.use(compress());
    }

    app.use(bodyParser.urlencoded({
      extended: true
    }));
    app.use(bodyParser.json());
    app.use(methodOverride());

    app.use(session({
      saveUninitialized: true,
      resave: true,
      secret: config.sessionSecret
    }));

    app.set('views', './app/views');
    app.set('view engine', 'ejs');

    require('../app/routes/index.server.routes.js')(app);
    require('../app/routes/users.server.routes.js')(app);

    app.use(express.static('./public'));

    return app;
};
```

That's it! To test it out, go to your root application folder and execute the following command:

$ node server

Your application should be running. To create a new user, perform an HTTP POST request to the base `users` route and make sure that the request body includes the following JSON:

```
{
  "firstName": "First",
  "lastName": "Last",
  "email": "user@example.com",
  "username": "username",
  "password": "password"
}
```

Another way to test your application would be to execute the following `curl` command in your command-line tool:

```
$ curl -X POST -H "Content-Type: application/json" -d
  '{"firstName":"First",
  "lastName":"Last","email":"user@example.com",
  "username":"username","password":"password"}' localhost:3000/users
```

 You are going to execute many different HTTP requests to test your application. For Mac OS X and Linux users, `curl` is a useful tool, but there are several other tools specifically designed for this task; we recommend that you find your favorite one and use it from now on.

Finding multiple user documents using find()

The `find()` method is a model method that retrieves multiple documents stored in the same collection using a query and is a Mongoose implementation of the MongoDB `find()` collection method. To understand this better, add the following `list()` method to your `app/controllers/users.server.controller.js` file:

```
exports.list = function(req, res, next) {
  User.find({}, (err, users) => {
    if (err) {
      return next(err);
    } else {
      res.status(200).json(users);
    }
  });
};
```

Note how the new `list()` method uses the `find()` method to retrieve an array of all the documents in the `users` collection. To use the new method you created, you'll need to register a route for it, so go to your `app/routes/users.server.routes.js` file and change it to look like what is shown in the following code snippet:

```
const users =
  require('../../app/controllers/users.server.controller');

module.exports = function(app) {
  app.route('/users')
    .post(users.create)
    .get(users.list);
};
```

All you have left to do is run your application by executing the following command:

```
$ node server
```

Then, you will be able to retrieve a list of your users by visiting `http://localhost:3000/users` in your browser.

Advanced querying using find()

In the preceding code example, the `find()` method accepted two arguments, a MongoDB query object and a callback function, but it can accept up to four parameters:

- `Query`: This is a MongoDB query object
- `[Fields]`: This is an optional string object that represents the document fields to be returned
- `[Options]`: This is an optional `options` object
- `[Callback]`: This is an optional callback function

For instance, in order to retrieve only the usernames and e-mails of your users, you will need to modify your call to look like what is shown in the following lines of code:

```
User.find({}, 'username email', (err, users) => {
  ...
});
```

Furthermore, you can also pass an `options` object when calling the `find()` method, which will manipulate the query result. For instance, to paginate through the `users` collection and retrieve only a subset of your `users` collection, you can use the `skip` and `limit` options, as follows:

```
User.find({}, 'username email', {
  skip: 10,
  limit: 10
}, (err, users) => {
  ...
});
```

This will return a subset of up to 10 user documents while skipping the first 10 documents.

 To learn more about query options, it is recommended that you visit the official Mongoose documentation at `http://mongoosejs.com/docs/api.html`.

Reading a single user document using findOne()

Retrieving a single user document is done using the `findOne()` method, which is very similar to the `find()` method, but it retrieves only the first document of the subset. To start working with a single user document, we'll have to add two new methods. Add the following lines of code to the end of your `app/controllers/users.server.controller.js` file:

```
exports.read = function(req, res) {
  res.json(req.user);
};

exports.userByID = function(req, res, next, id) {
  User.findOne({
    _id: id
  }, (err, user) => {
    if (err) {
      return next(err);
    } else {
      req.user = user;
      next();
    }
  });
};
```

The `read()` method is simple to understand; it is just responding with a JSON representation of the `req.user` object, but what is creating the `req.user` object? Well, the `userById()` method is the one responsible for populating the `req.user` object. You will use the `userById()` method as a middleware to deal with the manipulation of single documents when performing read, delete, and update operations. To do this, you will have to modify your `app/routes/users.server.routes.js` file to look like what is shown in the following lines of code:

```
const users =
  require('../../app/controllers/users.server.controller');
```

```
module.exports = function(app) {
  app.route('/users')
    .post(users.create)
    .get(users.list);

  app.route('/users/:userId')
    .get(users.read);

  app.param('userId', users.userByID);
};
```

Note how you added the `users.read()` method with a request path containing `userId`. In Express, adding a colon before a substring in a route definition means that this substring will be handled as a request parameter. To handle the population of the `req.user` object, you use the `app.param()` method, which defines a middleware to be executed before any other middleware that uses that parameter. Here, the `users.userById()` method will be executed before any other middleware registered with the `userId` parameter, which is the `users.read()` middleware in this case. This design pattern is useful when building a RESTful API, where you often add request parameters to the routing string.

To test this out, run your application using the following command:

$ node server

Then, navigate to `http://localhost:3000/users` in your browser, grab one of your users' `_id` values, and navigate to `http://localhost:3000/users/[id]`, replacing the `[id]` part with the user's `_id` value.

Updating an existing user document

The Mongoose model has several available methods to update an existing document. Among these are the `update()`, `findOneAndUpdate()`, and `findByIdAndUpdate()` methods. Each of the methods serves a different level of abstraction, easing the `update` operation when possible. In our case, and since we already use the `userById()` middleware, the easiest way to update an existing document would be to use the `findByIdAndUpdate()` method. To do this, go back to your app/controllers/users.server.controller.js file and add a new `update()` method:

```
exports.update = function(req, res, next) {
  User.findByIdAndUpdate(req.user.id, req.body, {
    'new': true
  }, (err, user) => {
    if (err) {
      return next(err);
```

```
      } else {
        res.status(200).json(user);
      }
    });
  };
```

Observe how you used the user's `id` field to find and update the correct document. Note that the default Mongoose behavior is to pass the callback to the document before it was updated; by setting the `new` option to `true`, we're making sure that we're receiving the updated document. The next thing you should do is wire your new `update()` method in your users' routing module. Go back to your `app/routes/users.server.routes.js` file and change it to look like what is shown in the following code snippet:

```
const users =
  require('../../app/controllers/users.server.controller');

module.exports = function(app) {
  app.route('/users')
      .post(users.create)
      .get(users.list);

  app.route('/users/:userId')
      .get(users.read)
      .put(users.update);

  app.param('userId', users.userByID);
};
```

Note how you used the route you had previously created and how you just chained the `update()` method using the route's `put()` method. To test your `update()` method, run your application using the following command:

$ node server

Then, use your favorite REST tool to issue a PUT request, or use `curl` and execute this command, replacing the `[id]` part with a real document's `_id` property:

$ curl -X PUT -H "Content-Type: application/json" -d '{"lastName": "Updated"}' localhost:3000/users/[id]

Deleting an existing user document

The Mongoose model has several available methods for removing an existing document. Among these are the remove(), findOneAndRemove(), and findByIdAndRemove() methods. In our case, and since we already use the userById() middleware, the easiest way to remove an existing document would be to simply use the remove() method. To do this, go back to your app/controllers/ users.server.controller.js file and add the following delete() method:

```
exports.delete = function(req, res, next) {
  req.user.remove(err => {
    if (err) {
      return next(err);
    } else {
      res.status(200).json(req.user);
    }
  })
};
```

Note how you used the user object to remove the correct document. The next thing you should do is use your new delete() method in your user's routing file. Go to your app/routes/users.server.routes.js file and change it to look like what is shown in the following code snippet:

```
const users =
  require('../../app/controllers/users.server.controller');

module.exports = function(app) {
  app.route('/users')
    .post(users.create)
    .get(users.list);

  app.route('/users/:userId')
    .get(users.read)
    .put(users.update)
    .delete(users.delete);

  app.param('userId', users.userByID);
};
```

Note how you used the route you had previously created and how you just chained the delete() method using the route's delete() method. To test your delete method, run your application using the following command:

```
$ node server
```

Then, use your favorite REST tool to issue a DELETE request, or use curl and execute the following command, replacing the [id] part with a real document's _id property:

```
$ curl -X DELETE localhost:3000/users/[id]
```

This completes the implementation of the four CRUD operations, providing you with a brief understanding of the Mongoose model capabilities. However, these methods are just examples of the vast features included with Mongoose. In the next section, you'll learn how to define default values, power your schema fields with modifiers, and validate your data.

Extending your Mongoose schema

Performing data manipulations is great, but in order to develop complex applications, you will need your ODM module to do more. Luckily, Mongoose supports various other features that help you safely model your documents and keep your data consistent.

Defining default values

Defining default field values is a common feature for data-modeling frameworks. You can add this functionality directly to your application's logic layer, but that would be messy and is generally a bad practice. Mongoose offers to define the default values at the schema level, helping you organize your code better and guaranteeing your documents' validity.

Let's say you want to add a created date field to your UserSchema. The created date field should be initialized at creation time and the time at which the user document was initially created should be saved—a perfect example of when you can utilize a default value. To do this, you'll have to change your UserSchema; so, go back to your app/models/user.server.model.js file and change it to look like what is shown in the following code snippet:

```
const mongoose = require('mongoose');
const Schema = mongoose.Schema;

const UserSchema = new Schema({
  firstName: String,
  lastName: String,
  email: String,
  username: String,
  password: String,
  created: {
```

```
        type: Date,
        default: Date.now
    }
});
```

```
mongoose.model('User', UserSchema);
```

Note how the created field is added and its default value defined. From now on, every new user document will be created with a default creation date that represents the moment the document was created. You should also note that every user document created prior to this schema change would be assigned a created field representing the moment you queried for it, since these documents don't have the created field initialized.

To test your new changes, run your application using the following command:

```
$ node server
```

Then, use your favorite REST tool to issue a POST request or use `curl` and execute the following command:

```
$ curl -X POST -H "Content-Type: application/json"
  -d '{"firstName":"First",
  "lastName":"Last","email":"user@example.com",
  "username":"username","password":"password"}' localhost:3000/users
```

A new user document will be created with a default created field initialized at the moment of creation.

Using schema modifiers

Sometimes, you may want to perform a manipulation over schema fields before saving them or presenting them to the client. For this purpose, Mongoose uses a feature called *modifiers*. A modifier can either change the field's value before saving the document, or it can represent it differently at query time.

Predefined modifiers

The simplest modifiers are the predefined ones included with Mongoose. For instance, string-type fields can have a trim modifier to remove whitespaces, an uppercase modifier to uppercase the field value, and so on. To understand how predefined modifiers work, let's make sure the username of your users is clear from a leading and trailing whitespace. To do this, all you have to do is change your app/models/user.server.model.js file to look like what is shown in the following code snippet:

```
const mongoose = require('mongoose');
const Schema = mongoose.Schema;

const UserSchema = new Schema({
  firstName: String,
  lastName: String,
  email: String,
  username: {
    type: String,
    trim: true
  },
  password: String,
  created: {
    type: Date,
    default: Date.now
  }
});

mongoose.model('User', UserSchema);
```

Note the `trim` property added to the `username` field. This will make sure your username data will be kept trimmed.

Custom setter modifiers

Predefined modifiers are great, but you can also define your own custom setter modifiers to handle data manipulation before saving the document. To understand this better, let's add a new `website` field to your User model. The `website` field should begin with `http://` or `https://`, but instead of forcing your customer to add this in the UI, you can simply write a custom modifier that validates the existence of these prefixes and adds them when required. To add your custom modifier, you will need to create the new `website` field with a `set` property, as follows:

```
const UserSchema = new Schema({
  ...
```

```
website: {
  type: String,
  set: function(url) {
    if (!url) {
      return url;
    } else {
      if (url.indexOf('http://') !== 0    &&
        url.indexOf('https://') !== 0) {
        url = 'http://' + url;
      }

      return url;
    }
  }
},
...
});
```

Now, every user created will have a properly formed website URL that is modified at creation time. However, what if you already have a big collection of user documents? You can, of course, migrate your existing data, but when dealing with big datasets, it would have a serious performance impact, so you can simply use getter modifiers.

Custom getter modifiers

Getter modifiers are used to modify existing data before outputting the documents to the next layer. For instance, in our previous example, a getter modifier would sometimes be better for changing the already existing user documents by modifying their website field at query time instead of going over your MongoDB collection and updating each document. To do this, all you have to do is change your UserSchema, as shown in the following code snippet:

```
const UserSchema = new Schema({
  ...
  website: {
    type: String,
    get: function(url) {
      if (!url) {
        return url;
      } else {
        if (url.indexOf('http://') !== 0 &&
          url.indexOf('https://') !== 0) {
            url = 'http://' + url;
          }
```

```
            return url;
        }
      }
    },
    …
});
```

```
UserSchema.set('toJSON', { getters: true });
```

You simply changed the setter modifier to a getter modifier by changing the set property to get. However, the important thing to notice here is how you configured your schema using UserSchema.set(). This will force Mongoose to include getters when converting the MongoDB document to a JSON representation and will allow the output of documents using res.json() in order to include the getter's behavior. If you didn't include this, you would have your document's JSON representation ignoring the getter modifiers.

> Modifiers are powerful and can save you a lot of time, but they should be used with caution in order to prevent unpredicted application behavior. It is recommended that you visit http://mongoosejs.com/docs/api.html for more information.

Adding virtual attributes

Sometimes, you may want to have dynamically calculated document properties, which are not really presented in the document. These properties are called *virtual attributes*, and they can be used to address several common requirements. For instance, let's say you want to add a new fullName field, which will represent the concatenation of the user's first and last names. To do this, you will have to use the virtual() schema method; so, a modified UserSchema would include the following code snippet:

```
UserSchema.virtual('fullName').get(function(){
  return this.firstName + ' ' + this.lastName;
});
```

```
UserSchema.set('toJSON', { getters: true, virtuals: true });
```

In the preceding code example, you added a virtual attribute named fullName to your UserSchema, added a getter method to that virtual attribute, and then configured your schema to include virtual attributes when converting the MongoDB document to a JSON representation.

However, virtual attributes can also have setters in order to help you save your documents they way you prefer instead of just adding more field attributes. In this case, let's say you wanted to break an input's `fullName` field into your first and last name fields. To do this, a modified virtual declaration would look like what is shown in the following code snippet:

```
UserSchema.virtual('fullName').get(function() {
  return this.firstName + ' ' + this.lastName;
}).set(function(fullName) {
  const splitName = fullName.split(' ');
  this.firstName = splitName[0] || '';
  this.lastName = splitName[1] || '';
});
```

Virtual attributes are a great feature of Mongoose, allowing you to modify document representation as they're being moved through your application's layers without getting persisted to MongoDB.

Optimizing queries using indexes

As we previously discussed, MongoDB supports various types of indexes to optimize query execution. Mongoose also supports the indexing functionality and even allows you to define secondary indexes.

The basic example of indexing is the unique index, which validates the uniqueness of a `document` field across a collection. In our example, it is common to keep usernames unique, so in order to convey this to MongoDB, you will need to modify your `UserSchema` definition to include the following code snippet:

```
const UserSchema = new Schema({
  ...
  username: {
    type: String,
    trim: true,
    unique: true
  },
  ...
});
```

This will tell MongoDB to create a unique index for the `username` field of the `users` collections. Mongoose also supports the creation of secondary indexes using the `index` property. So, if you know that your application will use a lot of queries involving the `email` field, you can optimize these queries by creating an e-mail secondary index, as follows:

```
const UserSchema = new Schema({
  …
  email: {
    type: String,
    index: true
  },
  …
});
```

Indexing is a wonderful feature of MongoDB, but you should keep in mind that it might cause you some trouble. For example, if you define a unique index on a collection where data is already stored, you might encounter some errors while running your application until you fix the issues with your collection data. Another common issue is Mongoose's automatic creation of indexes when the application starts, a feature that can cause major performance issues when running in a production environment.

Defining custom model methods

Mongoose models are quite packed with both static and instance predefined methods, some of which you have already used. However, Mongoose also lets you define your own custom methods to empower your models, giving you a modular tool to separate your application logic properly. Let's go over the proper way of defining these methods.

Defining custom static methods

Model static methods give you the liberty to perform model-level operations, such as adding extra `find` methods. For instance, let's say you want to search users by their username. You could, of course, define the `this` method in your controller, but that wouldn't be the right place for it. What you're looking for is a static model method. To add a static method, you will need to declare it as a member of your schema's `statics` property. In our case, adding a `findOneByUsername()` method would look like what is shown in the following code snippet:

```
UserSchema.statics.findOneByUsername = function(username,
   callback) {
     this.findOne({ username: new RegExp(username, 'i') },
   callback);
};
```

This method is using the model's findOne() method to retrieve a user document that has a certain username. Using the new findOneByUsername() method would be similar to using a standard static method by calling it directly from the User model, as follows:

```
User.findOneByUsername('username', (err, user) => {
   ...
});
```

You can, of course, come up with many other static methods; you'll probably need them when developing your application, so don't be afraid to add them.

Defining custom instance methods

Static methods are great, but what if you need methods that perform instance operations? Well, Mongoose offers support for those too, helping you slim down your code base and properly reuse your application code. To add an instance method, you will need to declare it as a member of your schema's methods property. Let's say you want to validate your user's password with an authenticate() method. Adding this method would then be similar to what is shown in the following code snippet:

```
UserSchema.methods.authenticate = function(password) {
   return this.password === password;
};
```

This will allow you to call the authenticate() method from any User model instance, as follows:

```
user.authenticate('password');
```

As you can see, defining custom model methods is a great way to keep your project properly organized while reusing common code. In the upcoming chapters, you'll discover how both instance and static methods can be very useful.

Model validation

One of the major issues when dealing with data marshaling is validation. When users input information to your application, you'll often have to validate that information before passing it on to MongoDB. While you can validate your data at the logic layer of your application, it is more useful to do this at the model level. Luckily, Mongoose supports both simple predefined validators and more complex custom validators. Validators are defined at the field level of a document and are executed when the document is being saved. If a validation error occurs, the save operation is aborted and the error is passed to the callback.

Predefined validators

Mongoose supports different types of predefined validators, most of which are type-specific. The basic validation of any application is, of course, the existence of a value. To validate field existence in Mongoose, you'll need to use the `required` property in the field you want to validate. Let's say you want to verify the existence of a `username` field before you save the user document. To do this, you'll need to make the following changes to your `UserSchema`:

```
const UserSchema = new Schema({
  ...
  username: {
    type: String,
    trim: true,
    unique: true,
    required: true
  },
  ...
});
```

This will validate the existence of the `username` field when saving the document, thus preventing the saving of any document that doesn't contain that field.

Besides the `required` validator, Mongoose also includes type-based predefined validators, such as the `enum` and `match` validators for strings. For instance, to validate your `email` field, you will need to change your `UserSchema` as follows:

```
const UserSchema = new Schema({
  ...
  email: {
    type: String,
    index: true,
    match: /.+\@.+\..+/
  },
```

```
...
});
```

The usage of a `match` validator here will make sure that the `email` field value matches the given `regex` expression, thus preventing the saving of any document where the e-mail doesn't conform to the right pattern.

Another example is the `enum` validator, which can help you define a set of strings that are available for that field value. Let's say you add a `role` field. A possible validation would look like this:

```
const UserSchema = new Schema({
  ...
  role: {
    type: String,
    enum: ['Admin', 'Owner', 'User']
  },
  ...
});
```

The preceding condition will allow the insertion of only these three possible strings, thus preventing you from saving the document.

 To learn more about predefined validators, it is recommended that you visit http://mongoosejs.com/docs/validation.html.

Custom validators

Other than predefined validators, Mongoose also enables you to define your own custom validators. Defining a custom validator is done using the `validate` property. The `validate` property value should be an array consisting of a **validation** function and an error message. Let's say you want to validate the length of your user password. To do this, you would have to make these changes in your `UserSchema`:

```
const UserSchema = new Schema({
  ...
  password: {
    type: String,
    validate: [
      function(password) {
        return password.length >= 6;
      },
      'Password should be longer'
```

```
      ]
    },
    ...
  });
```

This validator will make sure your user password is at least six characters long, or else it will prevent the saving of documents and pass the error message you defined to the callback.

Mongoose validation is a powerful feature that allows you to control your model and supply proper error handling, which you can use to help your users understand what went wrong. In the upcoming chapters, you'll learn how you can use Mongoose validators to handle users input and prevent common data inconsistencies.

Using Mongoose middleware

Mongoose middleware are functions that can intercept the process of the init, validate, save, and remove instance methods. Middleware are executed at the instance level and have two types: pre middleware and post middleware.

Using pre middleware

Pre middleware gets executed before the operation happens. For instance, a pre-save middleware will get executed before the saving of the document. This functionality makes pre middleware perfect for more complex validations and default values assignments.

A pre middleware is defined using the pre() method of the schema object, so validating your model using a pre middleware will look like what is shown in the following code snippet:

```
UserSchema.pre('save', function(next){
  if (...) {
    next()
  } else {
    next(new Error('An Error Occurred'));
  }
});
```

Using post middleware

A post middleware gets executed after the operation happens. For instance, a post-save middleware will get executed after saving the document. This functionality makes post middleware perfect for logging your application logic.

A post middleware is defined using the post() method of the schema object, so logging your model's save() method using a post middleware will look something like what is shown in the following code snippet:

```
UserSchema.post('save', function(next){
    console.log('The user "' + this.username +  '"
      details were saved.');
});
```

Mongoose middleware are great for the performing of various operations, including logging, validation, and performing various data consistency manipulations. Don't worry if you feel overwhelmed right now because later on in this book, you'll understand these better.

 To learn more about middleware, it is recommended that you visit http://mongoosejs.com/docs/middleware.html.

Using Mongoose ref fields

Although MongoDB doesn't support joins, it supports the reference from a document to another document using a convention named **DBRef**. DBRef enables the reference from one document to another using a special field that contains the collection name and the document ObjectId field. Mongoose implements a similar behavior for supporting document referral using the ObjectID schema type and the use of the ref property. It also supports the population of the parent document with the child document when querying the database.

To understand this better, let's say you create another schema for blog posts called PostSchema. Because a user authors a blog post, PostSchema will contain an author field that will be populated by a User model instance. So, a PostSchema will look like what is shown in the following code snippet:

```
const PostSchema = new Schema({
  title: {
    type: String,
    required: true
  },
```

```
  content: {
    type: String,
    required: true
  },
  author: {
    type: Schema.ObjectId,
    ref: 'User'
  }
});
```

```
mongoose.model('Post', PostSchema);
```

Note the `ref` property telling Mongoose that the `author` field will use the `User` model to populate the value.

Using this new schema is a simple task. To create a new blog post, you will need to retrieve or create an instance of the `User` model, create an instance of the `Post` model, and then assign the `post author` property with the `user` instance. An example of this is as follows:

```
const user = new User();
user.save();

const post = new Post();
post.author = user;
post.save();
```

Mongoose will create a reference in the MongoDB `post` document and will later use it to retrieve the referenced user document.

Since it is only an `ObjectID` reference to a real document, Mongoose will have to populate the `post` instance with the `user` instance. To do this, you'll have to tell Mongoose to use the `populate()` method when retrieving the document. For instance, a `find()` method that populates the `author` property will look like what is shown in the following code snippet:

```
Post.find().populate('author').exec((err, posts) => {
  ...
});
```

Mongoose will then retrieve all the documents in the `posts` collection and populate their `author` attribute.

Mongoose's support for this feature enables you to calmly rely on object references to keep your data models organized. Later in this book, you'll learn how to reference in order to support your application logic.

To find out more about reference fields and population, it is recommended that you visit `http://mongoosejs.com/docs/populate.html`.

Summary

In this chapter, you were introduced to the robust Mongoose model. You connected to your MongoDB instance and created your first Mongoose schema and model. You also learned how to validate your data and modify it using schema modifiers and Mongoose middleware. You discovered virtual attributes and modifiers, and you learned how to use them in order to change the representation of your documents. You also discovered how to use Mongoose to implement a reference between documents. In the next chapter, we'll go through the **Passport** authentication module, which will use your User model to address user authentication.

6
Managing User Authentication Using Passport

Passport is a robust piece of Node.js authentication middleware that helps you to authenticate requests sent to your Express application. Passport uses strategies to utilize both local authentication and OAuth authentication providers, such as Facebook, Twitter, and Google. Using Passport strategies, you'll be able to seamlessly offer different authentication options to your users while maintaining a unified User model. In this chapter, you'll go through the following basic features of Passport:

- Understanding Passport strategies
- Integrating Passport into your user's MVC architecture
- Using Passport's local strategy to authenticate users
- Utilizing Passport OAuth strategies
- Offering authentication through social OAuth providers

Introducing Passport

Authentication is a vital part of most web applications. Handling user registration and sign-in is an important feature that can sometimes present a development overhead. Express, with its lean approach, lacks this feature, so, as is usual with node, an external module is needed. Passport is a Node.js module that uses the middleware design pattern to authenticate requests. It allows developers to offer various authentication methods using a mechanism called **strategies**, which allows you to implement a complex authentication layer while keeping your code clean and simple. Just as with any other Node.js module, before you can start using it in your application, you will first need to install it. The examples in this chapter will continue directly from those in previous chapters. So, for this chapter, copy the final example from *Chapter 5*, *Introduction to Mongoose*, and let's start from there.

Installing Passport

Passport uses different modules, each representing a different authentication strategy, but all of which depend on the base Passport module. To install the Passport base module, change your `package.json` file as follows:

```json
{
  "name": "MEAN",
  "version": "0.0.6",
  "dependencies": {
    "body-parser": "1.15.2",
    "compression": "1.6.0",
    "ejs": "2.5.2",
    "express": "4.14.0",
    "express-session": "1.14.1",
    "method-override": "2.3.6",
    "mongoose": "4.6.5",
    "morgan": "1.7.0",
    "passport": "0.3.2"
  }
}
```

Before you continue developing your application, make sure you install the new Passport dependency. To do so, go to your application's folder, and issue the following command in your command-line tool:

```
$ npm install
```

This will install the specified version of Passport in your `node_modules` folder. Once the installation process has successfully finished, you will need to configure your application to load the Passport module.

Configuring Passport

To configure Passport, you will need to set it up in a few steps. To create the Passport configuration file, go to the `config` folder and create a new file named `passport.js`. Leave it empty for now; we will return to it in a bit. Next, you'll need to require the file you just created, so change your `server.js` file, as follows:

```
process.env.NODE_ENV = process.env.NODE_ENV || 'development';

const configureMongoose = require('./config/mongoose');
const configureExpress = require('./config/express');
const configurePassport = require('./config/passport');

const db = configureMongoose();
const app = configureExpress();
const passport = configurePassport();
app.listen(3000);

module.exports = app;

console.log('Server running at http://localhost:3000/');
```

Next, you'll need to register the Passport middleware in your Express application. To do so, change your `config/express.js` file, as follows:

```
const config = require('./config');
const express = require('express');
const morgan = require('morgan');
const compress = require('compression');
const bodyParser = require('body-parser');
const methodOverride = require('method-override');
const session = require('express-session');
const passport = require('passport');

module.exports = function() {
  const app = express();

  if (process.env.NODE_ENV === 'development') {
    app.use(morgan('dev'));
  } else if (process.env.NODE_ENV === 'production') {
    app.use(compress());
  }

  app.use(bodyParser.urlencoded({
    extended: true
  }));
  app.use(bodyParser.json());
```

```
        app.use(methodOverride());

        app.use(session({
          saveUninitialized: true,
          resave: true,
          secret: config.sessionSecret
        }));
        app.set('views', './app/views');
        app.set('view engine', 'ejs');

        app.use(passport.initialize());
        app.use(passport.session());

        require('../app/routes/index.server.routes.js')(app);
        require('../app/routes/users.server.routes.js')(app);

        app.use(express.static('./public'));

        return app;
    };
```

Let's go over the code you just added. First, you required the Passport module, and then you registered two middleware: the `passport.initialize()` middleware, which is responsible for bootstrapping the Passport module, and the `passport.session()` middleware, which is using the Express session to keep track of your user's session.

Passport is now installed and configured, but to start using it, you will have to install at least one authentication strategy. We'll begin with the local strategy, which provides a simple username/password authentication layer; but first, let's discuss how Passport strategies work.

Understanding Passport strategies

To offer its various authentication options, Passport uses separate modules that implement different authentication strategies. Each module provides a different authentication method, such as username/password authentication and OAuth authentication. So, in order to offer Passport-supported authentication, you'll need to install and configure the strategies modules that you'd like to use. Let's begin with the local authentication strategy.

Using Passport's local strategy

Passport's local strategy is a Node.js module that allows you to implement a username/password authentication mechanism. You'll need to install it like any other module and configure it to use your User Mongoose model. Let's begin by installing the local strategy module.

Installing Passport's local strategy module

To install Passport's local strategy module, you'll need to add `passport-local` to your `package.json` file, as follows:

```
{
  "name": "MEAN",
  "version": "0.0.6",
  "dependencies": {
    "body-parser": "1.15.2",
    "compression": "1.6.0",
    "ejs": "2.5.2",
    "express": "4.14.0",
    "express-session": "1.14.1",
    "method-override": "2.3.6",
    "mongoose": "4.6.5",
    "morgan": "1.7.0",
    "passport": "0.3.2",
    "passport-local": "1.0.0"
  }
}
```

Then, go to your application's `root` folder, and issue the following command in your command-line tool:

```
$ npm install
```

This will install the specified version of the local strategy module in your `node_modules` folder. When the installation process has successfully finished, you'll need to configure Passport to use the local strategy.

Configuring Passport's local strategy

Each authentication strategy you'll use is basically a node module that lets you define how that strategy will be used. In order to maintain a clear separation of logic, each strategy should be configured in its own separated file. In your `config` folder, create a new folder named `strategies`. Inside this new folder, create a file named `local.js` that contains the following code snippet:

```
const passport = require('passport');
const LocalStrategy = require('passport-local').Strategy;
const User = require('mongoose').model('User');

module.exports = function() {
  passport.use(new LocalStrategy((username, password, done) => {
    User.findOne({
      username: username
    }, (err, user) => {
      if (err) {
        return done(err);
      }

      if (!user) {
        return done(null, false, {
          message: 'Unknown user'
        });
      }

      if (!user.authenticate(password)) {
        return done(null, false, {
          message: 'Invalid password'
        });
      }

      return done(null, user);
    });
  }));
};
```

The preceding code begins by requiring the `Passport` module, the local strategy module's `Strategy` object, and your `User` Mongoose model. Then, you register the strategy using the `passport.use()` method, which uses an instance of the `LocalStrategy` object. Notice how the `LocalStrategy` constructor takes a callback function as an argument. It will later call this callback when trying to authenticate a user.

The callback function accepts three arguments—username, password, and a done callback—which will be called when the authentication process is over. Inside the callback function, you will use the User Mongoose model to find a user with that username and try to authenticate it. In the event of an error, you will pass the error object to the done callback. When the user is authenticated, you will call the done callback with the user Mongoose object.

Remember the empty config/passport.js file? Well, now that you have your local strategy ready, you can go back and use it to configure the local authentication. To do so, go back to your config/passport.js file and paste the following lines of code:

```
const passport = require('passport');
const mongoose = require('mongoose');

module.exports = function() {
  const User = mongoose.model('User');

  passport.serializeUser((user, done) => {
    done(null, user.id);
  });

  passport.deserializeUser((id, done) => {
    User.findOne({
      _id: id
    }, '-password -salt', (err, user) => {
      done(err, user);
    });
  });

  require('./strategies/local.js')();
};
```

In the preceding code snippet, the passport.serializeUser() and passport.deserializeUser() methods are used to define how Passport will handle user serialization. When a user is authenticated, Passport will save its _id property to the session. Later on, when the user object is needed, Passport will use the _id property to grab the user object from the database. Notice how we used the field options argument to make sure Mongoose doesn't fetch the user's password and salt properties. The second thing the preceding code does is include the local strategy configuration file. This way, your server.js file will load the Passport configuration file, which in turn will load its strategies configuration file. Next, you'll need to modify your User model to support Passport's authentication.

Adapting the User model

In the previous chapter, we started discussing the User model and created its basic structure. In order to use the User model in your MEAN application, you'll have to modify it to address a few authentication process requirements. These changes will include modifying UserSchema, adding some pre middleware, and adding some new instance methods. To do so, go to your app/models/user.js file, and change it as follows:

```
const mongoose = require('mongoose');
const crypto = require('crypto');
const Schema = mongoose.Schema;
const UserSchema = new Schema({
    firstName: String,
    lastName: String,
    email: {
        type: String,
        match: [/.+\@.+\..+/, "Please fill a valid e-mail address"]
    },
    username: {
        type: String,
        unique: true,
        required: 'Username is required',
        trim: true
    },
    password: {
        type: String,
        validate: [(password) => {
            return password && password.length > 6;
        }, 'Password should be longer']
    },
    salt: {
        type: String
    },
    provider: {
        type: String,
        required: 'Provider is required'
    },
    providerId: String,
    providerData: {},
    created: {
        type: Date,
        default: Date.now
```

```
    }
});

UserSchema.virtual('fullName').get(function() {
    return this.firstName + ' ' + this.lastName;
}).set(function(fullName) {
    const splitName = fullName.split(' ');
    this.firstName = splitName[0] || '';
    this.lastName = splitName[1] || '';
});

UserSchema.pre('save', function(next) {
    if (this.password) {
        this.salt = new
        Buffer(crypto.randomBytes(16).toString('base64'), 'base64');
        this.password = this.hashPassword(this.password);
    }
    next();
});

UserSchema.methods.hashPassword = function(password) {
    return crypto.pbkdf2Sync(password, this.salt, 10000,
        64).toString('base64');
};

UserSchema.methods.authenticate = function(password) {
    return this.password === this.hashPassword(password);
};

UserSchema.statics.findUniqueUsername = function(username, suffix,
    callback) {
    var possibleUsername = username + (suffix || '');
    this.findOne({
        username: possibleUsername
    }, (err, user) => {
        if (!err) {
            if (!user) {
                callback(possibleUsername);
            } else {
                return this.findUniqueUsername(username, (suffix || 0)
+
                    1, callback);
            }
        } else {
            callback(null);
        }
    });
};
```

```
UserSchema.set('toJSON', {
    getters: true,
    virtuals: true
});

mongoose.model('User', UserSchema);
```

Let's go over these changes. First, you added four fields to your UserSchema object: a salt property, which you'll use to hash your password; a provider property, which will indicate the strategy used to register the user; a providerId property, which will indicate the user identifier for the authentication strategy; and a providerData property, which you'll later use to store the user object retrieved from OAuth providers.

Next, you created some pre-save middleware to handle the hashing of your user's passwords. It is widely known that storing a clear text version of your user's passwords is a very bad practice that can result in the leakage of your users' passwords. To handle this issue, your pre-save middleware performs two important steps: first, it creates an auto-generated pseudo-random hashing salt, and then it replaces the current user password with a hashed password using the hashPassword() instance method.

You also added two instance methods: a hashPassword() instance method, which is used to hash a password string by utilizing Node.js, crypto module; and an authenticate() instance method, which accepts a string argument, hashes it, and compares it to the current user's hashed password. Finally, you added the findUniqueUsername() static method, which is used to find an available unique username for new users. You'll use this method later in this chapter when you deal with OAuth authentication.

That completes the modifications in your User model, but there are a few other things to take care of before you can test your application's authentication layer.

Creating the authentication views

Just as with any web application, you will need to have signup and signin pages in order to handle user authentication. We'll create those views using the **EJS** template engine, so in your app/views folder, create a new file named signup.ejs. In your newly created file, paste the following code snippet:

```
<!DOCTYPE html>
<html>
<head>
  <title>
    <%=title %>
  </title>
```

```
    </head>
    <body>
      <% for(var i in messages) { %>
        <div class="flash"><%= messages[i] %></div>
      <% } %>
      <form action="/signup" method="post">
        <div>
          <label>First Name:</label>
          <input type="text" name="firstName" />
        </div>
        <div>
          <label>Last Name:</label>
          <input type="text" name="lastName" />
        </div>
        <div>
          <label>Email:</label>
          <input type="text" name="email" />
        </div>
        <div>
          <label>Username:</label>
          <input type="text" name="username" />
        </div>
        <div>
          <label>Password:</label>
          <input type="password" name="password" />
        </div>
        <div>
          <input type="submit" value="Sign up" />
        </div>
      </form>
    </body>
    </html>
```

The `signup.ejs` view simply contains an HTML form; an EJS tag, which renders the title variable; and an EJS loop, which renders the `messages` list variable. Go back to your `app/views` folder and create another file, named `signin.ejs`. Inside this file, paste the following code snippet:

```
<!DOCTYPE html>
<html>
<head>
  <title>
    <%=title %>
  </title>
</head>
```

```
<body>
  <% for(var i in messages) { %>
    <div class="flash"><%= messages[i] %></div>
  <% } %>
  <form action="/signin" method="post">
    <div>
      <label>Username:</label>
      <input type="text" name="username" />
    </div>
    <div>
      <label>Password:</label>
      <input type="password" name="password" />
    </div>
    <div>
      <input type="submit" value="Sign In" />
    </div>
  </form>
</body>
</html>
```

As you can see, the `signin.ejs` view is even simpler and also contains an HTML form; an EJS tag, which renders the `title` variable; and an EJS loop, which renders the `messages` list variable. Now that you have your model and views set, it's time to connect them using your Users controller.

Modifying the Users controller

To alter the Users controller, go to your `app/controllers/users.server.controller.js` file, and change its content as follows:

```
const User = require('mongoose').model('User');
const passport = require('passport');

function getErrorMessage(err) {
  let message = '';

  if (err.code) {
    switch (err.code) {
      case 11000:
      case 11001:
        message = 'Username already exists';
        break;
      default:
        message = 'Something went wrong';
    }
  } else {
```

```
      for (var errName in err.errors) {
        if (err.errors[errName].message) message =
err.errors[errName].message;
      }
    }
  }

  return message;
};

exports.renderSignin = function(req, res, next) {
  if (!req.user) {
    res.render('signin', {
      title: 'Sign-in Form',
      messages: req.flash('error') || req.flash('info')
    });
  } else {
    return res.redirect('/');
  }
};

exports.renderSignup = function(req, res, next) {
  if (!req.user) {
    res.render('signup', {
      title: 'Sign-up Form',
      messages: req.flash('error')
    });
  } else {
    return res.redirect('/');
  }
};

exports.signup = function(req, res, next) {
  if (!req.user) {
    const user = new User(req.body);
    user.provider = 'local';

    user.save((err) => {
      if (err) {
        const message = getErrorMessage(err);

        req.flash('error', message);
        return res.redirect('/signup');
      }
      req.login(user, (err) => {
        if (err) return next(err);
        return res.redirect('/');
      });
    });
  } else {
    return res.redirect('/');
```

```
    }
  };

  exports.signout = function(req, res) {
    req.logout();
    res.redirect('/');
  };
```

The `getErrorMessage()` method is a private method that returns a unified error message from a Mongoose `error` object. It is worth noticing that there are two possible errors here: a MongoDB indexing error handled using the error code, and a Mongoose validation error handled using the `err.errors` object.

The next two controller methods are quite simple and will be used to render the sign-in and signup pages. The `signout()` method is also simple and uses the `req.logout()` method, which is provided by the Passport module to invalidate the authenticated session.

The `signup()` method uses your `User` model to create new users. As you can see, it first creates a user object from the HTTP request body. Then, try saving it to MongoDB. If an error occurs, the `signup()` method will use the `getErrorMessage()` method to provide the user with an appropriate error message. If the user creation was successful, the user session will be created using the `req.login()` method. The `req.login()` method is exposed by the `Passport` module and is used to establish a successful login session. After the login operation is completed, a user object will be signed to the `req.user` object.

 The `req.login()` method will be called automatically while using the `passport.authenticate()` method, so a manual call for `req.login()` is primarily used when registering new users.

In the preceding code, though, a module you're not yet familiar with is used. When an authentication process is failing, it is common to redirect the request back to the signup or sign-in pages. This is done here when an error occurs, but how can your user tell what exactly went wrong? The problem is that when redirecting to another page, you cannot pass variables to that page. The solution is to use some sort of mechanism to pass temporary messages between requests. Fortunately, that mechanism already exists in the form of a node module named `Connect-Flash`.

Displaying flash error messages

The Connect-Flash module is a node module that allows you to store temporary messages in an area of the session object called flash. Messages stored on the flash object will be cleared once they are presented to the user. This architecture makes the Connect-Flash module perfect for transferring messages before redirecting the request to another page.

Installing the Connect-Flash module

To install the Connect-Flash module in your application's modules folders, you'll need to change your package.json file as follows:

```
{
  "name": "MEAN",
  "version": "0.0.6",
  "dependencies": {
    "body-parser": "1.15.2",
    "compression": "1.6.0",
    "connect-flash": "0.1.1",
    "ejs": "2.5.2",
    "express": "4.14.0",
    "express-session": "1.14.1",
    "method-override": "2.3.6",
    "mongoose": "4.6.5",
    "morgan": "1.7.0",
    "passport": "0.3.2",
    "passport-local": "1.0.0"
  }
}
```

As usual, before you can continue developing your application, you will need to install your new dependency. Go to your application's folder, and issue the following command in your command-line tool:

```
$ npm install
```

This will install the specified version of the Connect-Flash module in your node_modules folder. When the installation process is successfully finished, your next step is to configure your Express application to use the Connect-Flash module.

Configuring Connect-Flash module

To configure your Express application to use the new Connect-Flash module, you'll have to require the new module in your Express configuration file and use the app.use() method to register it with your Express application. To do so, make the following changes in your config/express.js file:

```javascript
const config = require('./config');
const express = require('express');
const morgan = require('morgan');
const compress = require('compression');
const bodyParser = require('body-parser');
const methodOverride = require('method-override');
const session = require('express-session');
const flash = require('connect-flash');
const passport = require('passport');

module.exports = function() {
  const app = express();

  if (process.env.NODE_ENV === 'development') {
    app.use(morgan('dev'));
  } else if (process.env.NODE_ENV === 'production') {
    app.use(compress());
  }

  app.use(bodyParser.urlencoded({
    extended: true
  }));

  app.use(bodyParser.json());
  app.use(methodOverride());

  app.use(session({
    saveUninitialized: true,
    resave: true,
    secret: config.sessionSecret
  }));
  app.set('views', './app/views');
  app.set('view engine', 'ejs');

  app.use(flash());
  app.use(passport.initialize());
  app.use(passport.session());

  require('../app/routes/index.server.routes.js')(app);
  require('../app/routes/users.server.routes.js')(app);

  app.use(express.static('./public'));

  return app;
};
```

This will tell your Express application to use the Connect-Flash module and create the new flash area in the application session.

Using Connect-Flash module

Once installed, the Connect-Flash module exposes the req.flash() method, which allows you to create and retrieve flash messages. To understand it better, let's observe the changes you've made to your Users controller. First, let's take a look at the renderSignup() and renderSignin() methods, which are responsible for rendering the sign-in and signup pages:

```
exports.renderSignin = function(req, res, next) {
  if (!req.user) {
    res.render('signin', {
      title: 'Sign-in Form',
      messages: req.flash('error') || req.flash('info')
    });
  } else {
    return res.redirect('/');
  }
};

exports.renderSignup = function(req, res, next) {
  if (!req.user) {
    res.render('signup', {
      title: 'Sign-up Form',
      messages: req.flash('error')
    });
  } else {
    return res.redirect('/');
  }
};
```

As you can see, the res.render() method is executed with the title and messages variables. The messages variable uses req.flash() to read the messages written to the flash. Now if you go over the signup() method, you'll notice the following line of code:

```
req.flash('error', message);
```

This is how error messages are written to the flash, again using the `req.flash()` method. After you learned how to use the `Connect-Flash` module, you might have noticed that we're lacking a `signin()` method. This is because Passport provides you with an authentication method, which you can use directly in your routing definition. To wrap up, let's proceed to the last part that needs to be modified: the user's routing definition file.

Wiring the user's routes

Once you have your model, controller, and views configured, all that is left to do is define the user's routes. To do so, make the following changes in your `app/routes/users.server.routes.js` file:

```
const users = require('../../app/controllers/users.server.
controller');
const passport = require('passport');

module.exports = function(app) {
  app.route('/signup')
      .get(users.renderSignup)
      .post(users.signup);

  app.route('/signin')
      .get(users.renderSignin)
      .post(passport.authenticate('local', {
        successRedirect: '/',
        failureRedirect: '/signin',
        failureFlash: true
      }));

  app.get('/signout', users.signout);
};
```

As you can see, most of the route definitions here are basically directing to methods from your user controller. The only different route definition is the one where you're handling any POST request made to the `/signin` path using the `passport.authenticate()` method.

When the `passport.authenticate()` method is executed, it will try to authenticate the user request using the strategy defined by its first argument. In this case, it will try to authenticate the request using the local strategy. The second parameter this method accepts is an `options` object, which contains three properties:

- `successRedirect`: This property tells Passport where to redirect the request once it has successfully authenticated the user

- `failureRedirect`: This property tells Passport where to redirect the request once it has failed to authenticate the user

- `failureFlash`: This property tells Passport whether or not to use flash messages

You've almost completed the basic authentication implementation. To test it out, make the following changes to the `app/controllers/index.server.controller.js` file:

```
exports.render = function(req, res) {
  res.render('index', {
    title: 'Hello World',
    userFullName: req.user ? req.user.fullName : ''
  });
};
```

This will pass the authenticated user's full name to your home page template. You will also have to make the following changes in your `app/views/index.ejs` file:

```
<!DOCTYPE html>
<html>
  <head>
      <title><%= title %></title>
  </head>
  <body>
    <% if ( userFullName ) { %>
      <h2>Hello <%=userFullName%> </h2>
      <a href="/signout">Sign out</a>
    <% } else { %>
      <a href="/signup">Signup</a>
      <a href="/signin">Signin</a>
    <% } %>
    <br>
      <img src="img/logo.png" alt="Logo">
  </body>
</html>
```

That's it! Everything is ready to test your new authentication layer. Go to your root application folder and use the node command-line tool to run your application and type the following command:

```
$ node server
```

Test your application by visiting `http://localhost:3000/signin` and `http://localhost:3000/signup`. Try signing up, and then sign in and don't forget to go back to your home page to see how the user details are saved through the session.

Understanding Passport OAuth strategies

OAuth is an authentication protocol that allows users to register with your web application using an external provider, without the need to input their username and password. OAuth is mainly used by social platforms, such as Facebook, Twitter, and Google, to allow users to register with other websites using their social account.

[

To learn more about how OAuth works, visit the OAuth protocol website at `http://oauth.net/`.
]

Setting up OAuth strategies

Passport supports the basic OAuth strategy, which enables you to implement any OAuth-based authentication. However, it also supports user authentication through major OAuth providers using wrapper strategies that help you avoid the need to implement a complex mechanism by yourself. In this section, we'll review the top OAuth providers and how to implement their Passport authentication strategy.

[

Before you begin, you will have to contact the OAuth provider and create a developer application. This application will have both an OAuth client ID and an OAuth client secret, which will allow you to verify your application against the OAuth provider.
]

Handling OAuth user creation

The OAuth user creation should be a bit different from the local `signup()` method. Since users are signing up using their profile from other providers, the profile details are already present, which means you will need to validate them differently. To do so, go back to your `app/controllers/users.server.controller.js` file, and add the following method:

```
exports.saveOAuthUserProfile = function(req, profile, done) {
  User.findOne({
    provider: profile.provider,
    providerId: profile.providerId
  }, (err, user) => {
    if (err) {
      return done(err);
    } else {
      if (!user) {
        const possibleUsername = profile.username ||
          ((profile.email) ? profile.email.split(@''@')[0] : '');

        User.findUniqueUsername(possibleUsername, null,
            (availableUsername) => {
          const newUser = new User(profile);
          newUser.username = availableUsername;

          newUser.save((err) => {

            return done(err, newUser);
          });
        });
      } else {
        return done(err, user);
      }
    }
  });
};
```

This method accepts a user profile, and then looks for an existing user with these
`providerId` and `provider` properties. If it finds the user, it calls the `done()`
callback method with the user's MongoDB document. However, if it cannot
find an existing user, it will find a unique username using the User model's
`findUniqueUsername()` static method and save a new user instance. If an error
occurs, the `saveOAuthUserProfile()` method will use the `done()` methods to report
the error; otherwise, it will pass the user object to the `done()` callback method. Once
you have figured out the `saveOAuthUserProfile()` method, it is time to implement
the first OAuth authentication strategy.

Using Passport's Facebook strategy

Facebook is probably the world's largest OAuth provider. Many modern web applications offer their users the ability to register with the web application using their Facebook profile. Passport supports Facebook OAuth authentication using the passport-facebook module. Let's see how you can implement Facebook-based authentication in a few simple steps.

Installing Passport's Facebook strategy

To install Passport's Facebook module in your application's modules folders, you'll need to change your package.json file as follows:

```
{
  "name": "MEAN",
  "version": "0.0.6",
  "dependencies": {
    "body-parser": "1.15.2",
    "compression": "1.6.0",
    "connect-flash": "0.1.1",
    "ejs": "2.5.2",
    "express": "4.14.0",
    "express-session": "1.14.1",
    "method-override": "2.3.6",
    "mongoose": "4.6.5",
    "morgan": "1.7.0",
    "passport": "0.3.2",
    "passport-facebook": "2.1.1",
    "passport-local": "1.0.0"
  }
}
```

Before you can continue developing your application, you will need to install the new Facebook strategy dependency. To do so, go to your application's root folder, and issue the following command in your command-line tool:

```
$ npm install
```

This will install the specified version of Passport's Facebook strategy in your node_modules folder. Once the installation process has successfully finished, you will need to configure the Facebook strategy.

Configuring Passport's Facebook strategy

Before you begin configuring your Facebook strategy, you will have to go to Facebook's developers' home page at `https://developers.facebook.com/`, create a new Facebook application, and set the local host as the application domain. After configuring your Facebook application, you will get a Facebook application ID and secret. You'll need those to authenticate your users via Facebook, so let's save them in our environment configuration file. Go to the `config/env/development.js` file and change it as follows:

```
module.exports = {
  db: 'mongodb://localhost/mean-book',
  sessionSecret: 'developmentSessionSecret',
  facebook: {
    clientID: 'Application Id',
    clientSecret: 'Application Secret',
    callbackURL: 'http://localhost:3000/oauth/facebook/callback'
  }
};
```

Don't forget to replace `Application Id` and `Application Secret` with your Facebook application's ID and secret. The `callbackURL` property will be passed to the Facebook OAuth service, which will redirect to that URL after the authentication process is over. Make sure the `callbackURL` property matches the callback settings that you've set in the developer's home page.

Now, go to your `config/strategies` folder, and create a new file named `facebook.js` that contains the following code snippet:

```
const passport = require('passport');
const url = require('url');
const FacebookStrategy = require('passport-facebook').Strategy;
const config = require('../config');
const users = require('../../app/controllers/users.server.
controller');

module.exports = function() {
  passport.use(new FacebookStrategy({
    clientID: config.facebook.clientID,
    clientSecret: config.facebook.clientSecret,
    callbackURL: config.facebook.callbackURL,
    profileFields: ['id', 'name', 'displayName', 'emails'],
    passReqToCallback: true
  }, (req, accessToken, refreshToken, profile, done) => {
    const providerData = profile._json;
    providerData.accessToken = accessToken;
```

```
      providerData.refreshToken = refreshToken;

      const providerUserProfile = {
        firstName: profile.name.givenName,
        lastName: profile.name.familyName,
        fullName: profile.displayName,
        email: profile.emails[0].value,
        username: profile.name.givenName + profile.name.familyName,
        provider: 'facebook',
        providerId: profile.id,
        providerData: providerData
      };

      users.saveOAuthUserProfile(req, providerUserProfile, done);
   }));
};
```

Let's go over the preceding code snippet for a moment. You begin by requiring the `passport` module, the Facebook Strategy object, your environmental configuration file, your `User` Mongoose model, and the Users controller. Then, you register the strategy using the `passport.use()` method and creating an instance of a `FacebookStrategy` object. The `FacebookStrategy` constructor takes two arguments: the Facebook application information and a callback function that it will call later when trying to authenticate a user.

Take a look at the callback function you defined. It accepts five arguments: the HTTP `request` object, an `accessToken` object to validate future requests, a `refreshToken` object to grab new access tokens, a `profile` object containing the user profile, and a `done` callback to be called when the authentication process is over.

Inside the callback function, you will create a new user object using the Facebook profile information and the controller's `saveOAuthUserProfile()` method, which you previously created, to authenticate the current user.

Remember the `config/passport.js` file? Well, now that you have your Facebook strategy configured, you can go back to it and load the strategy file. To do so, go back to the `config/passport.js` file and change it, as follows:

```
const passport = require('passport');
const mongoose = require('mongoose');

module.exports = function() {
  const User = mongoose.model('User');

  passport.serializeUser((user, done) => {
    done(null, user.id);
  });

  passport.deserializeUser((id, done) => {
```

```
    User.findOne({
      _id: id
    }, '-password -salt', (err, user) => {
      done(err, user);
    });
  });

  require('./strategies/local.js')();
  require('./strategies/facebook.js')();
};
```

This will load your Facebook strategy configuration file. Now, all that is left to do is set the routes needed to authenticate users via Facebook and include a link to those routes in your sign-in and signup pages.

Wiring Passport's Facebook strategy routes

Passport OAuth strategies support the ability to authenticate users directly using the passport.authenticate() method. To do so, go to app/routes/users.server. routes.js, and append the following lines of code after the local strategy routes definition:

```
app.get('/oauth/facebook', passport.authenticate('facebook', {
  failureRedirect: '/signin'
}));

app.get('/oauth/facebook/callback', passport.authenticate('facebook',
{
  failureRedirect: '/signin',
  successRedirect: '/'
}));
```

The first route will use the passport.authenticate() method to start the user authentication process, while the second route will use the passport. authenticate() method to finish the authentication process once the user has linked their Facebook profile.

That's it! Everything is set up for your users to authenticate via Facebook. All you have to do now is go to your app/views/signup.ejs and app/views/signin.ejs files, and add the following line of code right before the closing BODY tag:

```
<a href="/oauth/facebook">Sign in with Facebook</a>
```

This will allow your users to click on the link and register with your application via their Facebook profile.

Using Passport's Twitter strategy

Another popular OAuth provider is Twitter, and a lot of web applications offer their users the ability to register with the web application using their Twitter profile. Passport supports the Twitter OAuth authentication method using the `passport-twitter` module. Let's see how you can implement a Twitter-based authentication in a few simple steps.

Installing Passport's Twitter strategy

To install Passport's Twitter strategy module in your application's modules folders, you'll need to change your `package.json` file as follows:

```json
{
    "name": "MEAN",
    "version": "0.0.6",
    "dependencies": {
        "body-parser": "1.15.2",
        "compression": "1.6.0",
        "connect-flash": "0.1.1",
        "ejs": "2.5.2",
        "express": "4.14.0",
        "express-session": "1.14.1",
        "method-override": "2.3.6",
        "mongoose": "4.6.5",
        "morgan": "1.7.0",
        "passport": "0.3.2",
        "passport-facebook": "2.1.1",
        "passport-local": "1.0.0",
        "passport-twitter": "1.0.4"
    }
}
```

Before you continue developing your application, you will need to install the new Twitter strategy dependency. Go to your application's `root` folder, and issue the following command in your command-line tool:

```
$ npm install
```

This will install the specified version of Passport's Twitter strategy in your `node_modules` folder. Once the installation process has successfully finished, you will need to configure the Twitter strategy.

Configuring Passport's Twitter strategy

Before we begin configuring your Twitter strategy, you will have to go to the Twitter developers' home page at `https://dev.twitter.com/` and create a new Twitter application. After configuring your Twitter application, you will get a Twitter application ID and secret. You'll need them to authenticate your users via Twitter, so let's add them in our environment configuration file. Go to the `config/env/development.js` file, and change it as follows:

```
module.exports = {
  db: 'mongodb://localhost/mean-book',
  sessionSecret: 'developmentSessionSecret',
  facebook: {
    clientID: 'Application Id',
    clientSecret: 'Application Secret',
    callbackURL: 'http://localhost:3000/oauth/facebook/callback'
  },
  twitter: {
    clientID: 'Application Id',
    clientSecret: 'Application Secret',
    callbackURL: 'http://localhost:3000/oauth/twitter/callback'
  }
};
```

Don't forget to replace `Application Id` and `Application Secret` with your Twitter application's ID and secret. The `callbackURL` property will be passed to the Twitter OAuth service, which will redirect the user to that URL after the authentication process is over. Make sure the `callbackURL` property matches the callback settings that you've set in the developer's home page.

As stated earlier, in your project, each strategy should be configured in its own separate file, which will help you keep your project organized. Go to your `config/strategies` folder, and create a new file named `twitter.js` containing the following lines of code:

```
const passport = require('passport');
const url = require('url');
const TwitterStrategy = require('passport-twitter').Strategy;
const config = require('../config');
const users = require('../../app/controllers/users.server.
controller');

module.exports = function() {
  passport.use(new TwitterStrategy({
    consumerKey: config.twitter.clientID,
    consumerSecret: config.twitter.clientSecret,
    callbackURL: config.twitter.callbackURL,
```

```
        passReqToCallback: true
    }, (req, token, tokenSecret, profile, done) => {
      const providerData = profile._json;
      providerData.token = token;
      providerData.tokenSecret = tokenSecret;

      const providerUserProfile = {
        fullName: profile.displayName,
        username: profile.username,
        provider: 'twitter',
        providerId: profile.id,
        providerData: providerData
      };

      users.saveOAuthUserProfile(req, providerUserProfile, done);
    }));
  };
```

You begin by requiring the passport module, the Twitter Strategy object,
your environmental configuration file, your User Mongoose model, and the Users
controller. Then, you register the strategy using the passport.use() method, and
create an instance of a TwitterStrategy object. The TwitterStrategy constructor
takes two arguments: the Twitter application information and a callback function
that it will call later when trying to authenticate a user.

Take a look at the callback function you defined. It accepts five arguments: the HTTP
request object, a token object and a tokenSecret object to validate future requests,
a profile object containing the user profile, and a done callback to be called when
the authentication process is over.

Inside the callback function, you will create a new user object using the Twitter
profile information and the controller's saveOAuthUserProfile() method, which
you created previously, to authenticate the current user.

Now that you have your Twitter strategy configured, you can go back to the config/
passport.js file and load the strategy file as follows:

```
const passport = require('passport');
const mongoose = require('mongoose');

module.exports = function() {
  const User = mongoose.model('User');

  passport.serializeUser((user, done) => {
    done(null, user.id);
  });
```

```
passport.deserializeUser((id, done) => {
  User.findOne({
    _id: id
  }, '-password -salt, ', (err, user) => {
    done(err, user);
  });
});

require('./strategies/local.js')();
require('./strategies/facebook.js')();
require('./strategies/twitter.js')();
};
```

This will load your Twitter strategy configuration file. Now all that is left to do is set the routes needed to authenticate users via Twitter and include a link to those routes in your sign-in and signup pages.

Wiring Passport's Twitter strategy routes

To add Passport's Twitter routes, go to your app/routes/users.server.routes.js file, and paste the following code after the Facebook strategy routes:

```
app.get('/oauth/twitter', passport.authenticate('twitter', {
  failureRedirect: '/signin'
}));

app.get('/oauth/twitter/callback', passport.authenticate('twitter', {
  failureRedirect: '/signin',
  successRedirect: '/'
}));
```

The first route will use the passport.authenticate() method to start the user authentication process, while the second route will use the passport.authenticate() method to finish the authentication process once the user has used their Twitter profile to connect.

That's it! Everything is set up for your user's Twitter-based authentication. All you have to do is go to your app/views/signup.ejs and app/views/signin.ejs files and add the following line of code right before the closing BODY tag:

```
<a href="/oauth/twitter">Sign in with Twitter</a>
```

This will allow your users to click on the link and register with your application via their Twitter profile.

Using Passport's Google strategy

The last OAuth provider we'll implement is Google as a lot of web applications offer their users the ability to register with the web application using their Google profile. Passport supports the Google OAuth authentication method using the `passport-google-oauth` module. Let's see how you can implement a Google-based authentication in a few simple steps.

Installing Passport's Google strategy

To install Passport's Google strategy module in your application's modules folders, you'll need to change your `package.json` file, as follows:

```json
{
  "name": "MEAN",
  "version": "0.0.6",
  "dependencies": {
    "body-parser": "1.15.2",
    "compression": "1.6.0",
    "connect-flash": "0.1.1",
    "ejs": "2.5.2",
    "express": "4.14.0",
    "express-session": "1.14.1",
    "method-override": "2.3.6",
    "mongoose": "4.6.5",
    "morgan": "1.7.0",
    "passport": "0.3.2",
    "passport-facebook": "2.1.1",
    "passport-google-oauth": "1.0.0",
    "passport-local": "1.0.0",
    "passport-twitter": "1.0.4"
  }
}
```

Before you can continue developing your application, you will need to install the new Google strategy dependency. Go to your application's `root` folder, and issue the following command in your command-line tool:

```
$ npm install
```

This will install the specified version of Passport's Google strategy in your `node_modules` folder. Once the installation process has successfully finished, you will need to configure the Google strategy.

Configuring Passport's Google strategy

Before we begin configuring your Google strategy, you will have to go to the Google developers' home page at `https://console.developers.google.com/`and create a new Google application. In your application's settings, set the JAVASCRIPT ORIGINS property to `http://localhost` and the REDIRECT URLs property to `http://localhost/oauth/google/callback`. After configuring your Google application, you will get a Google application ID and secret. You'll need them to authenticate your users via Google, so let's add them in our environment configuration file. Go to the `config/env/development.js` file, and change it as follows:

```
module.exports = {
  db: 'mongodb://localhost/mean-book',
  sessionSecret: 'developmentSessionSecret',
  facebook: {
    clientID: 'Application Id',
    clientSecret: 'Application Secret',
    callbackURL:
      'http://localhost:3000/oauth/facebook/callback'
  },
  twitter: {
    clientID: 'Application Id',
    clientSecret: 'Application Secret',
    callbackURL: 'http://localhost:3000/oauth/twitter/callback'
  },
  google: {
    clientID: 'Application Id',
    clientSecret: 'Application Secret',
    callbackURL: 'http://localhost:3000/oauth/google/callback'
  }
};
```

Don't forget to replace `Application Id` and `Application Secret` with your Google application's ID and secret. The `callbackURL` property will be passed to the Google OAuth service, which will redirect the user to that URL after the authentication process is over. Make sure the `callbackURL` property matches the callback settings that you've set in the developers' home page.

To implement the Google authentication strategy, go to your `config/strategies` folder, and create a new file named `google.js` containing the following lines of code:

```
const passport = require('passport');
const url = require('url');;
const GoogleStrategy = require('passport-google-oauth').
  OAuth2Strategy;
const config = require(../config');
```

```
const users = require('../../app/controllers/users.server.
 controller');

module.exports = function() {
  passport.use(new GoogleStrategy({
    clientID: config.google.clientID,
    clientSecret: config.google.clientSecret,
    callbackURL: config.google.callbackURL,
    passReqToCallback: true
  }, (req, accessToken, refreshToken, profile, done) => {
    const providerData = profile._json;
    providerData.accessToken = accessToken;
    providerData.refreshToken = refreshToken;

    const providerUserProfile = {
      firstName: profile.name.givenName,
      lastName: profile.name.familyName,
      fullName: profile.displayName,
      email: profile.emails[0].value,
      username: profile.username,
      provider: 'google''google',
      providerId: profile.id,
      providerData: providerData
    };

    users.saveOAuthUserProfile(req, providerUserProfile, done);
  }));
};
```

Let's go over the preceding code snippet for a moment. You begin by requiring the
passport module, the Google Strategy object, your environmental configuration file,
your User Mongoose model, and the Users controller. Then, you register the strategy
using the passport.use() method and create an instance of a GoogleStrategy
object. The GoogleStrategy constructor takes two arguments: the Google
application information and a callback function that it will later call when trying to
authenticate a user.

Take a look at the callback function you defined. It accepts five arguments: the HTTP
request object, an accessToken object to validate future requests, a refreshToken
object to grab new access tokens, a profile object containing the user profile, and a
done callback to be called when the authentication process is over.

Inside the callback function, you will create a new user object using the Google
profile information and the controller's saveOAuthUserProfile() method, which
you previously created, to authenticate the current user.

Now that you have your Google strategy configured, you can go back to the `config/` `passport.js` file and load the strategy file, as follows:

```
const passport = require('passport');
const mongoose = require('mongoose');

module.exports = function() {
  const User = mongoose.model('User');

  passport.serializeUser((user, done) => {
    done(null, user.id);
  });

  passport.deserializeUser((id, done) => {
    User.findOne({
      _id: id
    }, '-password -salt', function(err, user) => {
      done(err, user);
    });
  });

  require('./strategies/local.js')();
  require('./strategies/facebook.js')();
  require('./strategies/twitter.js')();
  require('./strategies/google.js')();
};
```

This will load your Google strategy configuration file. Now all that is left to do is set the routes required to authenticate users via Google and include a link to those routes in your sign-in and signup pages.

Wiring Passport's Google strategy routes

To add Passport's Google routes, go to your `app/routes/users.server.routes.js` file, and paste the following lines of code after the Twitter strategy routes:

```
app.get('/oauth/google', passport.authenticate('google', {
  failureRedirect: '/signin',
  scope: [
    'https://www.googleapis.com/auth/userinfo.profile',
    'https://www.googleapis.com/auth/userinfo.email'
  ],
}));
```

```
app.get('/oauth/google/callback', passport.authenticate('google', {
  failureRedirect: '/signin',
  successRedirect: '/'
}));
```

The first route will use the `passport.authenticate()` method to start the user authentication process, while the second route will use the `passport.authenticate()` method to finish the authentication process once the user has used their Google profile to connect.

That's it! Everything is set up for your user's Google-based authentication. All you have to do is go to your `app/views/signup.ejs` and `app/views/signin.ejs` files and add the following line of code right before the closing BODY tag:

```
<a href="/oauth/google">Sign in with Google</a>
```

This will allow your users to click on the link and register with your application via their Google profile. To test your new authentication layers, go to your application's `root` folder and use the node command-line tool to run your application:

$ node server

Test your application by visiting `http://localhost:3000/signin` and `http://localhost:3000/signup`. Try signing up and signing in using the new OAuth methods. Don't forget to visit your home page to see how the user details are saved throughout the session.

 Passport has similar support for many additional OAuth providers. To learn more, it is recommended that you visit `http://passportjs.org/guide/providers/`.

Summary

In this chapter, you learned about the Passport authentication module. You discovered its strategies and how to handle their installation and configuration. You also learned how to properly register your users and how to authenticate their requests. You went through Passport's local strategy and learned how to authenticate users using a username and password and how Passport supports the different OAuth authentication providers. In the next chapter, you'll discover the last piece of the MEAN puzzle, when we introduce you to **Angular**.

7
Introduction to Angular

The last piece of the MEAN puzzle is, of course, Angular. Back in 2009, while building their JSON as platform service, developers Miško Hevery and Adam Abrons noticed that the common JavaScript libraries weren't enough. The nature of their rich web applications raised the need for a more structured framework that would reduce redundant work and keep the project code organized. Abandoning their original idea, they decided to focus on the development of their framework, naming it AngularJS and releasing it under an open source license. The idea was to bridge the gap between JavaScript and HTML and help popularize single-page application development. In the years to come, AngularJS—now referred to as Angular—became one of the most popular frameworks in the JavaScript ecosystem, and it completely changed the frontend development world. However, in the past few years, there were a few major paradigm shifts. So, when the Google-sponsored team decided to work on Angular's next version, they introduced a whole set of new ideas. In this chapter, we'll cover the following topics:

- Introducing TypeScript
- Introducing Angular 2
- Understanding the building blocks of Angular 2
- Installing and configuring TypeScript and Angular 2
- Creating and organizing the Angular 2 application
- Utilizing Angular's components architecture
- Implementing the Authentication component

Introducing Angular 2

AngularJS was a frontend JavaScript framework designed to build single-page applications using an MVC-like architecture. The Angular approach was to extend the functionality of HTML using special attributes that bind JavaScript logic with HTML elements. AngularJS's ability to extend HTML allowed cleaner DOM manipulation through client-side templating and two-way data binding that seamlessly synchronized between models and views. AngularJS also improved the application's code structure and testability using MVC and dependency injection. AngularJS 1 was and still is a great framework, but it was built with the concepts of ES5 in mind, and with the huge improvements brought by the new ES2015 specification coming up, the team had to rethink the entire approach.

From Angular 1.x to Angular 2.x

If you're already familiar with Angular 1, moving to Angular 2 might seem like a big step. However, the Angular team made sure to keep the good parts of Angular 1 while leveraging ES2015's new capabilities and maintaining a clearer path toward an improved framework. Here's a quick summary of the changes made from Angular 1:

- **Syntax**: Angular 2 relies on the new ECMAScript specification formerly known as ES6 and now renamed ES2015. However, the specification is still a work in progress and browser support is still lacking. To overcome this issue, the Angular 2 team decided to use TypeScript.

- **TypeScript**: TypeScript is a superset of ES2015, which means that it allows you to write strongly typed ES2015 code, which will later be compiled into the ES5 or ES2015 source depending on your needs and platform support. Angular 2 is pushing hard for TypeScript usage in their documentation and code examples, and so will we. Don't worry, though; as vast and terrifying as TypeScript might seem, by the end of this chapter, you'll be able to use it.

- **Modules**: Angular 1 introduced a modular architecture that required the usage of the `angular#module()` custom method. However, ES2015 introduced a built-in module system very similar to the one used in Node.js. So Angular 2 modules are much easier to create and use.

- **Controllers**: Angular 1 was all about controllers. In the first version of this book, this chapter was mainly focused on the Angular 1 MVC approach, but in Angular 2, the basic building block is components. This shift also represents a bigger shift in the JavaScript ecosystem, especially regarding web components.

- **Scopes**: The famous $scope object is now obsolete. In Angular 2, the component model is cleaner and more readable. Generally, the introduction of classes in ES2015 and its support in TypeScript allows better design patterns.

- **Decorators**: Decorators is a design feature implemented in TypeScript and is probably going to be implemented in ES2016(ES7). Decorators allow developers to annotate classes and members in order to add features or data while not extending the entity. Angular 2 relies on decorators to implement certain features, and you're going to deal with them later in this chapter.

- **Dependency Injection**: Angular 1 used the Dependency Injection paradigm quite intensively. Angular 2 made Dependency Injection simpler and now supports multiple injectors instead of one.

All of these features mark a new era for Angular and JavaScript in general and it all starts with TypeScript.

Introduction to TypeScript

TypeScript is a typed programming language created by Microsoft, which uses the object-oriented foundations of C#, Java, and now ES2015. Code written in TypeScript is transpiled into JavaScript code either in ES3, ES5 or ES2015 and can be run on any of the modern web browsers. It is also a superset of ES2015, so basically, any JavaScript code is valid TypeScript code. The idea behind this was to create a strongly typed programming language for big projects that will allow big teams to better communicate the interface between their software components. As derived from its name, TypeScript has an optional type system that allows developers to enforce limits on their code in order to have better clarity. Since a lot of the features in TypeScript were already implemented in ES2015, we'll touch a few basic features that we'll need and didn't get in the current specifications.

Types

Types are a major part of every programming language, including JavaScript. Unfortunately, static typing was not introduced in ES2015; however, TypeScript support the basic JavaScript types and also allows developers to create and use their own types.

Basic types

Types can be JavaScript primitive types, as shown in the following code:

```
let firstName: string = "John";
let lastName = 'Smith';
let height: number = 6;
let isDone: boolean = false;
```

Moreover, TypeScript also allows you to work with arrays:

```
var numbers:number[] = [1, 2, 3];
var names:Array<string> = ['Alice', 'Helen', 'Claire'];
```

Both ways are then transpiled into the familiar JavaScript array declaration.

The any type

The `any` type represents any freeform JavaScript value. The value of `any` will go through a minimal static type checking by the transpiler and will support all operations as a JavaScript value. All properties on an `any` value can be accessed, and an `any` value can also be called as a function with an argument list. Actually, `any` is a supertype of all types, and whenever TypeScript cannot infer a type, the `any` type will be used. You'll be able to use the `any` type either explicitly or not:

```
var x: any;
var y;
```

Interfaces

As TypeScript is about keeping the structure of your project, highly important parts of the language are interfaces. An interface allows you shape your objects and keep your code solid and clear. Classes can implement interfaces, which means that they will have to conform to the properties or methods declared in the interface. Interfaces can also inherit from other interfaces, which means that their implementing classes will be able to implement the extended interfaces. An example TypeScript interface will look similar to this:

```
interface IVehicle {
  wheels: number;
  engine: string;
  drive();
}
```

Here, we have an `IVehicle` interface with two properties and one method. An implementing class would look like this:

```
class Car implements IVehicle  {
    wheels: number;
    engine: string;

    constructor(wheels: number, engine: string) {
        this.wheels = wheels;
        this.engine = engine;
    }

    drive() {
        console.log('Driving...');
    }
}
```

As you can see, the `Car` class implements the `IVehicle` interface and follows the structure set by it.

 Interfaces are a powerful feature of TypeScript and are an important part of OOP. It is recommended that you continue reading about them here: https://www.typescriptlang.org/docs/handbook/interfaces.html.

Decorators

While it's still in the proposal stage for the new ES7 specifications, Angular 2 relies heavily on decorators. A decorator is a special kind of declaration that can be attached to various entities, such as classes, methods, or properties. Decorators provide developers with a reusable way to annotate and modify classes and members. A decorator uses the `@decoratorName` form, where the `decoratorName` parameter must be a function that will be called at runtime with the decorated entity. A simple decorator would look as follows:

```
function Decorator(target: any) {

}
@Decorator
class MyClass {

}
```

At runtime, the decorator will be executed with the target parameter populated with the `MyClass` constructor. Moreover, the decorator can also have arguments as follows:

```
function DecoratorWithArgs(options: Object) {
  return (target: Object) => {

  }
}

@DecoratorWithArgs({ type: 'SomeType' })
class MyClass {

}
```

This pattern is also know as a decorator factory. Decorators may seem a bit odd, but as soon as we dive into Angular 2, you'll begin to understand their robustness.

Summary

TypeScript has been around for years and is being developed by a very strong team. This means that we've barely scratched the surface of its endless features and abilities. However, this introduction will provide us with the skills and knowledge required for diving into the great framework that Angular 2 is.

Angular 2 Architecture

The goal of Angular 2 is simple: bring HTML and JavaScript together in a manageable and scalable way in order to build a client application. To do that, Angular 2 uses a component-based approach with supporting entities, such as services and directives being injected into the components at runtime. This approach may seem a bit odd at first, but it allows us to keep a clear separation of concerns and generally maintain a clearer project structure. In order to understand the basics of Angular 2, take a look at the following figure:

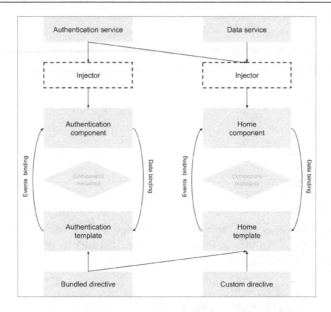

The preceding figure presents a simplistic architecture for an Angular 2 application consisting of two components. The center entities are the components. Each component performs data binding and event handling with its template in order to present the user with an interactive UI. Services are created for any other task, such as loading data, performing calculations, and so on. The services are then consumed by the components that delegate these tasks. Directives are the instructions for the rendering of the component's templates. In order to understand this better, let's dive in a little deeper.

Angular 2 Modules

Angular 2 applications are usually modular applications. This means that an Angular 2 application consists of multiple modules, and each one is a piece of code usually dedicated to a single task. In fact, the entire framework is built in a modular way that allows developer to import only the features they need. Fortunately, Angular 2 uses the ES2015 module syntax we covered earlier. Our application will be built of custom modules as well, and a sample application module would look as follows:

```
import { NgModule }       from '@angular/core';
import { CommonModule }   from '@angular/common';
import { RouterModule }   from '@angular/router';

import { AppComponent }     from './app.component';
import { AppRoutes }      from './app.routes';
```

```
@NgModule({
  imports: [
    CommonModule,
    RouterModule.forRoot(AppRoutes),
  ],
  declarations: [
    AppComponent
  ],
  bootstrap: [AppComponent]
})
export class AppModule { }
```

As you can see, we use the @NgModule decorator to create the application module, which uses the application component and routes to bootstrap our application. To understand this better, let's take a look at the first and foremost building block of an Angular 2 application: the component.

Angular 2 Components

A component is the essential building block of an Angular 2 application. Its job is to control a dedicated part of a user interface usually referred to as a view. Most applications will consist of at least one root application component and, usually, multiple components that control different views. Components are usually defined as a regular ES2015 class with a @Component decorator that defines it as a component and includes the component metadata. The component class is then exported as a module that can be imported and used in other parts of your application. A simple application component will be as follows:

```
import { Component } from '@angular/core';

@Component({
  selector: 'mean-app',
  template: '<h1>I AM AN APPLICATION COMPONENT</h1>'
})
export class AppComponent {    }
```

Note how we import the @Component decorator from the @angular/core module library and then use it to define our component DOM selector and the template we want to use. In the end, we export a class called AppComponent. Components are one side of the view management, and we have the template on the other side.

Angular 2 Templates

Templates are used by the components to render a component view. They are formed from a mix of basic HTML combined with Angular-dedicated annotations, which tells the component how to render the final view. In the previous example, you can see that a simple template is passed directly to the `AppComponent` class. However, you can also save your template in an external template file and change your component as follows:

```
import { Component } from '@angular/core';

@Component({
  selector: 'mean-app',
  templateUrl: 'app.template.html'
})
export class AppComponent {    }
```

As you can see here, our current template is static, so in order to create more useful templates, it's time to discuss data binding.

Angular 2 data binding

One of Angular's greatest features is its sophisticated data binding abilities. If you're used to working outside a framework, you know the nightmare that it is to manage data updates between the view and your data model. Luckily, Angular's data binding provides you with a straightforward way of managing the binding between your component class and the rendered view.

Interpolation binding

The simplest way of binding data from your component class to your template is called interpolation. An interpolation binds a value of the class property with your template using the double curly brackets syntax. A simple example of this mechanism will be as follows:

```
import { Component } from '@angular/core';

@Component({
  selector: 'mean-app',
  template: '<h1>{{title}}</h1>'
})
export class AppComponent {
  title = 'MEAN Application';
}
```

Note how we bind the `title` property of our `AppComponent` class inside the template HTML.

Property binding

Another example of one-way data binding would be property binding, which allows you to bind an HTML element property value with a component property value or any other template expression. This is done using square brackets, as follows:

```
import { Component } from '@angular/core';

@Component({
  selector: 'mean-app',
  template: '<button [disabled]="isButtonDisabled">My
    Button</button>'
})
export class AppComponent {
  isButtonDisabled = true;
}
```

In this example, Angular will render the button as disabled since we set the `isButtonDisabled` property to `true`.

Event binding

In order for your component to respond to the DOM event generated from the view, Angular 2 provides you with the mechanism of event binding. To bind a DOM event to a component method, all you have to do is set the event name inside round brackets, as shown in the following example:

```
import { Component } from '@angular/core';

@Component({
  selector: 'mean-app',
  template: '<button (click)="showMessage()">Show Message</button>'
})
export class AppComponent {
  showMessage() {
    alert('This is a message!')
  }
}
```

In this example, a click event of the view button will call the `showMessage()` method inside our `AppComponent` class.

Two-way binding

Up until now, we've only discussed one-way data binding where either the view calls a component function or the component changes the view. However, when dealing with user inputs, we'll need to be able to do two-way data binding in a seamless way. This can be done by adding the ngModel property to your input HTML element and binding it to a component property. To do that, we'll need to use a combination syntax of round and square brackets, as shown in the following example:

```
import { Component } from '@angular/core';

@Component({
  selector: 'mean-app',
  template: '<h1>Hello {{name}}</h1><br><input
    [(ngModel)]="name">'
})
export class AppComponent {
  name = ''
}
```

In this example, a user will see a title element that will be updated live according to the input. The input binds the name property both ways, so every change to the input value will be updated in the AppComponent class and rendered into the view. The ngModel property we used here is called a directive, so naturally, it's time to discuss directives.

Angular 2 Directives

Angular's basic operation is to transform our dynamic templates into views using a set of instructions that are usually directives. There are several types of directives, but the most basic and surprising one is the component. The @Component decorator actually extends the @Directive decorator by adding a template to it. Remember the selector property in previous examples? If you use this selector as a tag inside another component, it will render our component inside. But this is just one type of a directive; the other would be our ngModel directive in the previous example. All in all, we have three types of directives.

Attribute directives

Attribute directives change the behavior or appearance of a DOM element. We use these directives as HTML attributes on the given DOM element that we want to change. Angular 2 comes with several prebuilt attribute directives, such as the following:

- `ngClass`: Provides a way to bind singular or multiple classes to an element
- `ngStyle`: Provides a way to bind singular or multiple inline styles to an element
- `ngModel`: Creates a two-way data binding over form elements

These are just a few examples, but you should keep in mind that you can and should write your own custom directives.

Structural directives

Structural directives change our application's DOM layout by removing and adding DOM elements. Angular 2 contains three major structural directives you should know about:

- `ngIf`: Provides a way to add or remove elements according to the condition
- `ngFor`: Provides a way to create copies of an element based on a list of objects
- `ngSwitch`: Provides a way to display a single element out of a list of elements based on a property value

All structural directives use a mechanism called the HTML5 template, which allows our DOM to hold an HTML template without rendering using the template tag. This has a consequence that we'll discuss when we use these directives.

Component directives

As described previously, every component is basically a directive. For instance, let's say we have component called `SampleComponent`:

```
import { Component } from '@angular/core';

@Component({
  selector: 'sample-component',
  template: '<h1>I'm a component</h1>'
})
export class SampleComponent {

}
```

We can use it as a directive in our `AppComponent` class, as follows:

```
import { Component } from '@angular/core';
import { SampleComponent } from 'sample.component';

@Component({
  selector: 'mean-app',
  template: '<sample-component></sample-component>',
  directives: [SampleComponent]
})
export class AppComponent {

}
```

Notice how we use the sample-component tag and include our `SampleComponent` module in the `AppComponent` list of directives.

To conclude, directives used to be a frightening concept for many Angular 1 developers, but now they're simple, easy to understand, and fun to use. Later in this book, you'll learn how to use the majority of the concepts presented in this section.

Angular 2 Services

Services are an essential part of Angular 2. They are basically just classes that a single purpose or feature needs in the application. Since we want to keep our components clean and focused on the user experience, services come with pretty much everything else. For instance, any data management, logging, application configuration, or otherwise a functionality that does not belong in a component will be implemented as a service. It is also worth noting that there is absolutely nothing special about Angular 2 services; they are just plain classes with a defined functionality. What is special about them is that we can make these services available for components using a mechanism called Dependency Injection.

Angular 2 Dependency Injection

A Dependency Injection is a software design pattern popularized by a software engineer named Martin Fowler. The main principle behind Dependency Injection is the inversion of control in a software development architecture. To understand this better, let's take a look at the following `notifier` example:

```
const Notifier = function() {
  this.userService = new UserService();
};
```

```
Notifier.prototype.notify = function() {
  const user = this.userService.getUser();

  if (user.role === 'admin') {
    alert('You are an admin!');
  } else {
    alert('Hello user!');
  }
};
```

Our `Notifier` class creates an instance of `userService`, and when the `notify()` method is called, it alerts a different message based on the user role. Now this can work pretty well, but what happens when you want to test your `Notifier` class? You will create a `Notifier` instance in your test, but you won't be able to pass a mock `userService` object to test the different results of the `notify` method. Dependency injection solves this by moving the responsibility of creating the `userService` object to the creator of the `Notifier` instance, whether it is another object or a test. This creator is often referred to as the injector. A revised, injection-dependent version of this example will be as follows:

```
const Notifier = function(userService) {
  this.userService = userService;
};

Notifier.prototype.notify = function() {
  const user = this.userService.getUser();

  if (user.role === 'admin') {
    alert('You are an admin!');
  } else {
    alert('Hello user!');
  }
};
```

Now whenever you create an instance of the `Notifier` class, the injector will be responsible for injecting a `userService` object into the constructor, making it possible to control the behavior of the `Notifier` instance outside of its constructor, a design often described as the inversion of control.

Using Dependency Injection in Angular 2

In Angular 2, Dependency Injection is used to inject services into components. Services are injected in the constructor function of the components, as follows:

```
import { Component } from '@angular/core';
import { SomeService } from '../users/services/some.service';

@Component({
  selector: 'some-component',
  template: 'Hello Services',
  providers: [SomeService]
})
export class SomeComponent {
  user = null;
  constructor (private _someService: SomeService) {
    this.user = _someService.user;
  }
}
```

When Angular 2 creates an instance of a component class, it will first request an injector that will resolve the needed services to call the constructor function. If an Injector contains a previous instance of the service, it will provide it; otherwise, the Injector will create a new instance. To do that, you'll need to provide the component injector with the service provider. This is why we add the providers property to the @Component decorator. Furthermore, we can register providers at any level of our component tree, and a common pattern is to register providers at the root level when the application is being bootstrapped, so the same instance of the service will be available throughout the application component tree.

Angular 2 Routing

Our last topic before we set out to implement our application would be navigation and routing. Using web applications, users expect a certain type of URL routing. For this purpose, the Angular team created a module called the component router. The component router interprets the browser URL and then looks up in its definition to find and load a component view. Supporting the modern browser's history API, the router will respond to any URL change whether it's coming from the browser URL bar or a user interaction. So let's see how it works.

Setup

Since the Angular 2 team is focused on the modular approach, you'll need to load the router file separately—either from a local file or using a CDN. Furthermore, you'll also have to set up the `<base href="/">` tag inside the head section of your main HTML file. But don't worry about it for now. We'll take care of these changes in the next section.

Routes

Every application will have one router, so when a URL navigation occurs, the router will look for the routing configuration made inside the application in order to determine which component to load. In order to configure the application routing, Angular provides a special array class called `Routes`, which includes a list mapping between URLs and components. An example for this mechanism is as follows:

```
import { Routes } from '@angular/router';
import { HomeComponent } from './home.component';

export const HomeRoutes: Routes = [{
  path: '',
  component: HomeComponent,
}];
```

Router outlet

The component router uses a hierarchical component structure which means that every component decorated and loaded by the component router can have child paths configured. So, the root component is loaded, and it renders its view in the main application tag; however, when child components are loaded, how and where are they going to be rendered? To solve this, the router module includes a directive called `RouterOutlet`. To render your child components, all you have to do is include the `RouterOutlet` directive inside your parent component's template. An example component is as follows:

```
import { Component } from '@angular/core';

@Component({
  selector: 'mean-app',
  template: '<h1>Application Title</h1>
    <br>
    <router-outlet></router-outlet>'
})
export class AppComponent { ... }
```

Note that the `router-outlet` tag will be replaced with your child component's view.

Router links

After we configure our application routes, we'll be able to navigate through our application either by changing the browser URL or using the `RouterLink` directive to generate anchor tags pointing to a link inside our app. The `RouterLink` directive uses an array of link parameters, which the router will later resolve into a URL matching a component mapping. An example anchor with the `RouterLink` directive will look like this:

```
<a [routerLink]="['/about']">Some</a>
```

Summary

As we've progressed in this chapter, we've learned about TypeScript and Angular 2. We've now covered everything we need in order create an Angular application inside our MEAN application. So let's start by setting up our project.

The project setup

In order to use Angular in our project, we'll need to install both TypeScript and Angular. We'll need to use the TypeScript transpiler to convert our TypeScript files into valid ES5 or ES6 JavaScript files. Furthermore, since Angular is a frontend framework, installing it requires the inclusion of JavaScript files in the main page of your application. This can be done in various ways, and the easiest one would be to download the files you need and store them in the `public` folder. Another approach is to use Angular's CDN and load the files directly from the CDN server. While these two approaches are simple and easy to understand, they both have a strong flaw. Loading a single third-party JavaScript file is readable and direct, but what happens when you start adding more vendor libraries to your project? More importantly, how can you manage your dependencies' versions?

The answer to all of these questions is NPM! NPM will allow us to install all of our dependencies and run the TypeScript transpiler while we develop our application. In order to do that, you'll need to change your `package.json` file, as follows:

```
{
  "name": "MEAN",
  "version": "0.0.7",
  "scripts": {
    "tsc": "tsc",
    "tsc:w": "tsc -w",
    "app": "node server",
```

```
            "start": "concurrently \"npm run tsc:w\" \"npm run app\" ",
            "postinstall": "typings install"
        },
        "dependencies": {
            "@angular/common": "2.1.1",
            "@angular/compiler": "2.1.1",
            "@angular/core": "2.1.1",
            "@angular/forms": "2.1.1",
            "@angular/http": "2.1.1",
            "@angular/platform-browser": "2.1.1",
            "@angular/platform-browser-dynamic": "2.1.1",
            "@angular/router": "3.1.1",
            "body-parser": "1.15.2",
            "core-js": "2.4.1",
            "compression": "1.6.0",
            "connect-flash": "0.1.1",
            "ejs": "2.5.2",
            "express": "4.14.0",
            "express-session": "1.14.1",
            "method-override": "2.3.6",
            "mongoose": "4.6.5",
            "morgan": "1.7.0",
            "passport": "0.3.2",
            "passport-facebook": "2.1.1",
            "passport-google-oauth": "1.0.0",
            "passport-local": "1.0.0",
            "passport-twitter": "1.0.4",
            "reflect-metadata": "0.1.8",
            "rxjs": "5.0.0-beta.12",
            "systemjs": "0.19.39",
            "zone.js": "0.6.26"
        },
        "devDependencies": {
            "concurrently": "3.1.0",
            "traceur": "0.0.111",
            "typescript": "2.0.3",
            "typings": "1.4.0"
        }
    }
```

In our new `package.json` file, we did a few things; first, we added our project's Angular dependencies, including a few supportive libraries:

- **CoreJS**: This will provide us with some ES6 polyfills
- **ReflectMetadata**: This will provide us with some a metadata reflection polyfill
- **Rx.JS**: This is a Reactive framework that we'll use later
- **SystemJS**: This will help with loading our application modules
- **Zone.js**: This allows the creation of different execution context zones and is used by the Angular library
- **Concurrently**: This will allow us to run both the TypeScript transplier and our server concurrently
- **Typings**: This will help us with downloading predefined TypeScript definitions for our external libraries

At the top, we added a scripts property, where we defined different scripts we would like npm to run for us. For instance, we have a script that installs our typings for third-party libraries, another one that runs the TypeScript compiler called `tsc`, a script called `app` that we use to run our node server, and one called `start` to run both of these scripts together using the concurrency tool.

Next, we're going to configure the way we want the TypeScript compiler to run.

Configuring TypeScript

In order to configure the way TypeScript works, we'll need to add a new file called `tsconfig.json` to our application's root folder. In your new file, paste the following JSON:

```
{
  "compilerOptions": {
    "target": "es5",
    "module": "system",
    "moduleResolution": "node",
    "sourceMap": true,
    "emitDecoratorMetadata": true,
    "experimentalDecorators": true,
    "removeComments": false,
    "noImplicitAny": false
  },
  "exclude": [
    "node_modules",
```

```
        "typings/main",
        "typings/main.d.ts"
    ]
}
```

In our `tsconfig.json` file, we configured the TypeScript compiler to:

- Compile our TypeScript code into ES5 code
- Compile our modules into a system module pattern
- Use Node for module resolution
- Generate source maps
- Include decorators and emit their metadata
- Keep comments
- Cancel the error for any implicit declarations
- Not include the `node_modules` folder and typings files

When we run our application, the TypeScript will use the `tsconfig.json` configuration file by default. Next, you'll need to add a new file called `typings.json` to your application's root folder. In your new file, paste the following JSON:

```
{
    "globalDependencies": {
    "core-js": "registry:dt/core-js#0.0.0+20160914114559",
        "jasmine": "registry:dt/jasmine#2.5.0+20161025102649",
        "socket.io-client":
            "registry:dt/socket.io-client#1.4.4+20160317120654",
        "node": "registry:dt/node#6.0.0+20161102143327"
    }
}
```

As you can see, we've added all third-party libraries we need in order for the TypeScript transpiler to compile our code properly. Once you're done, go ahead and install your new dependencies:

```
$ npm install
```

All the packages we need will be installed along with external type definitions we'll need in order to support the TypeScript compiling. Now that we have installed our new packages and configured our TypeScript implementation, it is time to set up Angular.

It is recommended that you continue reading about Typings at the official documentation at https://github.com/typings/typings.

Configuring Express

To start using Angular, you will need to include the new JavaScript library files in our main EJS view. So, we will use the `app/views/index.ejs` file as the main application page. However, NPM installed all of our dependencies in the `node_module` folder, which is not accessible to our client side. To solve this issue, we'll have to change our `config/express.js` file as follows:

```
const path = require('path'),
const config = require('./config'),
const express = require('express'),
const morgan = require('morgan'),
const compress = require('compression'),
const bodyParser = require('body-parser'),
const methodOverride = require('method-override'),
const session = require('express-session'),
const flash = require('connect-flash'),
const passport = require('passport');

module.exports = function() {
  const app = express();

  if (process.env.NODE_ENV === 'development') {
    app.use(morgan('dev'));
  } else if (process.env.NODE_ENV === 'production') {
    app.use(compress());
  }

  app.use(bodyParser.urlencoded({
    extended: true
  }));
  app.use(bodyParser.json());
  app.use(methodOverride());

  app.use(session({
    saveUninitialized: true,
    resave: true,
    secret: config.sessionSecret
  }));
```

```
    app.set('views', './app/views');
    app.set('view engine', 'ejs');

    app.use(flash());
    app.use(passport.initialize());
    app.use(passport.session());

    app.use('/', express.static(path.resolve('./public')));
    app.use('/lib', express.static(
      path.resolve('./node_modules')));

    require('../app/routes/users.server.routes.js')(app);
    require('../app/routes/index.server.routes.js')(app);

    return app;
};
```

A major change here involves the creation of a /lib static route that directs to our node_modules folder. While we were here, we also switched the order of the routes users and index routes. This will come in handy when we start dealing with Angular's routing mechanism. In this regard, there is one more thing we have to do, and that is making sure our Express application always return the main application view when receiving routes that are not defined. This is for the case where the browser's initial request is made using a URL that was generated by the Angular Router and is not supported by our Express configuration. To do this, go back to the app/routes/index.server.routes.js file, and change it as follows:

```
module.exports = function(app) {
    const index = require('../controllers/index.server.controller');

    app.get('/*', index.render);
};
```

Now, that we have configured TypeScript and Express, it is time to set up Angular, but before we do that, let's talk a bit about our application structure.

Restructuring the application

As you might remember from *Chapter 3, Building an Express Web Application*, your application's structure depends on the complexity of your application. We previously decided to use the horizontal approach for the entire MEAN application; however, as we stated earlier, MEAN applications can be constructed in various ways, and an Angular application structure is a different topic, which is often discussed by the community and the Angular development team. There are many doctrines for different purposes, some of which are a bit more complicated, while others offer a simpler approach. In this section, we'll introduce a recommended structure. With the move from Angular 1 to Angular 2, this discussion is now even more complicated. For us, the easiest approach would be to start by using the `public` folder of our Express application as the root folder for the Angular application so that every file is available statically.

There are several options to structure your application according to its complexity. A simple application can have a horizontal structure where entities are arranged in folders according to their type, and a main application file is placed at the root folder of the application. An example application structure of this kind can be seen in the following screenshot:

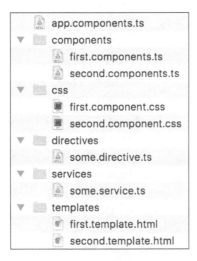

As you can see, this is a very comfortable solution for small applications with a few entities. However, your application might be more complex with several different features and many more entities. This structure cannot handle an application of this sort since it obfuscates the behavior of each application file, will have a bloated folder with too many files, and will generally be very difficult to maintain. For this purpose, there is a different approach to organizing your files in a vertical manner. A vertical structure positions every file according to its functional context, so different types of entities can be sorted together according to their role in a feature or a section. This is similar to the vertical approach we introduced in *Chapter 3, Building an Express Web Application*. However, the difference is that only Angular's logical units will have a standalone module folder structure, usually with a component and a template files. An example of an Angular application vertical structure can be seen in the following screenshot:

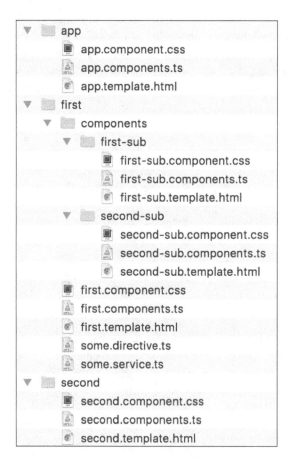

As you can see, each module has its own folder structure, which allows you to encapsulate each component. We're also using the file naming convention that we introduced in *Chapter 3, Building an Express Web Application*.

Now that you know the basic best practices of naming and structuring your application, let's continue and create the application module.

Creating the application module

To begin, clear the contents of the `public` folder and create the folder named `app` inside it. Inside your new folder, create a file named `app.module.ts`. In your file, add the following code:

```
import { NgModule }        from '@angular/core';
import { BrowserModule }   from '@angular/platform-browser';

import { AppComponent }       from './app.component';

@NgModule({
  imports: [
    BrowserModule
  ],
  declarations: [
    AppComponent
  ],
  bootstrap: [AppComponent]
})
export class AppModule { }
```

As you can see, we basically just created a simple module that declares the application component and uses it for bootstrapping. Next we'll need to create the application component.

Creating the application component

Inside your `public/app` folder, create a new file named `app.component.ts`. In your file, add the following code:

```
import { Component } from '@angular/core';

@Component({
  selector: 'mean-app',
  template: '<h1>Hello World</h1>',
})
export class AppComponent {}
```

As you can see, we basically just created the simplest component. Next we'll learn how to bootstrap our `AppModule` class.

Bootstrapping the application module

To bootstrap your application module, go to your `app` folder and create a new file named `bootstrap.ts`. In your file, add the following code:

```
import { platformBrowserDynamic } from
  '@angular/platform-browser-dynamic';
import { AppModule } from './app.module';

platformBrowserDynamic().bootstrapModule(AppModule);
```

Basically, this code is using the browser platform module to bootstrap the application module for browsers. Once we have these configured, it's time to learn how to load our bootstrap code using the SystemJS module loader.

Starting your Angular application

To use SystemJS as our module loader, we'll create a new file named `systemjs.config.js` inside our `public` folder. In your new file, paste the following code:

```
(function(global) {
  var packages = {
    app: {
      main: './bootstrap.js',
      defaultExtension: 'js'
    }
  };

  var map = {
    '@angular': 'lib/@angular',
    'rxjs': 'lib/rxjs'
  };

  var ngPackageNames = [
    'common',
    'compiler',
    'core',
    'forms',
    'http',
    'router',
```

```
    'platform-browser',
    'platform-browser-dynamic',
  ];

  ngPackageNames.forEach(function(pkgName) {
    packages['@angular/' + pkgName] = {
      main: '/bundles/' + pkgName + '.umd.js',
      defaultExtension: 'js' };
  });

  System.config({
    defaultJSExtensions: true,
    transpiler: null,
    packages: packages,
    map: map
  });
})(this);
```

In this file, we're telling SystemJS about our application package and from where to load the Angular and Rx modules. We then describe the main file for each package of Angular; in this case, we ask it to load the UMD file of each package. We then use the System.config method to configure SystemJS. Finally, we revisit our app/views/ index.ejs file and change it, as follows:

```
<!DOCTYPE html>
<html>
<head>
  <title><%= title %></title>
  <base href="/">
</head>
<body>
  <mean-app>
    <h1>Loading...</h1>
  </mean-app>

  <script src="lib/core-js/client/shim.min.js"></script>
  <script src="lib/zone.js/dist/zone.js"></script>
  <script src="lib/reflect-metadata/Reflect.js"></script>
  <script src="lib/systemjs/dist/system.js"></script>

  <script src="systemjs.config.js"></script>
  <script>
    System.import('app').catch(function(err){ console.error(err); });
  </script>
</body>
</html>
```

As you can see, we're loading our module files directly from the `node_modules` package folder and include our SystemJS configuration file. The last script tells SystemJS to load the application package we defined in the configuration file.

> To learn more about SystemJS, it is recommended that you visit the official documentation at `https://github.com/systemjs/systemjs`.

Now all you have left to do is run your application by invoking the following command in your command line:

```
$ npm start
```

When your application is running, use your browser and open your application URL at `http://localhost:3000`. You should see a header tag saying `Hello World` being rendered. Congratulations! You've created your first Angular 2 module and component and successfully bootstrapped your application. Next, we'll refactor the authentication part of our application and create a new authentication module.

Managing authentication

Managing an Angular application authentication is a complex issue. The problem is that while the server holds the information about the authenticated user, the Angular application is not aware of that information. One solution is to use a service and ask the server about the authentication status; however, this solution is flawed since all the Angular components will have to wait for the response to return, causing inconsistencies and development overhead. This can be solved using an advanced Angular router object; however, a simpler solution would be to make the Express application render the `user` object directly in the EJS view and then use an Angular service to serve the object.

Rendering the user object

To render the authenticated `user` object, you'll have to make several changes. Let's begin by changing the `app/controllers/index.server.controller.js` file, as follows:

```
exports.render = function(req, res) {
  const user = (!req.user) ? null : {
    _id: req.user.id,
    firstName: req.user.firstName,
    lastName: req.user.lastName
  };
```

```
res.render('index', {
  title: 'Hello World',
  user: JSON.stringify(user)
});
};
```

Next, go to your `app/views/index.ejs` file and make the following changes:

```
<!DOCTYPE html>
<html>
<head>
  <title><%= title %></title>
  <base href="/">
</head>
<body>
  <mean-app>
    <h1>Loading...</h1>
  </mean-app>

  <script type="text/javascript">
    window.user = <%- user || 'null' %>;
  </script>

  <script src="lib/core-js/client/shim.min.js"></script>
  <script src="lib/zone.js/dist/zone.js"></script>
  <script src="lib/reflect-metadata/Reflect.js"></script>
  <script src="lib/systemjs/dist/system.js"></script>

  <script src="systemjs.config.js"></script>

  <script>
    System.import('app').catch(function(err){
      console.error(err); });
  </script>
</body>
</html>
```

This will render the user object as a JSON representation right in your main view application. When the Angular application bootstraps, the authentication state will already be available. If the user is authenticated, the user object will become available; otherwise, the user object will be Null.

Modifying the users' server controller

To support our authentication refactoring, we'll need to make sure our user's server controller is able to process the Angular service requests. To do that, you'll need to change the code in your `app/controllers/users.server.controller.js` file to look like this:

```javascript
const User = require('mongoose').model('User'),
  passport = require('passport');

const getErrorMessage = function(err) {
  const message = '';

  if (err.code) {
    switch (err.code) {
      case 11000:
      case 11001:
      message = 'Username already exists';
      break;
      default:
      message = 'Something went wrong';
    }
  } else {
    for (let errName in err.errors) {
      if (err.errors[errName].message) message =
        err.errors[errName].message;
    }
  }

  return message;
};

exports.signin = function(req, res, next) {
  passport.authenticate('local', function(err, user, info) {
    if (err || !user) {
      res.status(400).send(info);
    } else {
      // Remove sensitive data before login
      user.password = undefined;
      user.salt = undefined;

      req.login(user, function(err) {
        if (err) {
          res.status(400).send(err);
        } else {
```

```
            res.json(user);
          }
        });
      }
    })(req, res, next);
};

exports.signup = function(req, res) {
  const user = new User(req.body);
  user.provider = 'local';

  user.save((err) => {
    if (err) {
      return res.status(400).send({
        message: getErrorMessage(err)
      });
    } else {
      // Remove sensitive data before login
      user.password = undefined;
      user.salt = undefined;

      req.login(user, function(err) {
        if (err) {
          res.status(400).send(err);
        } else {
          res.json(user);
        }
      });
    }
  });
};

exports.signout = function(req, res) {
  req.logout();
  res.redirect('/');
};

exports.saveOAuthUserProfile = function(req, profile, done) {
  User.findOne({
    provider: profile.provider,
    providerId: profile.providerId
  }, function(err, user) {
    if (err) {
      return done(err);
```

```
        } else {
          if (!user) {
            const possibleUsername = profile.username ||
              ((profile.email) ? profile.email.split('@')[0] : '');

            User.findUniqueUsername(possibleUsername, null,
            function(availableUsername) {
              profile.username = availableUsername;

              user = new User(profile);

              user.save((err) => {
                if (err) {
                  const message =
                    _this.getErrorMessage(err);

                  req.flash('error', message);
                  return res.redirect('/signup');
                }

                return done(err, user);
              });
            });
          } else {
            return done(err, user);
          }
        }
      });
    };
```

We basically just encapsulated the authentication logic inside two methods that can accept and respond with a JSON object. Now let's go ahead and change the app/ routes/users.server.routes.js directory as follows:

```
const users =
  require('../../app/controllers/users.server.controller'),
  passport = require('passport');

module.exports = function(app) {
  app.route('/api/auth/signup').post(users.signup);
  app.route('/api/auth/signin').post(users.signin);
  app.route('/api/auth/signout').get(users.signout);

  app.get('/api/oauth/facebook',
    passport.authenticate('facebook', {
```

```
      failureRedirect: '/signin'
  }));
  app.get('/api/oauth/facebook/callback',
    passport.authenticate('facebook', {
    failureRedirect: '/signin',
    successRedirect: '/'
  }));

    app.get('/api/oauth/twitter', passport.authenticate('twitter',
    {
      failureRedirect: '/signin'
  }));
  app.get('/api/oauth/twitter/callback',
    passport.authenticate('twitter', {
    failureRedirect: '/signin',
    successRedirect: '/'
  }));

    app.get('/api/oauth/google', passport.authenticate('google', {
      failureRedirect: '/signin',
      scope: [
        'https://www.googleapis.com/auth/userinfo.profile',
        'https://www.googleapis.com/auth/userinfo.email'
      ],
  }));
  app.get('/api/oauth/google/callback',
    passport.authenticate('google', {
    failureRedirect: '/signin',
    successRedirect: '/'
  }));

  };
```

Note how we removed the routes that we used to render our authentication views. More importantly, look at the way in which we added an /api prefix for all the routes. It is a very good practice to keep all your routes under one prefix, since we want the Angular router to be able to have routes that do not interfere with our server routes. Now that we have our server side ready, it's time to create our Angular authentication module.

Creating the authentication module

Now that we're done with laying the ground for our Angular application, we can move forward and refactor our authentication logic into a cohesive authentication module. To do that, we'll begin by creating a new folder inside our `public/` app folder, called `authentication`. In our new folder, create a file named `authentication.module.ts` with the following code:

```
import { NgModule }         from '@angular/core';
import { FormsModule }      from '@angular/forms';
import { RouterModule } from '@angular/router';

import { AuthenticationRoutes } from './authentication.routes';
import { AuthenticationComponent } from './authentication.component';
import { SigninComponent } from './signin/signin.component';
import { SignupComponent } from './signup/signup.component';

@NgModule({
  imports: [
    FormsModule,
    RouterModule.forChild(AuthenticationRoutes),
  ],
  declarations: [
    AuthenticationComponent,
    SigninComponent,
    SignupComponent,
  ]
})
export class AuthenticationModule {}
```

Our module consists of three components:

- An authentication component
- A signup component
- A signin component

We also included an authentication routing configuration and the Angular's Forms module to support our signin and signup forms. Let's begin by implementing the base authentication component.

Creating the authentication component

We'll begin by creating our authentication component hierarchy. Then, we will convert our server signin and signup views into Angular templates, add the authentication functionality to `AuthenticationService`, and refactor our server logic. Let's start by creating a file named `authentication.component.ts` inside our `public/app/authentication` folder. In the new file, paste the following code:

```
import { Component } from '@angular/core';
import { SigninComponent } from './signin/signin.component';
import { SignupComponent } from './signup/signup.component';

@Component({
  selector: 'authentication',
  templateUrl: 'app/authentication/authentication.template.html',
})
export class AuthenticationComponent { }
```

In this code, we implement our new authentication component. We begin by importing the authentication service and a signup and signin component, all of which we haven't created yet. Another thing to notice is that this time, we used an external template file for our component. We'll continue by creating a routing configuration for our authentication module.

Configuring the authentication routes

To do that, create a new file named `authentication.routes.ts` inside our `public/app/authentication` folder. In the new file, paste the following code:

```
import { Routes } from '@angular/router';

import { AuthenticationComponent } from './authentication.component';
import { SigninComponent } from './signin/signin.component';
import { SignupComponent } from './signup/signup.component';

export const AuthenticationRoutes: Routes = [{
  path: 'authentication',
  component: AuthenticationComponent,
  children: [
    { path: 'signin', component: SigninComponent },
    { path: 'signup', component: SignupComponent },
  ],
}];
```

As you can see, we create a new `Routes` instance with a parent route of `authentication` and two child routes for the `signin` and `signup` components. We'll continue by creating the template file named `authentication.template.html` inside our component's folder. In the new file, paste the following code:

```
<div>
  <a href="/api/oauth/google">Sign in with Google</a>
  <a href="/api/oauth/facebook">Sign in with Facebook</a>
  <a href="/api/oauth/twitter">Sign in with Twitter</a>
  <router-outlet></router-outlet>
</div>
```

Note how we used the `RouterOutlet` directive inside our code. This is where our subcomponents will be rendered. We'll continue with creating these subcomponents.

Creating the signin component

To implement the `signin` component, create a new folder named `signin` inside your `public/app/authentication` folder. Inside your new folder, create a new file named `signin.component.ts` with the following code:

```
import { Component } from '@angular/core';
import { Router } from '@angular/router';

import { AuthenticationService } from '../authentication.service';

@Component({
  selector: 'signin',
  templateUrl: 'app/authentication/signin/signin.template.html'
})
export class SigninComponent {
  errorMessage: string;
  credentials: any = {};

  constructor (private _authenticationService: AuthenticationService,
private _router: Router) {    }

  signin() {
    this._authenticationService.signin(
      this.credentials).subscribe(result  =>
      this._router.navigate(['/']),
      error =>  this.errorMessage = error );
  }
}
```

Note how our `signin` component uses the authentication service in order to perform a `signin` action. Don't worry; we'll implement this in the next section. Next, you'll need to create a file named `signin.template.html` in the same folder as your component. In your new file, add the following code:

```
<form (ngSubmit)="signin()">
  <div>
    <label>Username:</label>
    <input type="text" [(ngModel)]="credentials.username"
      name="username">
  </div>
  <div>
    <label>Password:</label>
    <input type="password" [(ngModel)]="credentials.password"
      name="password">
  </div>
  <div>
    <input type="submit" value="Sign In">
  </div>
  <span>{{errorMessage}}</span>
</form>
```

We've just created a new component to handle our authentication signin operation! The signup component will look quite similar.

Creating the signup component

To implement the signup component, create a new folder named `signup` inside your `public/app/authentication` folder. Inside your new folder, create a new file named `signup.component.ts` with the following code:

```
import { Component } from '@angular/core';
import { Router } from '@angular/router';

import { AuthenticationService } from '../authentication.service';

@Component({
  selector: 'signup',
  templateUrl: 'app/authentication/signup/signup.template.html'
})
export class SignupComponent {
  errorMessage: string;
  user: any = {};

  constructor (private _authenticationService:
```

```
      AuthenticationService,
      private _router: Router) {}

    signup() {
      this._authenticationService.signup(this.user)
      .subscribe(result  => this._router.navigate(['/']),
      error =>  this.errorMessage = error);
    }
  }
```

Note how our signup component uses the authentication service in order to perform a signup action. Next, you'll need to create a file named signup.template.html in the same folder as your component. In your new file, add the following code:

```html
<form (ngSubmit)="signup()">
  <div>
  <label>First Name:</label>
    <input type="text" [(ngModel)]="user.firstName"
      name="firstName">
  </div>
  <div>
    <label>Last Name:</label>
    <input type="text" [(ngModel)]="user.lastName"
      name="lastName">
  </div>
  <div>
    <label>Email:</label>
    <input type="text" [(ngModel)]="user.email" name="email">
  </div>
  <div>
    <label>Username:</label>
    <input type="text" [(ngModel)]="user.username"
      name="username">
  </div>
  <div>
    <label>Password:</label>
    <input type="password" [(ngModel)]="user.password"
      name="password">
  </div>
  <div>
    <input type="submit" value="Sign up" />
  </div>
  <span>{{errorMessage}}</span>
</form>
```

Now that we have our authentication components in place, let's go back and handle the authentication service.

Creating the authentication service

In order to support our new components, we would need to create an authentication service to provide them with the needed functionality. To do that, create a new file named `authentication.service.ts` inside your `public/app/authentication` folder. In your new file, paste the following code:

```
import 'rxjs/Rx';
import { Injectable } from '@angular/core';
import { Http, Response, Headers, RequestOptions } from
  '@angular/http';
import { Observable } from 'rxjs/Observable';

@Injectable()
export class AuthenticationService {
  public user = window['user'];

  private _signinURL = 'api/auth/signin';
  private _signupURL = 'api/auth/signup';

  constructor (private http: Http) {

  }
  isLoggedIn(): boolean {
    return (!!this.user);
  }

  signin(credentials: any): Observable<any> {
    let body = JSON.stringify(credentials);
    let headers = new Headers({ 'Content-Type':
      'application/json' });
    let options = new RequestOptions({ headers: headers });

    return this.http.post(this._signinURL, body, options)
    .map(res => this.user = res.json())
    .catch(this.handleError)
  }

  signup(user: any): Observable<any> {
    let body = JSON.stringify(user);
    let headers = new Headers({ 'Content-Type':
      'application/json' });
```

```
    let options = new RequestOptions({ headers: headers });

    return this.http.post(this._signupURL, body, options)
    .map(res => this.user = res.json())
    .catch(this.handleError)
  }

  private handleError(error: Response) {
    console.error(error);
    return Observable.throw(error.json().message ||
      'Server error');
  }
}
```

Note how we decorated the `AuthenticationService` class with an `@Injectable` decorator. While that's not needed in this case, it is a good practice to decorate your services that way. The reason is that if you'd like to inject a service with another service, you'll need to use this decorator, so for the sake of uniformity, it is better to stay safe and decorate all your services. Another thing to note is the way we get our user object from the window object.

We also added three methods to our service: one that handles signin, another that handles signup, and a last one for error handling. Inside our methods, we use the HTTP module provided by Angular to call our server endpoints. In the next chapter, we'll elaborate further on this module, but in the meantime, all you need to know is that we just used it to send POST a request to our server. To finish up the Angular part, our application will need to modify our application module and add a simple home component.

Creating the home module

To extend our simple example, we'll need to have a home component that will provide the view for our base root and will present different information for the logged-in and logged-out users. To do that, create a folder named `home` inside your `public/app` folder. Then, create a file inside this folder called `home.module.ts`, which contains the following code:

```
import { NgModule }       from '@angular/core';
import { CommonModule }   from '@angular/common';
import { RouterModule } from '@angular/router';

import { HomeRoutes } from './home.routes';
import { HomeComponent } from './home.component';
```

```
@NgModule({
  imports: [
    CommonModule,
    RouterModule.forChild(HomeRoutes),
  ],
  declarations: [
    HomeComponent,
  ]
})
export class HomeModule {}
```

As you may have probably noticed, our module is only importing a new home component and the routing configuration. Let's continue by creating our home component.

Creating the home component

Next, we'll create our home component. To do that, go to your public/app/home folder and create a new file called home.component.ts containing the following code:

```
import { Component } from '@angular/core';
import { AuthenticationService } from '../authentication/
authentication.service';

@Component({
  selector: 'home',
  templateUrl: './app/home/home.template.html'
})
export class HomeComponent {
  user: any;

  constructor (private _authenticationService:
    AuthenticationService) {
    this.user = _authenticationService.user;
  }
}
```

As you can see, this is just a simple component, which has the authentication service injected and which is used to provide the component with the user object. Next, we'll need to create our home component template. To do that, go to your `public/app/home` folder and create a file named `home.template.html` with the following code inside it:

```html
<div *ngIf="user">
  <h1>Hello {{user.firstName}}</h1>
  <a href="/api/auth/signout">Signout</a>
</div>

<div *ngIf="!user">
  <a [routerLink]="['/authentication/signup']">Signup</a>
  <a [routerLink]="['/authentication/signin']">Signin</a>
</div>
```

This template's code nicely demonstrates a few of the topics we previously discussed. Note the use of the `ngIf` and `routerLink` directives we talked about earlier in this chapter.

Configuring the home routes

To finish with our module, we'll need to create a routing configuration for our home component. To do that, create a new file named `home.routes.ts` inside your `public/app/home` folder. In your new file, paste the following code:

```typescript
import { Routes } from '@angular/router';
import { HomeComponent } from './home.component';

export const HomeRoutes: Routes = [{
  path: '',
  component: HomeComponent,
}];
```

As you can see, this is just a simple component routing. To complete our implementation, we'll need to modify our application module a bit.

Refactoring the application module

To include our authentication and home component modules, we'll need to change our `app.module.ts` file as follows:

```typescript
import { NgModule }       from '@angular/core';
import { BrowserModule }  from '@angular/platform-browser';
import { RouterModule }   from '@angular/router';
```

```
import { HttpModule } from '@angular/http';

import { AppComponent }        from './app.component';
import { AppRoutes }        from './app.routes';

import { HomeModule } from './home/home.module';
import { AuthenticationService } from './authentication/
authentication.service';
import { AuthenticationModule } from './authentication/authentication.
module';

@NgModule({
  imports: [
    BrowserModule,
    HttpModule,
    AuthenticationModule,
    HomeModule,
    RouterModule.forRoot(AppRoutes),
  ],
  declarations: [
    AppComponent
  ],
  providers: [
    AuthenticationService
  ],
  bootstrap: [AppComponent]
})
    export class AppModule { }
```

As you can see, this is quite a big change to our application module. First, we imported the HTTP module and our new home and authentication modules along with our new Application routing configuration. We injected the authentication service in the `providers` property so that it is available for all of our submodules. The last thing we have to do is implement our application routing configuration.

Configuring the application routes

To configure our application routes, we'll need to create a new file named `app.routes.ts` inside the `public/app` folder. In the new file, paste the following code:

```
import { Routes } from '@angular/router';

export const AppRoutes: Routes = [{
  path: '**',
  redirectTo: '/',
}];
```

As you can see, our application consists of a very simple, single configuration, which redirects any unknown routing requests to our home component.

That is it. Your application is ready for use! All you need to do is to run it by invoking the following command in your command line:

```
$ npm start
```

When your application is running, use your browser and open your application URL at `http://localhost:3000`. You should see two links for signing up and signing in. Use them and see what happens. Try to refresh your application and see how it keeps its state and route.

Summary

In this chapter, you learned about the basic principles of TypeScript. You went through Angular's building blocks and learned how they fit in the architecture of an Angular 2 application. You also learned how to use NPM to install frontend libraries and how to structure and bootstrap your application. You discovered Angular's entities and how they work together. You also used Angular's Router to configure your application routing scheme. Near the end of this chapter, we made use of all of this in order to refactor our authentication module. In the next chapter, you'll connect everything you learned so far to create your first MEAN CRUD module.

8

Creating a MEAN CRUD Module

In the previous chapters, you learned how to set up each framework and how to connect them all together. In this chapter, you're going to implement the basic operational building blocks of a MEAN application, the CRUD module. CRUD modules consist of a base entity with the basic functionality of creating, reading, updating, and deleting entity instances. In a MEAN application, your CRUD module is built from the server-side Express components and an Angular client module. In this chapter, we'll cover the following topics:

- Setting up the Mongoose model
- Creating the Express controller
- Wiring the Express routes
- Creating and organizing the Angular module
- Understanding Angular forms
- Introducing the Angular `http` client
- Implementing the Angular module service
- Implementing the Angular module components

Introducing CRUD modules

CRUD modules are the basic building blocks of a MEAN application. Each CRUD module consists of two structures supporting the Express and Angular functionalities. The Express part is built upon a Mongoose model, an Express controller, and an Express routes file. The Angular module is a bit more complex and contains a set of templates and a few Angular components, service, and the routing configuration. In this chapter, you'll learn how to combine these components in order to build an example `Article` CRUD module. The examples in this chapter will continue directly from those in previous chapters, so copy the final example from *Chapter 7, Introduction to Angular*, and let's start from there.

Setting up the Express components

Let's begin with the Express part of the module. First, you'll create a Mongoose model that will be used to save and validate your articles. Then, you'll move on to the Express controller that will deal with the business logic of your module. Finally, you'll wire the Express routes to produce a RESTful API for your controller methods. We'll begin with the Mongoose model.

Creating the Mongoose model

The Mongoose model will consist of four simple properties that will represent our `Article` entity. Let's begin by creating the Mongoose model file in the `app/models` folder; create a new file named `article.server.model.js`, which contains the following code snippet:

```
const mongoose = require('mongoose');
const Schema = mongoose.Schema;

const ArticleSchema = new Schema({
  created: {
    type: Date,
    default: Date.now
  },
  title: {
    type: String,
    default: '',
    trim: true,
    required: 'Title cannot be blank'
  },
  content: {
    type: String,
```

```
      default: '',
      trim: true
    },
    creator: {
      type: Schema.ObjectId,
      ref: 'User'
    }
});
```

```
mongoose.model('Article', ArticleSchema);
```

You should be familiar with this code snippet, so let's quickly go over this model. First, you included your model dependencies and then you used the Mongoose Schema object to create a new ArticleSchema. ArticleSchema defines four model fields:

- created: This is a date field that represents the time at which the article was created
- title: This is a string field that represents the article title; note how you used the required validation to make sure all articles have a title
- content: This is a string field that represents the article content
- creator: This is a reference object that represents the user who created the article

In the end, you registered the Article Mongoose model to allow you to use it in the Articles Express controller. Next, you'll need to make sure your application is loading the model file, so go back to the config/mongoose.js file and change it as follows:

```
const config = require('./config');
const mongoose = require('mongoose');

module.exports = function() {
  const db = mongoose.connect(config.db);

  require('../app/models/user.server.model');
  require('../app/models/article.server.model');

  return db;
};
```

This will load your new model file and make sure your application can use your Article model. Once you have your model configured, you'll be able to create your Articles controller.

Setting up the Express controller

The Express controller is responsible for managing articles-related functionalities on the server side. It is built to offer the basic CRUD operations to manipulate the MongoDB article documents. To begin writing the Express controller, go to your `app/controllers` folder and create a new file named `articles.server.controller.js`. In your newly created file, add the following dependencies:

```
const mongoose = require('mongoose');
const Article = mongoose.model('Article');
```

In the preceding lines of code, you basically just included your `Article` mongoose model. Now, before you begin creating the CRUD methods, it is recommended that you create an error handling method for validation and other server errors.

The error handling method of the Express controller

In order to handle Mongoose errors, it is preferable to write a simple error handling method that will take care of extracting a simple error message from the Mongoose error object and provide it to your controller methods. Go back to your `app/controllers/articles.server.controller.js` file and append the following lines of code:

```
function getErrorMessage (err) {
  if (err.errors) {
    for (let errName in err.errors) {
      if (err.errors[errName].message) return err.errors[errName].
        message;
    }
  } else {
    return 'Unknown server error';
  }
};
```

The `getErrorMessage()` method gets the Mongoose error object passed as an argument and then iterates over the error collection and extracts the first message. This is done because you don't want to overwhelm your users with multiple error messages at once. Now that you have error handling set up, it is time to write your first controller method.

The create() method of the Express controller

The `create()` method of the Express controller will provide the basic functionality to create a new article document. It will use the HTTP request body as the JSON base object for the document, and it will use the model `save()` method to save it to MongoDB. To implement the `create()` method, append the following lines of code to your `app/controllers/articles.server.controller.js` file:

```
exports.create = function(req, res) {
  const article = new Article(req.body);
  article.creator = req.user;

  article.save((err) => {
    if (err) {
      return res.status(400).send({
        message: getErrorMessage(err)
      });
    } else {
      res.status(200).json(article);
    }
  });
};
```

Let's go over the `create()` method code. First, you created a new `Article` model instance using the HTTP request body. Next, you added the authenticated `passport` user as the article `creator`. Finally, you used the Mongoose instance `save()` method to save the article document. In the `save()` callback function, it is worth noticing how you return either an error response and an appropriate HTTP error code or the new `article` object as a JSON response. Once you're done with the `create()` method, you will move on to implementing the read operation. The read operation consists of two methods: one that retrieves a list of articles and a second method that retrieves a particular article. Let's begin with the method that lists a collection of articles.

The list() method of the Express controller

The `list()` method of the Express controller will provide the basic functionality to retrieve a list of the existing articles. It will use the model's `find()` method to retrieve all the documents in the article collection and then output a JSON representation of this list. To implement the `list()` method, append the following lines of code to your `app/controllers/articles.server.controller.js` file:

```
exports.list = function(req, res) {
  Article.find().sort('-created').populate('creator', 'firstName
lastName fullName').exec((err, articles) => {
    if (err) {
```

```
            return res.status(400).send({
                message: getErrorMessage(err)
            });
        } else {
            res.status(200).json(articles);
        }
    });
};
```

In this controller method, note how you used the `find()` function of Mongoose to get the collection of article documents, and while we can add a MongoDB query of some sort, for now, we'll retrieve all the documents in the collection. Next, note how the article collection is sorted using the `created` property. Then, you can see how the `populate()` method of Mongoose was used to add some user fields to the `creator` property of the `articles` objects. In this case, you populated the `firstName`, `lastName`, and `fullName` properties of the `creator` user object.

The rest of the CRUD operations involve a manipulation of a single existing article document. You could, of course, implement the retrieval of the article document in each method by itself, basically repeating this logic. However, the Express router has a neat feature for the handling of route parameters, so before you'll implement the rest of your Express CRUD functionality, you'll first learn how to leverage the route parameter middleware to save some time and code redundancy.

The read() middleware of the Express controller

The `read()` method of the Express controller will provide the basic functionality to read an existing article document from the database. Since you're writing a sort of RESTful API, the common usage of this method will be handled by passing the article's ID field as a route parameter. This means that your requests to the server will contain an `articleId` parameter in their paths.

Fortunately, the Express router provides the `app.param()` method for the handling of route parameters. This method allows you to attach a middleware for all the requests containing the `articleId` route parameter. The middleware itself will then use the `articleId` provided to find the proper MongoDB document and add the retrieved `article` object to the request object. This will allow all the controller methods that manipulate an existing article to obtain the `article` object from the Express request object. To make this clearer, let's implement the route parameter middleware. Go to your `app/controllers/articles.server.controller.js` file and append the following lines of code:

```
exports.articleByID = function(req, res, next, id) {
    Article.findById(id).populate('creator', 'firstName lastName
fullName').exec((err, article) => {
```

```
    if (err) return next(err);
    if (!article) return next(new Error('Failed to load article '
      + id));

    req.article = article;
    next();
  });
};
```

As you can see, the middleware function signature contains all the Express middleware arguments and an `id` argument. It then uses the `id` argument to find an article and reference it using the `req.article` property. Note how the `populate()` method of the Mongoose model was used to add some user fields to the `creator` property of the `article` object. In this case, you populated the `firstName`, `lastName`, and `fullName` properties of the `creator` user object.

When you connect your Express routes, you'll learn how to add the `articleByID()` middleware to different routes, but for now, let's add the `read()` method of the Express controller, which will return an `article` object. To add the `read()` method, append the following lines of code to your `app/controllers/articles.server.controller.js` file:

```
exports.read = function(req, res) {
  res.status(200).json(req.article);
};
```

Quite simple, isn't it? That's because you already took care of obtaining the `article` object in the `articleByID()` middleware, so now all you have to do is just output the `article` object as a JSON representation. We'll connect the middleware and routes in the next sections, but before we do that, let's finish implementing the Express controller CRUD functionality.

The update() method of the Express controller

The `update()` method of the Express controller will provide the basic operations to update an existing article document. It will use the existing `article` object as the base object and then update the `title` and `content` fields using the HTTP request body. It will also use the model `save()` method to save the changes to the database. To implement the `update()` method, go to your `app/controllers/articles.server.controller.js` file and append the following lines of code:

```
exports.update = function(req, res) {
  const article = req.article;

  article.title = req.body.title;
```

```
      article.content = req.body.content;

      article.save((err) => {
        if (err) {
          return res.status(400).send({
            message: getErrorMessage(err)
          });
        } else {
          res.status(200).json(article);
        }
      });
    };
```

As you can see, the update() method also makes the assumption that you already obtained the article object in the articleByID() middleware. So, all you have to do is update the title and content fields, save the article, and then output the updated article object as a JSON representation. In case of an error, it will output the appropriate error message using the getErrorMessage() method you wrote earlier and an HTTP error code. The last CRUD operation left to implement is the delete() method; so let's look at how you can add a simple delete() method to your Express controller.

The delete() method of the Express controller

The delete() method of the Express controller will provide the basic operations to delete an existing article document. It will use the model remove() method to delete the existing article from the database. To implement the delete() method, go to your app/controllers/articles.server.controller.js file and append the following lines of code:

```
    exports.delete = function(req, res) {
      const article = req.article;

      article.remove((err) => {
        if (err) {
          return res.status(400).send({
            message: getErrorMessage(err)
          });
        } else {
          res.status(200).json(article);
        }
      });
    };
```

Again, you can see how the delete() method also makes use of the already obtained article object by the articleByID() middleware. So, all you have to do is invoke the Mongoose model's remove() method and then output the deleted article object as a JSON representation. In case of an error, it will output the appropriate error message using the getErrorMessage() method you wrote earlier and an HTTP error code instead.

Congratulations! You just finished implementing your Express controller's CRUD functionality. Before you continue to wire the Express routes that will invoke these methods, let's take some time to implement two authorization middleware.

Implementing an authentication middleware

When building your Express controller, you probably noticed that most methods require your user to be authenticated. For instance, the create() method won't be operational if the req.user object is not assigned. While you can check this assignment inside your methods, this will enforce you to implement the same validation code over and over. Instead, you can just use the Express middleware chaining to block unauthorized requests from executing your controller methods. The first middleware you should implement will check whether a user is authenticated at all. Since this is an authentication-related method, it would be best to implement it in the Express users controller, so go to the app/controllers/users.server.controller.js file and append the following lines of code:

```
exports.requiresLogin = function(req, res, next) {
  if (!req.isAuthenticated()) {
    return res.status(401).send({
      message: 'User is not logged in'
    });
  }

  next();
};
```

The requiresLogin() middleware uses the Passport-initiated req.isAuthenticated() method to check whether a user is currently authenticated. If it finds out that the user is indeed signed in, it will call the next middleware in the chain; otherwise, it will respond with an authentication error and an HTTP error code. This middleware is great, but if you want to check whether a specific user is authorized to perform a certain action, you will need to implement an article-specific authorization middleware.

Implementing an authorization middleware

In your CRUD module, there are two methods that edit an existing article document. Usually, the update() and delete() methods should be restricted so that only the user who created the article will be able to use them. This means that you need to authorize any request made to these methods to validate whether the current article is being edited by its creator. To do this, you will need to add an authorization middleware to your Articles controller, so go to the app/controllers/articles. server.controller.js file and append the following lines of code:

```javascript
exports.hasAuthorization = function(req, res, next) {
    if (req.article.creator.id !== req.user.id) {
        return res.status(403).send({
            message: 'User is not authorized'
        });
    }

    next();
};
```

The hasAuthorization() middleware uses the req.article and req.user objects to verify that the current user is the creator of the current article. This middleware also assumes that it gets executed only for requests that contain the articleId route parameter. Now that you have all your methods and middleware in place, it is time to wire the routes that enable their execution.

Wiring the Express routes

Before we begin wiring the Express routes, let's do a quick overview of the RESTful API architectural design. The RESTful API provides a coherent service structure that represents a set of actions that you can perform on an application resource. This means that the API uses a predefined route structure along with the HTTP method name in order to provide context for HTTP requests. Though the RESTful architecture can be applied in different ways, a RESTful API usually complies with a few simple rules:

- A base URI per resource, in our case, http://localhost:3000/articles
- A data structure, usually JSON, passed in the request body
- The usage of standard HTTP methods (for example, GET, POST, PUT, and DELETE)

Using these three rules, you'll be able to properly route HTTP requests to use the right controller method. So, your articles API will consist of five routes:

- GET http://localhost:3000/articles: This will return a list of articles
- POST http://localhost:3000/articles : This will create and return a new article
- GET http://localhost:3000/articles/:articleId: This will return a single existing article
- PUT http://localhost:3000/articles/:articleId: This will update and return a single existing article
- DELETE http://localhost:3000/articles/:articleId: This will delete and return a single article

As you probably noticed, these routes already have corresponding controller methods. You even have the articleId route parameter middleware already implemented, so all that is left to do is implement the Express routes. To do that, go to the app/routes folder and create a new file named articles.server. routes.js. In your newly created file, paste the following code snippet:

```
const users = require('../../app/controllers/users.server.
controller');
const articles = require('../../app/controllers/articles.server.
controller');

module.exports = function(app) {
  app.route('/api/articles')
     .get(articles.list)
     .post(users.requiresLogin, articles.create);

  app.route('/api/articles/:articleId')
     .get(articles.read)
     .put(users.requiresLogin, articles.hasAuthorization, articles.
update)
     .delete(users.requiresLogin, articles.hasAuthorization, articles.
delete);

  app.param('articleId', articles.articleByID);
};
```

In the preceding code snippet, you did several things. First, you required the users and articles controllers, and then you used the Express `app.route()` method to define the base routes for your CRUD operations. You used the Express routing methods to wire each controller method to a specific HTTP method. You may also notice how the POST method uses the `users.requiresLogin()` middleware, since a user needs to log in before they can create a new article. In the same way, the PUT and DELETE methods use both `users.requiresLogin()` and `articles.hasAuthorization()` middleware, since users can only edit and delete the articles they created. Finally, you used the `app.param()` method to make sure that every route that has the `articleId` parameter will first call the `articles.articleByID()` middleware. Next, you'll need to configure your Express application to load your new Article model and routes file.

Configuring the Express application

In order to use your new Express assets, you have to configure your Express application to load your route file. To do that, go back to your `config/express.js` file and change it, as follows:

```
const path = require('path');
const config = require('./config');
const express = require('express');
const morgan = require('morgan');
const compress = require('compression');
const bodyParser = require('body-parser');
const methodOverride = require('method-override');
const session = require('express-session');
const flash = require('connect-flash');
const passport = require('passport');

module.exports = function() {
  const app = express();

  if (process.env.NODE_ENV === 'development') {
    app.use(morgan('dev'));
  } else if (process.env.NODE_ENV === 'production') {
    app.use(compress());
  }

  app.use(bodyParser.urlencoded({
    extended: true
  }));
  app.use(bodyParser.json());
  app.use(methodOverride());
```

```
app.use(session({
  saveUninitialized: true,
  resave: true,
  secret: config.sessionSecret
}));

app.set('views', './app/views');
app.set('view engine', 'ejs');

app.use(flash());
app.use(passport.initialize());
app.use(passport.session());

app.use('/', express.static(path.resolve('./public')));
app.use('/lib', express.static(path.resolve('./node_modules')));

require('../app/routes/users.server.routes.js')(app);
require('../app/routes/articles.server.routes.js')(app);
require('../app/routes/index.server.routes.js')(app);

return app;
};
```

This is it; your article's RESTful API is ready! Next, you'll learn how simple it is to use the HTTP client to let your Angular components communicate with it.

Using the HTTP client

In *Chapter 7, Introduction to Angular*, we mentioned the http client as a means of communication between the Angular 2 application and your backend API. Since the REST architecture is well structured, it would be quite easy to implement a service for our Angular module, which we'll provide to our components with an API in order to communicate with the server. To do that, the Angular http client utilizes the Observable pattern to deal with its asynchronous nature, so before we continue, it would be best to quickly review this powerful pattern.

Reactive programming and Observables

In programming, we mostly expect things to run in a serial way, where all of our instructions occur in an order. Alas, from its beginning, web application development suffered from a lack of synchronicity. This is especially a problem when dealing with data and, more specifically in our case, data that is retrieved from the server. To solve this issue, various different patterns were created, from which now we mostly use the callback and promise patterns. Callbacks were the go-to for most of JavaScript's lifetime, and more recently, Promises started gaining some traction. However, Promises suffer from a short, onetime lifespan. To be more precise, a Promise can be set up and then can only be differed once, but our data can change over time, so we'll need to create more and more promises. For instance, let's say we want to track all the changes made to a text field and implement an 'undo' functionality; to do that, we can use a callback to our text change event and then record all of the changes and do something with it. This might seem simple, but what if we have hundreds of objects or what if our text field value is changed programmatically? This is a very simplistic example, but this scenario repeats itself in various ways across modern application development, and to solve it, a new methodology has emerged, a methodology called Reactive Programming. You might have heard about reactive programming or you might have not, but the easiest way to understand it is to realize that it's all about tracking asynchronous data that is changing over time, and the way it does this is by using Observables. Observables are streams of data that can be observed by one or multiple observers. An Observable emits values over time and notifies the "subscribed" observers with a new value, an error, or a completion event. A visual representation of this mechanism can be seen in the following figure:

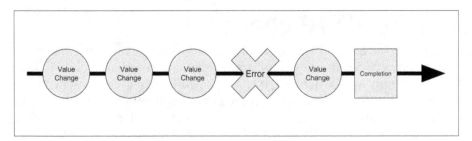

In this diagram, you can see that the Observables keeps emitting value changes, an error, another value change, and then a completion event when the Observable finishes its life cycle. Reactive programming might seem complicated, but fortunately, the ReactiveX library allows us to deal with observables in a very simple way.

It is recommended that you continue reading about reactive programming, since it's rapidly becoming a dominant approach to modern web application development.

The ReactiveX library

The Rx library is a cross-platform library that uses the observer pattern to help developers manage asynchronous data changes over time. Simply put, ReactiveX is a library that allows us to create and manipulate Observable objects. In Angular 2 projects, we use the RxJS library, which is basically a JavaScript version of the ReactiveX library. If you look closely at the previous chapter, you'll be able to see that we already set it up and even used it in our authentication service. We did that by installing it using npm:

```
...
"rxjs": "5.0.0-beta.12",
...
```

We imported it in our entities as follows:

```
...
import 'rxjs/Rx';
...
```

We had to do this because the Angular team chose to use Observables quite extensively. And one of our first encounters with it was using the http client.

Using the http client

The http module provides us with a standardized way to communicate with our RESTful endpoints. To use the http client, we'll have to import and inject it into our entities and then use our http client instance to perform different HTTP requests. A simple example of using the http client to perform a POST request was presented in *Chapter 7, Introduction to Angular*, where we used it in our signin method:

```
signin(credentials: any): Observable<any> {
    let body = JSON.stringify(credentials);
    let headers = new Headers({ 'Content-Type': 'application/json'
});
    let options = new RequestOptions({ headers: headers });

  return this.http.post(this._signinURL, body, options)
                      .map(res => this.user = res.json())
                      .catch(this.handleError)
  }
```

As you can see, we created a JSON string and set the request headers using the RequestOptions object before we called the http client post() methods. The http client method returns an Observable object that tracks an HTTP Response object. But since we want our service to provide data, we used the map() method to extract the response JSON object.

 We need to use the json() method since Angular follows the ES2015 specification for the HTTP response object.

Note that we also catch any error using our handleError() method. So how do we use the Observable object returned from this method? If you look back at our signin component, you'll be able to see how we used our authentication service:

```
signin() {
  this._authenticationService.signin(this.credentials).subscribe(
  result  => this._router.navigate(['/']),
  error =>  this.errorMessage = error );
  }
}
```

In this method, we called the authentication service's signin method and then subscribed to the returned Observable. We then handled any value event with the first arrow function and any error with the second arrow function. That's basically the way we work the HTTP client!

The HTTP client offers various methods to handle different HTTP requests:

- request(url, options): This method allows us to perform any HTTP request defined by the options object.
- get(): This method performs a GET HTTP request.
- post(): This method performs a POST HTTP request.
- put(): This method performs a PUT HTTP request.
- delete(): This method performs a DELETE HTTP request.

All these methods return a Response Observable object that can be subscribed or manipulated.

 An important thing to notice is that the HTTP client always returns a "cold" observable. This means that the request itself will not be sent until someone subscribes to the observable.

In the next section, you'll learn how to use the `http` client to communicate with your Express API.

Implementing the Angular module

The second part of your CRUD module is the Angular module. This module will contain an Angular service that will communicate with the Express API using the `http` client, an Angular Article component that will contain four subcomponents with a set of templates that provide your users with an interface to perform CRUD operations. Before you begin creating your Angular entities, let's first create the initial module structure. Go to your application's `public/app` folder and create a new folder named `articles`. In this new folder, create the module file named `articles.module.ts` and paste the following lines of code:

```
import { NgModule }        from '@angular/core';
import { CommonModule }    from '@angular/common';
import { FormsModule }     from '@angular/forms';
import { RouterModule } from '@angular/router';

import { ArticlesRoutes } from './articles.routes';
import { ArticlesComponent } from './articles.component';
import { CreateComponent } from './create/create.component';
import { ListComponent } from './list/list.component';
import { ViewComponent } from './view/view.component';
import { EditComponent } from './edit/edit.component';

@NgModule({
  imports: [
    CommonModule,
    FormsModule,
    RouterModule.forChild(ArticlesRoutes),
  ],
  declarations: [
    ArticlesComponent,
    CreateComponent,
    ListComponent,
    ViewComponent,
    EditComponent,
  ]
})
export class ArticlesModule {}
```

As you can see, we simply imported the modules we needed from the Angular packages and the components, service, and routes definition of our new module. Next, we created a new Angular module that imports the Angular modules and our routing configuration as a child router and then declares our new module components. Now, we can continue by creating our main component file. To do that, create a file named `articles.component.ts` inside your `public/app` folder and paste the following lines of code:

```
import { Component } from '@angular/core';
import { ArticlesService } from './articles.service';

@Component({
  selector: 'articles',
  template: '<router-outlet></router-outlet>',
  providers: [ArticlesService]
})
export class ArticlesComponent {}
```

In this file, we imported the basic Angular modules and the articles service we'll shortly create. We then created a new component that uses `router-outlet` and injects our service. Next, we'll need to create a routing configuration for our `articles` component. To do that, create a file named `articles.routes.ts` and paste the following lines of code:

```
import { Routes } from '@angular/router';

import { ArticlesComponent } from './articles.component';
import { CreateComponent } from './create/create.component';
import { ListComponent } from './list/list.component';
import { ViewComponent } from './view/view.component';
import { EditComponent } from './edit/edit.component';

export const ArticlesRoutes: Routes = [{
  path: 'articles',
  component: ArticlesComponent,
  children: [
    {path: '', component: ListComponent},
    {path: 'create', component: CreateComponent},
    {path: ':articleId', component: ViewComponent},
    {path: ':articleId/edit', component: EditComponent}
  ],
}];
```

As you can see, we simply created a routing configuration for our component and its subcomponents. The code should be familiar, since it resembles the authentication routing we implemented in the previous chapter. Moreover, in our update and view paths, we defined a URL parameter in the form of a colon followed by the name of our parameter, in this case, the `articleId` parameter.

Next, you'll need to import our articles module in our application module configuration. To do that, go back to your `public/app/app.module.ts` file and change it as follows:

```
import { NgModule }          from '@angular/core';
import { BrowserModule }     from '@angular/platform-browser';
import { FormsModule }       from '@angular/forms';
import { RouterModule }      from '@angular/router';
import { HttpModule, RequestOptions } from '@angular/http';
import { LocationStrategy, HashLocationStrategy } from '@angular/common';

import { AppComponent }      from './app.component';
import { AppRoutes }         from './app.routes';

import { HomeModule } from './home/home.module';
import { AuthenticationService } from './authentication/authentication.service';
import { AuthenticationModule } from './authentication/authentication.module';
import { ArticlesModule } from './articles/articles.module';

@NgModule({
  imports: [
    BrowserModule,
    HttpModule,
    FormsModule,
    AuthenticationModule,
    HomeModule,
    ArticlesModule,
    RouterModule.forRoot(AppRoutes),
  ],
  declarations: [
    AppComponent
  ],
  providers: [
    AuthenticationService
  ],
  bootstrap: [AppComponent]
})
export class AppModule { }
```

This concludes the configuration of our new module. Now we can move on to creating our module entities. We'll begin with our module service.

Creating the Angular module service

In order for your CRUD module to easily communicate with the API endpoints, it is recommended that you use a single Angular service that will utilize the `http` client methods. To do that, go to your `public/app/articles` folder and create a new file named `articles.service.ts` with the following lines of code:

```
import 'rxjs/Rx';
import {Observable} from 'rxjs/Observable';

import {Injectable} from '@angular/core';
import {Http, Headers, Request, RequestMethod, Response} from '@angular/http';


@Injectable()
export class ArticlesService {
  private _baseURL = 'api/articles';

  constructor (private _http: Http) {}

  create(article: any): Observable<any> {
    return this._http
      .post(this._baseURL, article)
      .map((res: Response) => res.json())
      .catch(this.handleError);
    }

  read(articleId: string): Observable<any> {
    return this._http
      .get(`${this._baseURL}/${articleId}`)
      .map((res: Response) => res.json())
      .catch(this.handleError);
  }

  update(article: any): Observable<any> {
    return this._http
      .put(`${this._baseURL}/${article._id}`, article)
```

```
      .map((res: Response) => res.json())
      .catch(this.handleError);
   }

  delete(articleId: any): Observable<any> {
    return this._http
      .delete(`${this._baseURL}/${articleId}`)
      .map((res: Response) => res.json())
      .catch(this.handleError);
  }

  list(): Observable<any> {
    return this._http
      .get(this._baseURL)
      .map((res: Response) => res.json())
      .catch(this.handleError);
  }

  private handleError(error: Response) {
    return Observable.throw(error.json().message || 'Server error');
  }
 }
}
```

Let's review this. First, we imported the `Observable` and `rxjs` library module. You might notice that we import the entire library, since we'll need to use various operators with our Observable object, for instance, the `map()` method.

Next, we imported the modules we needed from the Angular library and created our injectable service using the `@Injectable` decorator. Our service has one property to hold our API base URL and a constructor to inject the HTTP client. It contains an error handling method that deals with server errors. Our other methods are quite easy to understand:

- `create()`: Accepts an article object and sends it to the server using an HTTP POST request
- `read()`: Accepts an `article ID` string and asks for an article object from the server using an HTTP GET request
- `update ()`: Accepts an article object and sends it to the server for an update using an HTTP PUT request
- `delete()`: Accepts an `article ID` string and tries to delete it using an HTTP DELETE request
- `list()`: Requests for an array of article objects using an HTTP GET request

Note how we map the response object to only send the JSON object and how we catch any error to modify the response so that our components will only have to deal with the data itself.

That's it! Our module infrastructure is ready for our subcomponents. In the next sections, you'll be able to see how easy our implementation becomes using our previous preparations.

Implementing the Create subcomponent

Our "Create" subcomponent will be taking care of creating new articles. Begin by creating a new folder named `create` inside your `public/app/articles` folder. In this folder, create a new file named `create.component.ts` and paste the following code:

```
import { Component } from '@angular/core';
import { Router } from '@angular/router';

import { ArticlesService } from '../articles.service';

@Component({
  selector: 'create',
  templateUrl: 'app/articles/create/create.template.html'
})
export class CreateComponent {
  article: any = {};
  errorMessage: string;

  constructor(private _router:Router,
        private _articlesService: ArticlesService) {}

  create() {
    this._articlesService
      .create(this.article)
      .subscribe(createdArticle => this._router.navigate(['/articles',
createdArticle._id]),
            error =>  this.errorMessage = error);
  }
}
```

Let's review this. We started by importing the modules we need from the Angular library along with our `ArticlesService`. Then, we created our component with an empty article and `errorMessage` objects. Note how our Component's constructor injects the `Router` and our `ArticlesService` services. Then, we created a `create()` method that uses `ArticlesService` to create a new article object. In our observable subscription, we use the `Router` service to navigate to our View components along with the newly created `article` ID. In case of an error, we set our component's `errorMessage` property to the message. To finish up with our subcomponent, we'll need to create its template.

Adding the template

The `create` template will provide your user with an interface to create a new article. It will contain an HTML form and it will use your component's `create` method to save the new article. To create your template, go to the `public/app/articles/create` folder and create a new file named `create.template.html`. In your new file, paste the following code snippet:

```
<h1>New Article</h1>
<form (ngSubmit)="create()" novalidate>
  <div>
    <label for="title">Title</label>
    <div>
      <input type="text" required [(ngModel)]="article.title"
name="title" placeholder="Title">
    </div>
  </div>
  <div>
    <label for="content">Content</label>
    <div>
      <textarea type="text" required cols="30" rows="10"
[(ngModel)]="article.content" name="content" placeholder="Content"></
textarea>
    </div>
  </div>
  <div>
    <input type="submit">
  </div>

  <strong id="error">{{errorMessage}}</strong>
</form>
```

The `create` template contains a simple form with two text input fields and a submit button. The text fields use the `ngModel` directive to bind the user input to our component's properties. It is also important to note the `ngSubmit` directive you placed in the `form` element. This directive tells Angular to call a specific component method when the form is submitted. In this case, the form submission will execute your component's `create()` method. The last thing you should notice is the error message at the end of the form that will be shown in case of any error. Next, we're going to implement the View subcomponent.

Implementing the View subcomponent

Our "View" subcomponent will be taking care of presenting a single article. Our component will also contain a set of buttons that are visible only to the article creator, which will allow the creator to delete the article or navigate to the `edit` route. Begin by creating a new folder named `view` inside your `public/app/articles` folder. In this folder, create a new file named `view.component.ts` and paste the following code:

```
import { Component } from '@angular/core';
import { Router, ActivatedRoute } from '@angular/router';
import { AuthenticationService } from '../../authentication/
authentication.service';
import { ArticlesService } from '../articles.service';

@Component({
  selector: 'view',
  templateUrl: 'app/articles/view/view.template.html',
})
export class ViewComponent {
  user: any;
  article: any;
  paramsObserver: any;
  errorMessage: string;
  allowEdit: boolean = false;

  constructor(private _router:Router,
        private _route: ActivatedRoute,
        private _authenticationService: AuthenticationService,
        private _articlesService: ArticlesService) {}

  ngOnInit() {
    this.user = this._authenticationService.user

    this.paramsObserver = this._route.params.subscribe(params => {
```

```
      let articleId = params['articleId'];

    this._articlesService
      .read(articleId)
      .subscribe(
        article => {
          this.article = article;
          this.allowEdit = (this.user && this.user._id === this.
article.creator._id);
        },
        error => this._router.navigate(['/articles'])
      );
  });
}

ngOnDestroy() {
  this.paramsObserver.unsubscribe();
}

delete() {
  this._articlesService.delete(this.article._id).
subscribe(deletedArticle => this._router.navigate(['/articles']),
                          error => this.errorMessage = error);

}
}
```

We started by importing the modules we need from the Angular library along with our ArticlesService and AuthenticationService. Then, we created our component with an article property, a currentUser property, a paramsObserver property, an allowEdit flag, and an errorMessage property. Note how our component's constructor injects Router, RouteParams, and our ArticlesService and AuthenticationService services. Our constructor also sets the currentUser property using the AuthenticationService instance. In our ngOnInit method, which is being invoked when the component is initialized, we read the article ID parameter from the route parameters, and then we use the ArticlesService to fetch an existing article. We do this using ActivatedRoute, which supplies us with a params Observable. We unsubscribe to this Observable on our component's ngOnDestroy method. In our Observable subscription, we set the component's article property and determine whether the current user can edit the article. In case of an error, we use the Router service to navigate back to our List route. Lastly, we implemented a delete() method that uses ArticlesService to delete the viewed article and go back to the article list. To finish up with our subcomponent, we'll need to create its template.

Adding the template

The `view` template will provide your user with an interface to `view` an existing article. Your template will also contain a set of buttons only visible to the article creator, which will allow the creator to delete the article or navigate to the `edit` route. To create the template, go to the `public/app/articles/view` folder and create a new file named `view.template.html`. In your new file, paste the following code snippet:

```html
<section *ngIf="article && article.creator">
  <h1>{{article.title}}</h1>

  <div *ngIf="allowEdit">
      <a [routerLink]="['/articles', article._id, 'edit']">edit</a>
      <button (click)="delete()">delete</button>
  </div>
  <small>
      <em>Posted on {{article.created}} by {{article.creator.
fullName}}</em>
  </small>

  <p>{{article.content}}</p>
</section>
```

The `view` template contains a simple set of HTML elements presenting the article information using the `double curly braces` syntax. It is also important to note how you used the `ngIf` directive to present the article edit link and delete button only to the creator of the article. The edit link will direct the user to the `edit` subcomponent, while the delete button will call the `delete()` method of your controller. Next, we'll implement our edit component.

Implementing the Edit subcomponent

Our "Edit" subcomponent will be taking care of editing existing articles. Begin by creating a new folder named `edit` inside your `public/app/articles` folder. In this folder, create a new file named `edit.component.ts` and paste the following code:

```typescript
import { Component } from '@angular/core';
import { Router, ActivatedRoute } from '@angular/router';

import { ArticlesService } from '../articles.service';

@Component({
  selector: 'edit',
  templateUrl: 'app/articles/edit/edit.template.html'
```

```
})
export class EditComponent {
  article: any = {};
  errorMessage: string;
  paramsObserver: any;

  constructor(private _router:Router,
        private _route: ActivatedRoute,
        private _articlesService: ArticlesService) {}

  ngOnInit() {
    this.paramsObserver = this._route.params.subscribe(params => {
      let articleId = params['articleId'];

      this._articlesService.read(articleId).subscribe(article => {
                          this.article = article;
                        },
                      error => this._router.navigate(['/
articles']));
    });
  }

  ngOnDestroy() {
    this.paramsObserver.unsubscribe();
  }

  update() {
    this._articlesService.update(this.article).subscribe(savedArticle
=> this._router.navigate(['/articles', savedArticle._id]),
                        error =>  this.errorMessage =
error);
  }
}
```

Again, we started by importing the modules we need from the Angular library
along with our `ArticlesService`. Then, we created our component with an article
property and an `errorMessage` property. In our constructor, we read the `article`
ID from the route parameters and then we used `ArticlesService` to fetch an
existing article. In our Observables subscription, we set the component's article
property, and in case of an error, we use the `Router` service to navigate back to our
List route. Lastly, we implemented an `update()` method that uses `ArticlesService`
to update the viewed article and go back to the View route. To finish up with our
subcomponent, we'll need to create its template.

Adding the template

The `edit` template will provide your user with an interface to update an existing article. It will contain an HTML form and it will use your component's `update()` method to save the updated article. To create this template, go to the `public/app/articles/edit` folder and create a new file named `edit.template.html`. In your new file, paste the following HTML code:

```
<h1>Edit Article</h1>
<form (ngSubmit)="update()" novalidate>
    <div>
        <label for="title">Title</label>
        <div>
            <input type="text" required [(ngModel)]="article.title"
name="title" placeholder="Title">
        </div>
    </div>
    <div>
        <label for="content">Content</label>
        <div>
            <textarea type="text" required cols="30" rows="10"
[(ngModel)]="article.content" name="content" placeholder="Content"></
textarea>
        </div>
    </div>
    <div>
        <input type="submit" value="Update">
    </div>

    <strong>{{errorMessage}}</strong>
</form>
```

The `edit` template contains a simple form with two text input fields and a submit button. The text fields use the `ngModel` directive to bind the user input to the component's `article` property. It is also important to note the `ngSubmit` directive you placed in the `form` element. This time, the directive tells Angular that the form submission should execute your component's `update()` method. The last thing you should notice is the error message at the end of the form, which will be shown in the case of an editing error. Our final subcomponent is our List subcomponent.

Implementing the List subcomponent

Our "List" subcomponent will be taking care of presenting a list of articles. We'll begin by creating a new folder named `list` inside our `public/app/articles` folder. In this folder, create a new file named `list.component.ts` and paste the following code:

```
import { Component } from '@angular/core';
import { ArticlesService } from '../articles.service';

@Component({
  selector: 'list',
  templateUrl: 'app/articles/list/list.template.html'
})
export class ListComponent{
  articles: any;
  errorMessage: string;

  constructor(private _articlesService: ArticlesService) {}

  ngOnInit() {
    this._articlesService.list().subscribe(articles  => this.articles
= articles);
  }
}
```

We started by importing the modules we need from the Angular library along with our `ArticlesService`. Then, we created our component with an articles property and an `errorMessage` property. Note how our component's constructor injects `ArticlesService` and uses it to fetch a list of articles. Inside our Observables subscription, we set the component's articles property. Now all we have left to do is implement the component's template.

Adding the template

The `list` template will provide your user with an interface to view the list of existing articles. Our template will use the `ngFor` directive to render a list of HTML elements, each representing a single article. If there aren't any existing articles, the view will offer the user to navigate to the `create` route. To create your view, go to the `public/app/articles/list` folder and create a new file named `list.template.html`. In your new file, paste the following code snippet:

```
<h1>Articles</h1>
<ul>
  <li *ngFor="let article of articles">
    <a [routerLink]="['/articles', article._id]">{{article.title}}</a>
```

```
    <br>
    <small>{{article.created}}/{{article.creator.fullName}}</small>
    <p>{{article.content}}</p>
  </li>
</ul>

<div *ngIf="articles && articles.length === 0">
  No articles yet, why don't you <a [routerLink]="['/articles/
create']">create one</a>?
</div>
```

The `list` template contains a simple set of repeating HTML elements that represent the list of articles. It uses the `ngFor` directive to duplicate the list item for every article in the collection and displays each article's information. We then used `routerLink` to link to a single article view. It is also important to note how we used the `ngIf` directive to ask the user to create a new article in case there are no existing articles.

By implementing your Angular subcomponents, you practically finished your first CRUD module! All that is left to do is provide the user with links to our new routes.

Wrapping up

To finish our implementation, it would be great to provide the user with links to your new CRUD module routes. To do that, go to your `public/app/home/home.template.html` file and change it, as follows:

```
<div *ngIf="user">
  <h1>Hello {{user.firstName}}</h1>
  <a href="/api/auth/signout">Signout</a>
  <ul>
    <li><a [routerLink]="['/articles']">List Articles</a></li>
    <li><a [routerLink]="['/articles/create']">Create Article</a></li>
  </ul>
</div>

<div *ngIf="!user">
  <a [routerLink]="['/authentication/signup']">Signup</a>
  <a [routerLink]="['/authentication/signin']">Signin</a>
</div>
```

This change will present our users with links to the new `Articles` component routes only when they're logged in and hide it when they're not. This is it! Everything is ready for you to test your new CRUD module. Use your command-line tool and navigate to the MEAN application's root folder. Then, run your application:

```
$ npm start
```

Once your application is running, use your browser and navigate to `http://localhost:3000`. You will see the sign-up and sign-in links; try to sign in and watch how the home view changes. Then, try to navigate to the `http://localhost:3000/articles` URL and see how the `list` component suggests that you create a new article. Continue to create a new article and try to edit and delete it using the components you created previously. Your CRUD module should be fully operational.

Summary

In this chapter, you learned how to build your first CRUD module. You started by defining the Mongoose model and Express controller and learned how to implement each CRUD method. You also authorized your controller methods using Express middleware. Then, you defined a RESTful API for your module methods. You learned a bit about reactive programming and the observer pattern. You used the HTTP client to communicate with your API. Then, you created your Angular components and implemented the Angular CRUD functionality. After connecting the four parts of a MEAN application and creating your first CRUD module, in the next chapter, you'll use Socket.io in order to add real-time connectivity between your server and client applications.

9
Adding Real-time Functionality Using Socket.io

In previous chapters, you learned how to build your MEAN application and how to create CRUD modules. These chapters covered the basic functionalities of a web application; however, more and more applications require real-time communication between the server and the browser. In this chapter, you'll learn how to connect your Express and Angular applications in real time using the `Socket.io` module. Socket.io enables Node.js developers to support real-time communication using `WebSockets` in modern browsers and legacy fallback protocols in older browsers. In this chapter, we'll cover the following topics:

- Setting up the Socket.io module
- Configuring the Express application
- Setting up the Socket.io/Passport session
- Wiring Socket.io routes
- Using the Socket.io client object
- Building a simple chat room

Introducing WebSockets

Modern web applications, such as Facebook, Twitter, and Gmail, are incorporating real-time capabilities which enable applications to continuously present the user with recently updated information. Unlike traditional applications, in real-time applications, the common roles of the browser and the server can be reversed since the server needs to update the browser with new data regardless of the browser request state. This means that unlike the common HTTP behavior, the server won't wait for the browser's requests. Instead, it will send new data to the browser whenever this data becomes available.

This reverse approach is often called **Comet**, a term coined by a web developer named Alex Russel back in 2006 (the term was a word play on the AJAX term; both Comet and AJAX are common household cleaners in the US). In the past, there were several ways to implement a Comet functionality using the HTTP protocol.

The first and easiest way is **XMLHttpRequest** (**XHR**) polling. In XHR polling, the browser makes periodic requests to the server. The server then returns an empty response unless it has new data to send back. Upon a new event, the server will return the new event data to the next polling request. While this works quite well for most browsers, this method has two problems. The most obvious one is that using this method generates a large number of requests that hit the server with no particular reason, since a lot of requests return empty. The second problem is that the update time depends on the request period. This means that new data will only get pushed to the browser on the next request, causing delays in updating the client state. To solve these issues, a better approach was introduced: XHR long polling.

In XHR long polling, the browser makes an XHR request to the server, but a response is not sent back unless the server has new data. Upon an event, the server responds with the event data and the browser makes a new long polling request. This cycle enables better management of requests, since there is only a single request per session. Furthermore, the server can update the browser immediately with new information without having to wait for the browser's next request. Because of its stability and usability, XHR long polling has become the standard approach for real-time applications and was implemented in various ways, including Forever iFrame, multipart XHR, and JSONP long polling using script tags (for cross-domain, real-time support), and the common long-living XHR.

However, all these approaches were actually hacks using the HTTP and XHR protocols in a way they were not meant to be used. With the rapid development of modern browsers and the increased adoption of the new HTML5 specifications, a new protocol emerged in order to implement real-time communication: the full duplex `WebSockets` protocol.

In browsers that support the `WebSockets` protocol, the initial connection between the server and browser is made over HTTP and is called an HTTP handshake. Once the initial connection is made, the browser and server open a single ongoing communication channel over a TCP socket. Once the socket connection is established, it enables bidirectional communication between the browser and the server. This enables both parties to send and retrieve messages over a single communication channel. This also helps lower the server load, decrease message latency, and unify PUSH communication using a standalone connection.

However, `WebSockets` still suffers from two major problems. First and foremost is browser compatibility. The `WebSockets` specification is fairly new, so older browsers don't support it, and though most modern browsers implement the protocol now, a large group of users is still using these older browsers. The second problem is HTTP proxies, firewalls, and hosting providers. Since `WebSockets` uses a different communication protocol than HTTP, a lot of these intermediaries don't support it yet and block any socket communication. As it has always been with the Web, developers are left with a fragmentation problem, which can only be solved using an abstraction library that optimizes usability by switching between protocols according to the available resources. Fortunately, a popular library called Socket.io has been developed for this purpose, and it is freely available for the Node.js developer community.

Introducing Socket.io

Created in 2010 by the JavaScript developer Guillermo Rauch, Socket.io aimed at abstracting Node.js real-time application development. Since then, it has evolved dramatically and has been released in nine major versions before being broken in its latest version into two different modules: `engine.io` and `socket.io`.

Previous versions of Socket.io were criticized for being unstable since they first tried to establish the most advanced connection mechanisms and then fall back on more primitive protocols. This caused serious issues with using Socket.io in production environments and posed a threat to the adoption of Socket.io as a real-time library. To solve this, the Socket.io team redesigned it and wrapped the core functionality in a base module called Engine.io.

The idea behind Engine.io was to create a more stable real-time module, which first opens a long-polling XHR communication and then tries to upgrade the connection to a `WebSockets` channel. The new version of Socket.io uses the Engine.io module and provides the developer with various features, such as events, rooms, and automatic connection recovery, which you would otherwise implement by yourself. In this chapter's examples, we will use the new Socket.io 1.0, which is the first version to use the Engine.io module.

Older versions of Socket.io prior to version 1.x don't use the new Engine.io module and, therefore, are much less stable in production environments.

When you include the `socket.io` module, it provides you with two objects: a socket server object that is responsible for the server functionality and a socket client object that handles the browser's functionality. We'll begin by examining the server object.

The Socket.io server object

The Socket.io server object is where it all begins. You start by requiring the `socket.io` module and then use it to create a new Socket.io server instance that will interact with socket clients. The server object supports both a standalone implementation and the ability to use it in conjunction with the Express framework. The server instance then exposes a set of methods that allow you to manage the Socket.io server operations. Once the server object is initialized, it will also be responsible for serving the socket client JavaScript file for the browser.

A simple implementation of the standalone Socket.io server will look as follows:

```
const io = require('socket.io')();
io.on('connection', function(socket){ /* ... */ });
io.listen(3000);
```

This will open a Socket.io over the `3000` port and serve the socket client file at `http://localhost:3000/socket.io/socket.io.js`. Implementing the Socket.io server in conjunction with an Express application will be a bit different as shown in the following code:

```
const app = require('express')();
const server = require('http').Server(app);
const io = require('socket.io')(server);
io.on('connection', (socket) => { /* ... */ });
server.listen(3000);
```

This time, you first use the `http` module of Node.js to create a server and wrap the Express application. The server object is then passed to the `socket.io` module and serves both the Express application and the Socket.io server. Once the server is running, it will be available for socket clients to connect. A client trying to establish a connection with the Socket.io server will start by initiating the handshaking process.

Socket.io handshaking

When a client wants to connect the Socket.io server, it will first send a handshake HTTP request. The server will then analyze the request to gather the necessary information for the ongoing communication. It will then look for the configuration middleware that is registered with the server and execute it before firing the connection event. When the client is successfully connected to the server, the connection event listener is executed, exposing a new socket instance.

Once the handshaking process is over, the client is connected to the server, and all communication with it is handled through the socket instance object. For example, handling a client's disconnection event will be as follows:

```
const app = require('express')();
const server = require('http').Server(app);
const io = require('socket.io')(server);
io.on('connection', (socket) => {
  socket.on('disconnect', () => {
    console.log('user has disconnected');
  });
});
server.listen(3000);
```

Note how the `socket.on()` method adds an event handler to the disconnection event. Although the disconnection event is a predefined event, this approach works the same for custom events as well, as you will see in the following sections.

While the handshake mechanism is fully automatic, Socket.io provides you with a way to intercept the handshake process using a configuration middleware.

The Socket.io configuration middleware

Although the Socket.io configuration middleware existed in previous versions, in the new version, it is even simpler and allows you to manipulate socket communication before the handshake actually occurs. To create a configuration middleware, you will need to use the server's `use()` method, which is very similar to the Express application's `use()` method:

```
const app = require('express')();
const server = require('http').Server(app);
const io = require('socket.io')(server);
io.use((socket, next) => {
  /* ... */
  next(null, true);
});
io.on('connection', (socket) => {
```

```
    socket.on('disconnect', () => {
      console.log('user has disconnected');
    });
  });
  server.listen(3000);
```

As you can see, the `io.use()` method callback accepts two arguments: the `socket` object and a `next` callback. The `socket` object is the same socket object that will be used for the connection, and it holds some connection properties. An important property is the `socket.request` property, which represents the handshake HTTP request. In the following sections, you will use the handshake request to incorporate the Passport session with the Socket.io connection.

The `next` argument is a callback method that accepts two arguments: an error object and a Boolean value. The `next` callback tells Socket.io whether or not to proceed with the handshake process, so if you pass an error object or a false value to the `next` method, Socket.io will not initiate the socket connection. Now that you have a basic understanding of how handshaking works, it is time to discuss the Socket.io client object.

The Socket.io client object

The Socket.io client object is responsible for the implementation of the browser socket communication with the Socket.io server. You start by including the Socket.io client JavaScript file, which is served by the Socket.io server. The Socket.io JavaScript file exposes an `io()` method that connects to the Socket.io server and creates the client `socket` object. A simple implementation of the socket client will be as follows:

```
<script src="/socket.io/socket.io.js"></script>
<script>
  var socket = io();
  socket.on('connect', function() {
      /* ... */
  });
</script>
```

Note the default URL for the Socket.io client object. Although it can be altered, you can usually leave it like this and just include the file from the default Socket.io path. Another thing you should notice is that the `io()` method will automatically try to connect to the default base path when executed with no arguments; however, you can also pass a different server URL as an argument.

As you can see, the socket client is much easier to implement, so we can move on to discussing how Socket.io handles real-time communication using events.

Socket.io events

To handle the communication between the client and the server, Socket.io uses a structure that mimics the WebSockets protocol and fires event messages across the server and client objects. There are two types of events: system events, which indicate the socket connection status, and custom events, which you'll use to implement your business logic.

The system events on the socket server are as follows:

- `io.on('connection', ...)`: This is emitted when a new socket is connected
- `socket.on('message', ...)`: This is emitted when a message is sent using the `socket.send()` method
- `socket.on('disconnect', ...)`: This is emitted when the socket is disconnected

The system events on the client are as follows:

- `socket.io.on('open', ...)`: This is emitted when the socket client opens a connection with the server
- `socket.io.on('connect', ...)`: This is emitted when the socket client is connected to the server
- `socket.io.on('connect_timeout', ...)`: This is emitted when the socket client connection with the server is timed out
- `socket.io.on('connect_error', ...)`: This is emitted when the socket client fails to connect with the server
- `socket.io.on('reconnect_attempt', ...)`: This is emitted when the socket client tries to reconnect with the server
- `socket.io.on('reconnect', ...)`: This is emitted when the socket client is reconnected to the server
- `socket.io.on('reconnect_error', ...)`: This is emitted when the socket client fails to reconnect with the server
- `socket.io.on('reconnect_failed', ...)`: This is emitted when the socket client fails to reconnect with the server
- `socket.io.on('close', ...)`: This is emitted when the socket client closes the connection with the server

Handling events

While system events are helping us with connection management, the real magic of Socket.io lies in using custom events. In order to do that, Socket.io exposes two methods, both on the client and server objects. The first method is the on() method, which binds event handlers with events, and the second method is the emit() method, which is used to fire events between the server and client objects.

An implementation of the on() method in the socket server is very simple:

```
const app = require('express')();
const server = require('http').Server(app);
const io = require('socket.io')(server);
io.on('connection', function(socket){
  socket.on('customEvent', (customEventData) => {
    /* ... */
  });
});
server.listen(3000);
```

In the preceding code, you bound an event listener to the customEvent event. The event handler is called when the socket client object emits the customEvent event. Note how the event handler accepts the customEventData argument that is passed to the event handler from the socket client object.

An implementation of the on() method in the socket client is also straightforward:

```
<script src="/socket.io/socket.io.js"></script>
<script>
  var socket = io();
  socket.on('customEvent', function(customEventData) {
    /* ... */
  });
</script>
```

This time, the event handler is called when the socket server emits the customEvent event that sends customEventData to the socket client event handler.

Once you set your event handlers, you can use the emit() method to send events from the socket server to the socket client and vice versa.

Emitting events

On the socket server, the `emit()` method is used to send events to a single socket client or a group of connected socket clients. The `emit()` method can be called from the connected `socket` object, which will send the event to a single socket client, as follows:

```
io.on('connection', (socket) => {
  socket.emit('customEvent', customEventData);
});
```

The `emit()` method can also be called from the `io` object, which will send the event to all connected socket clients, as follows:

```
io.on('connection', (socket) => {
  io.emit('customEvent', customEventData);
});
```

Another option is to send the event to all connected socket clients except from the sender using the `broadcast` property, as shown in the following lines of code:

```
io.on('connection', (socket) => {
  socket.broadcast.emit('customEvent', customEventData);
});
```

On the socket client, things are much simpler. Since the socket client is only connected to the socket server, the `emit()` method will only send the event to the socket server:

```
const socket = io();
socket.emit('customEvent', customEventData);
```

Although these methods allow you to switch between personal and global events, they still lack the ability to send events to a group of connected socket clients. Socket. io offers two options to group sockets together: namespaces and rooms.

Socket.io namespaces

In order to easily control socket management, Socket.io allows developers to split socket connections according to their purpose using namespaces. So instead of creating different socket servers for different connections, you can just use the same server to create different connection endpoints. This means that socket communication can be divided into groups, which will then be handled separately.

Socket.io server namespaces

To create a socket server namespace, you will need to use the socket server `of()` method that returns a socket namespace. Once you retain the socket namespace, you can just use it the same way you use the socket server object:

```
const app = require('express')();
const server = require('http').Server(app);
const io = require('socket.io')(server);

io.of('/someNamespace').on('connection', (socket) => {
  socket.on('customEvent', (customEventData) => {
    /* ... */
  });
});

io.of('/someOtherNamespace').on('connection', (socket) => {
  socket.on('customEvent', (customEventData) => {
    /* ... */
  });
});
server.listen(3000);
```

In fact, when you use the `io` object, Socket.io actually uses a default empty namespace, as follows:

```
io.on('connection', (socket) => {
/* ... */
});
```

The preceding lines of code are actually equivalent to this:

```
io.of('').on('connection', (socket) => {
/* ... */
});
```

Socket.io client namespaces

On the socket client, the implementation is a little different:

```
<script src="/socket.io/socket.io.js"></script>
<script>
  var someSocket = io('/someNamespace');
  someSocket.on('customEvent', function(customEventData) {
    /* ... */
  });
```

```
var someOtherSocket = io('/someOtherNamespace');
someOtherSocket.on('customEvent', function(customEventData) {
  /* ... */
});
</script>
```

As you can see, you can use multiple namespaces on the same application without much effort. However, once sockets are connected to different namespaces, you will not be able to send an event to all these namespaces at once. This means that namespaces are not very good for a more dynamic grouping logic. For this purpose, Socket.io offers a different feature called **rooms**.

Socket.io rooms

Socket.io rooms allow you to partition connected sockets into different groups in a dynamic way. Connected sockets can join and leave rooms, and Socket.io provides you with a clean interface to manage rooms and emit events to the subset of sockets in a room. The rooms functionality is handled solely on the socket server but can easily be exposed to the socket client.

Joining and leaving rooms

Joining a room is handled using the socket `join()` method, while leaving a room is handled using the `leave()` method. So, a simple subscription mechanism can be implemented as follows:

```
io.on('connection', (socket) => {
    socket.on('join', (roomData) => {
        socket.join(roomData.roomName);
    })
    socket.on('leave', (roomData) => {
        socket.leave(roomData.roomName);
    })
});
```

Note that the `join()` and `leave()` methods both take the room name as the first argument.

Emitting events to rooms

To emit events to all the sockets in a room, you will need to use the `in()` method. So, emitting an event to all socket clients who joined a room is quite simple and can be achieved with the help of the following code snippets:

```
io.on('connection', (socket) => {
  io.in('someRoom').emit('customEvent', customEventData);
});
```

Another option is to send the event to all the connected socket clients in a room except the sender using the `broadcast` property and the `to()` method:

```
io.on('connection', (socket) => {
  socket.broadcast.to('someRoom').emit('customEvent',
customEventData);
});
```

This pretty much covers the simple yet powerful room functionality of Socket. io. In the next section, you will learn how to implement Socket.io in your MEAN application, and more importantly, how to use the Passport session to identify users in the Socket.io session. The examples in this chapter will continue directly from those in previous chapters, so copy the final example from *Chapter 8, Creating a MEAN CRUD Module*, and let's start from there.

> While we covered most of the Socket.io features, you can learn more about Socket.io by visiting the official project page at `https://socket.io`.

Installing Socket.io

Before you can use the `socket.io` module, you will need to install it using npm. To do that, change your `package.json` file as follows:

```
{
  "name": "MEAN",
  "version": "0.0.9",
  "scripts": {
    "tsc": "tsc",
    "tsc:w": "tsc -w",
    "app": "node server",
    "start": "concurrently \"npm run tsc:w\" \"npm run app\" ",
    "postinstall": "typings install"
  },
  "dependencies": {
```

```
    "@angular/common": "2.1.1",
    "@angular/compiler": "2.1.1",
    "@angular/core": "2.1.1",
    "@angular/forms": "2.1.1",
    "@angular/http": "2.1.1",
    "@angular/platform-browser": "2.1.1",
    "@angular/platform-browser-dynamic": "2.1.1",
    "@angular/router": "3.1.1",
    "body-parser": "1.15.2",
    "core-js": "2.4.1",
    "compression": "1.6.0",
    "connect-flash": "0.1.1",
    "ejs": "2.5.2",
    "express": "4.14.0",
    "express-session": "1.14.1",
    "method-override": "2.3.6",
    "mongoose": "4.6.5",
    "morgan": "1.7.0",
    "passport": "0.3.2",
    "passport-facebook": "2.1.1",
    "passport-google-oauth": "1.0.0",
    "passport-local": "1.0.0",
    "passport-twitter": "1.0.4",
    "reflect-metadata": "0.1.8",
    "rxjs": "5.0.0-beta.12",
    "socket.io": "1.4.5",
    "systemjs": "0.19.39",
    "zone.js": "0.6.26"
  },
  "devDependencies": {
    "concurrently": "3.1.0",
    "traceur": "0.0.111",
    "typescript": "2.0.3",
    "typings": "1.4.0"
  }
}
```

To install the socket.io module, go to your application's root folder and issue the following command in your command-line tool:

```
$ npm install
```

As usual, this will install the specified version of Socket.io in your `node_modules` folder. When the installation process is successfully over, you will need to configure your Express application to work in conjunction with the `socket.io` module and start your socket server.

Configuring the Socket.io server

After you've installed the `socket.io` module, you will need to start the socket server in conjunction with the Express application. For this, you will have to make the following changes in your `config/express.js` file:

```
const path = require('path');
const config = require('./config');
const http = require('http');
const socketio = require('socket.io');
const express = require('express');
const morgan = require('morgan');
const compress = require('compression');
const bodyParser = require('body-parser');
const methodOverride = require('method-override');
const session = require('express-session');
const flash = require('connect-flash');
const passport = require('passport');

module.exports = function() {
  const app = express();
  const server = http.createServer(app);
  const io = socketio.listen(server);

  if (process.env.NODE_ENV === 'development') {
    app.use(morgan('dev'));
  } else if (process.env.NODE_ENV === 'production') {
    app.use(compress());
  }

  app.use(bodyParser.urlencoded({
    extended: true
  }));
  app.use(bodyParser.json());
  app.use(methodOverride());

  app.use(session({
    saveUninitialized: true,
    resave: true,
```

```
    secret: config.sessionSecret
  }));

  app.set('views', './app/views');
  app.set('view engine', 'ejs');

  app.use(flash());
  app.use(passport.initialize());
  app.use(passport.session());

  app.use('/', express.static(path.resolve('./public')));
  app.use('/lib', express.static(path.resolve('./node_modules')));

  require('../app/routes/users.server.routes.js')(app);
  require('../app/routes/articles.server.routes.js')(app);
  require('../app/routes/index.server.routes.js')(app);

  return server;
};
```

Let's go over the changes you made to your Express configuration. After including the new dependencies, you used the `http` core module to create a `server` object that wraps your Express `app` object. You then used the `socket.io` module and its `listen()` method to attach the Socket.io server with your `server` object. Finally, you returned the new `server` object instead of the Express application object. When the server starts, it will run your Socket.io server along with your Express application.

While you can already start using Socket.io, there is still one major problem with this implementation. Since Socket.io is a standalone module, requests that are sent to it are detached from the Express application. This means that the Express session information is not available in a socket connection. This raises a serious obstacle when dealing with your Passport authentication in the socket layer of your application. To solve this issue, you will need to configure a persistent session storage, which will allow you to share your session information between the Express application and Socket.io handshake requests.

Configuring the Socket.io session

To configure your Socket.io session to work in conjunction with your Express sessions, you have to find a way to share session information between Socket.io and Express. Since the Express session information is being stored in the memory currently, Socket.io will not be able to access it properly. So, a better solution would be to store the session information in your MongoDB. Fortunately, there is a node module named `connect-mongo` that allows you to store the session information in a MongoDB instance almost seamlessly. To retrieve the Express session information, you will need a way to parse the signed session cookie information. For this purpose, you'll also need to install the `cookie-parser` module, which is used to parse the cookie header and populate the HTTP request object with cookies-related properties.

Installing the connect-mongo and cookie-parser modules

Before you can use the `connect-mongo` and `cookie-parser` modules, you will need to install them using npm. To do that, change your `package.json` file as follows:

```
{
  "name": "MEAN",
  "version": "0.0.9",
  "scripts": {
    "tsc": "tsc",
    "tsc:w": "tsc -w",
    "app": "node server",
    "start": "concurrently \"npm run tsc:w\" \"npm run app\" ",
    "postinstall": "typings install"
  },
  "dependencies": {
    "@angular/common": "2.1.1",
    "@angular/compiler": "2.1.1",
    "@angular/core": "2.1.1",
    "@angular/forms": "2.1.1",
    "@angular/http": "2.1.1",
    "@angular/platform-browser": "2.1.1",
    "@angular/platform-browser-dynamic": "2.1.1",
    "@angular/router": "3.1.1",
    "body-parser": "1.15.2",
    "core-js": "2.4.1",
    "compression": "1.6.0",
    "connect-flash": "0.1.1",
    "connect-mongo": "1.3.2",
    "cookie-parser": "1.4.3",
```

```
      "ejs": "2.5.2",
      "express": "4.14.0",
      "express-session": "1.14.1",
      "method-override": "2.3.6",
      "mongoose": "4.6.5",
      "morgan": "1.7.0",
      "passport": "0.3.2",
      "passport-facebook": "2.1.1",
      "passport-google-oauth": "1.0.0",
      "passport-local": "1.0.0",
      "passport-twitter": "1.0.4",
      "reflect-metadata": "0.1.8",
      "rxjs": "5.0.0-beta.12",
      "socket.io": "1.4.5",
      "systemjs": "0.19.39",
      "zone.js": "0.6.26"
    },
    "devDependencies": {
      "concurrently": "3.1.0",
      "traceur": "0.0.111",
      "typescript": "2.0.3",
      "typings": "1.4.0"
    }
  }
```

To install the new modules, go to your application's root folder and issue the following command in your command-line tool:

```
$ npm install
```

As usual, this will install the specified versions of the connect-mongo and cookie-parser modules in your node_modules folder. When the installation process is successfully over, your next step will be to configure your Express application to use connect-mongo as the session storage.

Configuring the connect-mongo module

To configure your Express application to store session information using the connect-mongo module, you will have to make a few changes. First, you will need to change your config/express.js file, as follows:

```
const path = require('path');
const config = require('./config');
const http = require('http');
const socketio = require('socket.io');
const express = require('express');
```

```javascript
const morgan = require('morgan');
const compress = require('compression');
const bodyParser = require('body-parser');
const methodOverride = require('method-override');
const session = require('express-session');
const MongoStore = require('connect-mongo')(session);
const flash = require('connect-flash');
const passport = require('passport');

module.exports = function(db) {
  const app = express();
  const server = http.createServer(app);
  const io = socketio.listen(server);

  if (process.env.NODE_ENV === 'development') {
    app.use(morgan('dev'));
  } else if (process.env.NODE_ENV === 'production') {
    app.use(compress());
  }

  app.use(bodyParser.urlencoded({
    extended: true
  }));
  app.use(bodyParser.json());
  app.use(methodOverride());

  const mongoStore = new MongoStore({
    mongooseConnection: db.connection
  });

  app.use(session({
    saveUninitialized: true,
    resave: true,
    secret: config.sessionSecret,
    store: mongoStore
  }));

  app.set('views', './app/views');
  app.set('view engine', 'ejs');

  app.use(flash());
  app.use(passport.initialize());
  app.use(passport.session());
```

```
app.use('/', express.static(path.resolve('./public')));
app.use('/lib', express.static(path.resolve('./node_modules')));

require('../app/routes/users.server.routes.js')(app);
require('../app/routes/articles.server.routes.js')(app);
require('../app/routes/index.server.routes.js')(app);

    return server;
};
```

In the preceding code snippet, you configured a few things. First, you loaded the
connect-mongo module and then passed the Express session module to it. Then, you
created a new connect-mongo instance and passed your Mongoose connection object
to it. Finally, you used the Express session store option to let the Express session
module know where to store the session information.

As you can see, your Express configuration method requires a db argument. This
argument is the Mongoose connection object, which will be passed to the Express
configuration method from the server.js file when it requires the express.js file.
So, go to your server.js file and change it as follows:

```
process.env.NODE_ENV = process.env.NODE_ENV || 'development';
const configureMongoose = require('./config/mongoose');
const configureExpress = require('./config/express');
const configurePassport = require('./config/passport');

const db = configureMongoose();
const app = configureExpress(db);
const passport = configurePassport();
app.listen(3000);

module.exports = app;

console.log('Server running at http://localhost:3000/');
```

Once the Mongoose connection is created, the server.js file will call the express.
js module method and pass the Mongoose database property to it. In this way,
Express will persistently store the session information in your MongoDB database
so that it will be available for the Socket.io session. Next, you will need to configure
your Socket.io handshake middleware to use the connect-mongo module and
retrieve the Express session information.

Configuring the Socket.io session

To configure the Socket.io session, you'll need to use the Socket.io configuration middleware and retrieve your session user. Begin by creating a new file named socketio.js in your config folder to store all your Socket.io-related configurations. In your new file, add the following lines of code:

```
const config = require('./config');
const cookieParser = require('cookie-parser');
const passport = require('passport');

module.exports = function(server, io, mongoStore) {
  io.use((socket, next) => {
    cookieParser(config.sessionSecret)(socket.request, {}, (err) => {
      const sessionId = socket.request.signedCookies['connect.sid'];

      mongoStore.get(sessionId, (err, session) => {
        socket.request.session = session;

        passport.initialize()(socket.request, {}, () => {
          passport.session()(socket.request, {}, () => {
            if (socket.request.user) {
              next(null, true);
            } else {
              next(new Error('User is not authenticated'), false);
            }
          })
        });
      });
    });
  });
  io.on('connection', (socket) => {
    /* ... */
  });
};
```

Let's go over the new Socket.io configuration file. First, you required the necessary dependencies, and then you used the io.use() configuration method to intercept the handshake process. In your configuration function, you used the Express cookie-parser module to parse the handshake request cookie and retrieve the Express sessionId. Then, you used the connect-mongo instance to retrieve the session information from the MongoDB storage.

Once you retrieved the session object, you used the `passport.initialize()` and `passport.session()` middleware to populate the session's `user` object according to the session information. If a user is authenticated, the handshake middleware will call the `next()` callback and continue with the socket initialization; otherwise, it will use the `next()` callback in a way that informs Socket.io that a socket connection cannot be opened. This means that only authenticated users can open a socket communication with the server and prevent unauthorized connections to your Socket.io server.

To complete your Socket.io server configuration, you will need to call the Socket.io configuration module from your `express.js` file. Go to your `config/express.js` file and change it, as follows:

```
const path = require('path');
const config = require('./config');
const http = require('http');
const socketio = require('socket.io');
const express = require('express');
const morgan = require('morgan');
const compress = require('compression');
const bodyParser = require('body-parser');
const methodOverride = require('method-override');
const session = require('express-session');
const MongoStore = require('connect-mongo')(session);
const flash = require('connect-flash');
const passport = require('passport');
const configureSocket = require('./socketio');

module.exports = function(db) {
  const app = express();
  const server = http.createServer(app);
  const io = socketio.listen(server);

  if (process.env.NODE_ENV === 'development') {
    app.use(morgan('dev'));
  } else if (process.env.NODE_ENV === 'production') {
    app.use(compress());
  }

  app.use(bodyParser.urlencoded({
    extended: true
  }));
  app.use(bodyParser.json());
  app.use(methodOverride());
```

```
const mongoStore = new MongoStore({
  mongooseConnection: db.connection
});

app.use(session({
  saveUninitialized: true,
  resave: true,
  secret: config.sessionSecret,
  store: mongoStore
}));

app.set('views', './app/views');
app.set('view engine', 'ejs');

app.use(flash());
app.use(passport.initialize());
app.use(passport.session());

app.use('/', express.static(path.resolve('./public')));
app.use('/lib', express.static(path.resolve('./node_modules')));

require('../app/routes/users.server.routes.js')(app);
require('../app/routes/articles.server.routes.js')(app);
require('../app/routes/index.server.routes.js')(app);

configureSocket(server, io, mongoStore);

return server;
};
```

This will execute your Socket.io configuration method and will take care of setting the Socket.io session. Now that you have everything configured, let's see how you can use Socket.io and MEAN to easily build a simple chat.

Building a Socket.io chat

To test your Socket.io implementation, build a simple chat application. Your chat will be constructed from several server event handlers, but most of the implementation will take place in your Angular application. We'll begin with setting the server event handlers.

Setting the event handlers of the chat server

Before implementing the chat client in your Angular application, you'll first need to create a few server event handlers. You already have a proper application structure, so you won't implement the event handlers directly in your configuration file. Instead, it would be better to implement your chat logic by creating a new file named `chat.server.controller.js` inside your `app/controllers` folder. In your new file, paste the following lines of code:

```
module.exports = function(io, socket) {
  io.emit('chatMessage', {
    type: 'status',
    text: 'connected',
    created: Date.now(),
    username: socket.request.user.username
  });

  socket.on('chatMessage', (message) => {
    message.type = 'message';
    message.created = Date.now();
    message.username = socket.request.user.username;

    io.emit('chatMessage', message);
  });

  socket.on('disconnect', () => {
    io.emit('chatMessage', {
    type: 'status',
    text: 'disconnected',
    created: Date.now(),
    username: socket.request.user.username
    });
  });
};
```

In this file, you implemented a couple of things. First, you used the `io.emit()` method to inform all the connected socket clients about the newly connected user. This was done by emitting the `chatMessage` event and passing a chat message object with the user information and the message text, time, and type. Since you took care of handling the user authentication in your socket server configuration, the user information is available from the `socket.request.user` object.

Next, you implemented the chatMessage event handler that will take care of messages sent from the socket client. The event handler will add the message type, time, and user information, and it will send the modified message object to all connected socket clients using the io.emit() method.

Our last event handler will take care of handling the disconnect system event. When a certain user is disconnected from the server, the event handler will notify all the connected socket clients about this event using the io.emit() method. This will allow the chat view to present the disconnection information to other users.

You now have your server handlers implemented, but how will you configure the socket server to include these handlers? To do that, you will need to go back to your config/socketio.js file and slightly modify it:

```
const config = require('./config');
const cookieParser = require('cookie-parser');
const passport = require('passport');
const configureChat = require('../app/controllers/chat.server.
controller');

module.exports = function(server, io, mongoStore) {
  io.use((socket, next) => {
    cookieParser(config.sessionSecret)(socket.request, {}, (err) => {
      const sessionId = socket.request.signedCookies['connect.sid'];

      mongoStore.get(sessionId, (err, session) => {
        socket.request.session = session;

        passport.initialize()(socket.request, {}, () => {
          passport.session()(socket.request, {}, () => {
            if (socket.request.user) {
              next(null, true);
            } else {
              next(new Error('User is not authenticated'), false);
            }
          })
        });
      });
    });
  });

  io.on('connection', (socket) => {
    configureChat(io, socket);
  });
};
```

Note how the socket server `connection` event is used to call the chat controller. This will allow you to bind your event handlers directly with the connected socket.

Congratulations; you've successfully completed your server implementation! Next, you'll see how easy it is to implement the Angular chat component.

Creating the Chat Angular module

In order to finish our chat implementation, we're going to create a new Angular chat module. Our module will include our component and template, a routing configuration, and a service wrapping the `socket.io` client functionality. Socket. io provides us with a client library to handle the socket communication; however, a best practice would be to obfuscate it using our own Angular service. We'll begin by configuring the Socket.io client library.

Setting up the Socket.io client library

To set up the Socket.io client library, we'll need to include the library JavaScript file in our `index.ejs` template. To do that, go to the `app/views/index.ejs` file and make the following change:

```
<!DOCTYPE html>
<html>
<head>
  <title><%= title %></title>
  <base href="/">
</head>
<body>
  <mean-app>
    <h1>Loading...</h1>
  </mean-app>

  <script type="text/javascript">
    window.user = <%- user || 'null' %>;
  </script>

  <script src="/socket.io/socket.io.js"></script>
  <script src="lib/core-js/client/shim.min.js"></script>
  <script src="lib/zone.js/dist/zone.js"></script>
  <script src="lib/reflect-metadata/Reflect.js"></script>
  <script src="lib/systemjs/dist/system.js"></script>

  <script src="systemjs.config.js"></script>
```

```
<script>
  System.import('app').catch(function(err){ console.error(err); });
</script>
</body>
</html>
```

As you can see, all that we did here was add the script tag to include Socket.io's client file in our main application page. Next, we'll need to create our Chat module.

Creating the Chat module

Once we are finished with the basic declaration setup for our client Socket.io implementation, we can continue with our chat implementation. To begin, create a folder named chat inside your public/app folder. Then, create a file inside this folder called chat.module.ts, which contains the following code:

```
import { NgModule }        from '@angular/core';
import { CommonModule }    from '@angular/common';
import { FormsModule }     from '@angular/forms';
import { RouterModule } from '@angular/router';

import { ChatRoutes } from './chat.routes';
import { ChatService } from './chat.service';
import { ChatComponent } from './chat.component';

@NgModule({
  imports: [
    CommonModule,
    FormsModule,
    RouterModule.forChild(ChatRoutes),
  ],
  declarations: [
    ChatComponent,
  ],
  providers: [
    ChatService
  ]
})
export class ChatModule {}
```

As you probably noticed, our module imports a new chat component and routing configuration and injects the chat service. Let's continue by creating our chat service.

Creating the Chat service

In order to obfuscate our component communication with the Socket.io client library, we'll need to create an Angular service. To do that, create a file named `chat.service.ts` inside your `public / app / chat` folder. In your new file, paste the following code:

```
import 'rxjs/Rx';
import { Observable } from 'rxjs/Observable';
import { Injectable } from '@angular/core';
import { Router } from '@angular/router';

import { AuthenticationService } from '../authentication/
authentication.service';

@Injectable()
export class ChatService {
  private socket: any;

  constructor(private _router:Router, private _authenticationService:
AuthenticationService) {
    if (this._authenticationService.isLoggedIn()) {
      this.socket = io();
    } else {
      this._router.navigate(['Home']);
    }
  }

  on(eventName, callback) {
    if (this.socket) {
      this.socket.on(eventName, function(data) {
        callback(data);
      });
    }
  };

  emit(eventName, data) {
    if (this.socket) {
      this.socket.emit(eventName, data);
    }
  };

  removeListener(eventName) {
    if (this.socket) {
      this.socket.removeListener(eventName);
```

```
        }
    };
    }
```

Let's review our new code for a moment. The basic structure should look familiar, since it is basically a regular Angular service. After injecting the Authentication and Router services in the constructor, you checked whether the user is authenticated using the Authentication service. If the user was not authenticated, you redirected the request back to the home page using the Router service. Since Angular services are lazily loaded, the Socket service will only load when requested. This will prevent unauthenticated users from using the Socket service. If the user is authenticated, the service socket property is set by calling the io() method of Socket.io.

Next, you wrapped the socket emit(), on(), and removeListener() methods with compatible service methods. In order to keep our example straightforward, we called our ChatService service. However, as you may notice by its structure, this service can easily become a general Socket service used across different components of our application. Now that the chat service is ready, all we have to do is implement the chat component and template. Let's begin by defining the chat component.

Creating the Chat component

Our chat component will contain the basic client-side chat functionality. To implement it, go to your public / app / chat folder and create a file named char.component.ts. In your new file, paste the following code:

```
import { Component } from '@angular/core';
import { ChatService } from './chat.service';

@Component({
  selector: 'chat',
  templateUrl: 'app/chat/chat.template.html',
  providers: [ChatService]
})
export class ChatComponent {
  messageText: string;
  messages: Array<any>;

  constructor(private _chatService: ChatService) {}

  ngOnInit() {
    this.messages = new Array();

    this._chatService.on('chatMessage', (msg) => {
```

```
            this.messages.push(msg);
        });
    }

    sendMessage() {
        const message = {
            text: this.messageText,
        };

        this._chatService.emit('chatMessage', message);
        this.messageText = ''
    }

    ngOnDestroy() {
        this._chatService.removeListener('chatMessage');
    }
}
```

In our component, you first created a message array and then used the ChatService on() method to implement the chatMessage event listener that will add retrieved messages to this array. Next, you created a sendMessage() method that will send new messages by emitting the chatMessage event to the socket server. Finally, you used the in-built ngOnInit directive to remove the chatMessage event listener from the socket client. The ngOnDestroy method will be emitted when the controller instance is deconstructed. This is important because the event handler will still get executed unless you remove it.

Creating the Chat template

The chat template will be constructed from a simple form and a list of chat messages. To implement your chat template, go to your public/app/chat folder and create a new file named chat.template.html, which contains the following code snippet:

```html
<div *ngFor="let message of messages" [ngSwitch]="message.type">
    <strong *ngSwitchCase="'status'">
        <span>{{message.created}}</span>
        <span>{{message.username}}</span>
        <span>is</span>
        <span>{{message.text}}</span>
    </strong>
    <span *ngSwitchDefault>
        <span>{{message.created}}</span>
        <span>{{message.username}}:</span>
        <span>{{message.text}}</span>
    </span>
```

```
</div>
<form (ngSubmit)="sendMessage()">
    <input type="text" name= "messageText" [(ngModel)]="messageText">
    <input type="submit">
</form>
```

In your template, you used the ngFor directive to render the message list and the ngSwitch directive to distinguish between status messages and regular messages. The template ends with a simple form that uses the ngSubmit directive to invoke the sendMessage() method. That is it! All you have to do is finalize your implementation by adding the Chat module to our application module.

Adding the Chat routing configuration

To add your Chat component route, go back to your public/app/chat folder and create a new file named chat.routes.ts, which contains the following code snippet:

```
import { Routes } from '@angular/router';
import { ChatComponent } from './chat.component';

export const ChatRoutes: Routes = [{
  path: 'chat',
  component: ChatComponent
}];
```

As you can see, we created a simple routing for our chat component. All we have left to do is include our chat module in our application module.

Using the Chat module

To finalize our Chat implementation, we'll need to include our module in the application module. To do that, go to your public/app/app.module.ts, as follows:

```
import { NgModule }         from '@angular/core';
import { BrowserModule }    from '@angular/platform-browser';
import { FormsModule }      from '@angular/forms';
import { RouterModule }     from '@angular/router';
import { HttpModule, RequestOptions } from '@angular/http';
import { LocationStrategy, HashLocationStrategy } from '@angular/
common';

import { AppComponent } from './app.component';
```

```
import { AppRoutes } from './app.routes';

import { HomeModule } from './home/home.module';
import { AuthenticationService } from './authentication/
authentication.service';
import { AuthenticationModule } from './authentication/authentication.
module';
import { ArticlesModule } from './articles/articles.module';
import { ChatModule } from './chat/chat.module';

@NgModule({
  imports: [
    BrowserModule,
    HttpModule,
    FormsModule,
    AuthenticationModule,
    HomeModule,
    ArticlesModule,
    ChatModule,
    RouterModule.forRoot(AppRoutes),
  ],
  declarations: [
    AppComponent
  ],
  providers: [
    AuthenticationService
  ],
  bootstrap: [AppComponent]
})
export class AppModule { }
```

Now, you'll need to add a link to our chat component in our home component.
To do that, go to your `public/app/home/home.template.html` file and make the
following changes:

```
<div *ngIf="user">
  <h1>Hello {{user.firstName}}</h1>
  <a href="/api/auth/signout">Signout</a>
  <ul>
    <li><a [routerLink]="['/articles']">List Articles</a></li>
    <li><a [routerLink]="['/articles/create']">Create Article</a></li>
    <li><a [routerLink]="['/chat']">Chat</a></li>
  </ul>
</div>
```

```
<div *ngIf="!user">
  <a [routerLink]="['/authentication/signup']">Signup</a>
  <a [routerLink]="['/authentication/signin']">Signin</a>
</div>
```

Once you are finished with these changes, your new chat component should be ready for use! Use your command-line tool and navigate to the MEAN application's root folder. Then, run your application by typing the following command:

```
$ npm start
```

Once your application is running, open two different browsers and sign up with two different users. Then, navigate to http://localhost:3000/ and click on your new Chat link. Try to send chat messages between your two clients, and you'll be able to see how chat messages are updated in real time. Your MEAN application now supports real-time communication!

Summary

In this chapter, you learned how the socket.io module works. You went over the key features of Socket.io and learned how the server and client communicate. You configured your Socket.io server and learned how to integrate it with your Express application. You also used the Socket.io handshake configuration to integrate the Passport session. Finally, you built a fully functional chat example and learned how to wrap the Socket.io client with an Angular service. In the next chapter, you'll learn how to write and run tests to cover your application code.

10
Testing MEAN Applications

In previous chapters, you learned to build your real-time MEAN application. You went through Express and Angular basics and learned to connect all the parts together. However, when your application becomes bigger and more complex, you'll soon find out that it's very difficult to manually verify your code. You will then need to start testing your application automatically. Fortunately, testing a web application, which was once a complicated task, has become much easier with the help of new tools and suitable testing frameworks. In this chapter, you'll learn to cover your MEAN application code using modern test frameworks and popular tools. We'll cover the following topics:

- Introducing JavaScript TDD and BDD
- Setting up your testing environment
- Installing and configuring the Mocha test framework
- Writing Express model and controller tests
- Installing and configuring the Karma test runner
- Using Jasmine to unit test your Angular entities
- Writing and running end-to-end Angular tests

Introducing JavaScript testing

As you already know, in the past couple of years, JavaScript has evolved dramatically. It was once a simple scripting language made for small web applications, but now it's the backbone for complex architectures, both in the server and the browser. However, this evolution has put developers in a situation where they need to manually manage a large code base that remained uncovered in terms of automated testing. While our fellow Java, .NET, or Ruby developers have been safely writing and running their tests, JavaScript developers remained in an uncharted territory, with the burden of figuring out how to properly test their applications. Lately, this void has been filled with the formation of new tools and testing frameworks written by the talented JavaScript community members. In this chapter, we'll cover some of these popular tools, but keep in mind that this field is fairly new and is constantly changing, so you'll also have to keep an eye out for newly emerging solutions.

In this chapter, we'll discuss two major types of tests: unit tests and **end-to-end(E2E)** tests. Unit tests are written to validate the functionality of isolated units of code. This means a developer should aspire to write each unit test to cover the smallest testable part of the application. For example, a developer might write unit tests to validate that an ORM method works properly and gives the right validation errors as output. However, quite often a developer will choose to write unit tests that verify bigger code units, mostly because these units perform an isolated operation together. If a developer wants to test a process that includes many of the software components combined, he will write an E2E test. E2E tests are written to validate cross-application functionality. These tests often force the developer to use more than one tool and cover different parts of the application in the same test, including UI, server, and database components. An example would be an E2E test that validates the signup process. Identifying the right tests is one of the crucial steps to writing a proper test suite for your application. However, setting appropriate conventions for the development team can make this process much easier.

Before we begin discussing JavaScript-specific tools, let's first look at a quick overview of the TDD paradigm and how it affects our daily development cycles.

TDD, BDD, and unit testing

Test-driven development (TDD) is a software-development paradigm developed by software engineer and agile methodology advocate Kent Beck. In TDD, the developer starts by writing a (initially failing) test, which defines what is expected from an isolated unit of code. The developer is then required to implement the minimum amount of code that passes the test.

When the test is successfully passed, the developer cleans up the code and verifies that all the tests are passing. The following diagram illustrates TDD cycles:

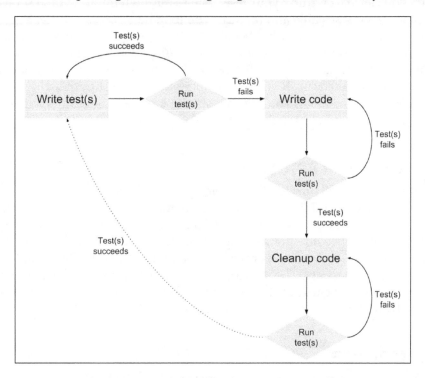

It is important to remember that although TDD has become a popular approach in modern software development, it is very difficult to implement in its purest form. To ease this process and improve team communication, a new approach was developed on top of TDD, called **Behavior-Driven Development (BDD)**. The BDD paradigm is a subset of TDD, created by Dan North, that helps developers identify the scope of their unit tests and express their test process in behavioral terminology. Basically, TDD provides the wireframe for writing tests, and BDD provides the vocabulary to shape the way tests are written. Usually, a BDD test framework provides the developer with a set of self-explanatory methods to describe the test process.

Although BDD provides us with a mechanism for writing tests, running these tests in a JavaScript environment is still a complicated task. Your application will probably run on different browsers and even different versions of the same browser. So, running the tests you wrote on a single browser will not provide you with proper coverage. To solve this issue, the JavaScript community has developed a diverse set of tools for writing, evaluating, and properly running tests.

Test frameworks

Although you can start writing your tests using your own library, you'll soon find out that it is not very scalable and requires you to build a complex infrastructure. Fortunately, considerable effort has been put into solving this issue, which has resulted in several popular test frameworks that allow you to write your tests in a structured and common way. These test frameworks usually provide a set of methods to encapsulate tests. It is also very common for a test framework to provide some sort of API that enables you to run tests and integrate the results with other tools in your development cycle.

Assertion libraries

Though test frameworks provide the developer with a way to create and organize tests, they often lack the ability to actually test a Boolean expression that represents the test result. For instance, the Mocha test framework, which we'll introduce in the next section, doesn't provide the developer with an assertion tool. For this purpose, the community has developed several assertion libraries, which allow you to examine a certain predicate. The developer uses assertion expressions to indicate a predicate that should be true in the test context. When running the test, the assertion is evaluated, and if it turns out to be false, the test fails.

Test runners

Test runners are utilities that enable the developer to easily run and evaluate tests. A test runner usually uses a defined testing framework along with a set of preconfigured properties to evaluate test results in different contexts. For instance, a test runner can be configured to run tests with different environment variables or run the same test on different testing platforms (usually browsers). We will look at two different test runners in the *Testing your Angular application* section.

Now that you have an overview of a set of terms associated with testing, you can finally learn how to test the different parts of your MEAN application. Although your code is written entirely in JavaScript, it does run on different platforms with different scenarios. In order to mitigate the testing process, I've divided it into two different sections: testing Express components and testing Angular components. Let's begin with testing your Express application components.

Testing your Express application

In the Express part of your MEAN application, your business logic is mostly encapsulated inside controllers; however, you also have Mongoose models that obfuscate many tasks, including data manipulation and validations. So, to properly cover your Express application code, you will need to write tests that cover both models and controllers. In order to do so, you will use Mocha as your test framework, the `Should.js` assertion library for your models, and the `SuperTest HTTP` assertion library for your controllers. You will also need to create a new test environment configuration file that will provide you with special configuration options for testing purposes, for example, a dedicated MongoDB connection string. By the end of this section, you will learn to use the Mocha command-line tool to run and evaluate your test results. We'll begin with presenting the Mocha test framework.

Introducing Mocha

Mocha is a versatile test framework developed by Express creator TJ Holowaychuk. It supports both BDD and TDD unit tests, uses Node.js to run the tests, and allows the developer to run both synchronous and asynchronous tests. Since Mocha is minimal by structure, it doesn't include a built-in assertion library; instead, it supports the integration of popular assertion frameworks. It comes packed with a set of different reporters to present the test results and includes many features, such as pending tests, excluding tests, and skipping tests. The main interaction with Mocha is done using the command-line tool provided, which lets you configure the way tests are executed and reported.

The BDD interface for Mocha tests includes several descriptive methods, which enable the developer to easily describe the test scenario. These methods are as follows:

- `describe(description, callback)`: This is the basic method that wraps each test suite with a description. The callback function is used to define test specifications or sub-suites.

- `it(description, callback)`: This is the basic method that wraps each test specification with a description. The callback function is used to define the actual test logic.

- `before(callback)`: This is a hook function that is executed once before all the tests in a test suite.

- `beforeEach(callback)`: This is a hook function that is executed before each test specification in a test suite.

- `after(callback)`: This is a hook function that is executed once after all the tests in a test suite are executed.

- `afterEach(callback)`: This is a hook function that is executed after each test specification in a test suite is executed.

Using these basic methods will allow you to define unit tests by utilizing the BDD paradigm. However, no test can be concluded without including an assertion expression that determines the developer's expectations from the covered code. To support assertions, you will need to use an assertion library.

 You can learn more about Mocha's features by visiting the official documentation at `http://visionmedia.github.io/mocha/`.

Introducing Should.js

The `Should.js` library, also developed by TJ Holowaychuk, aims to help developers write readable and expressive assertion expressions. Using `Should.js`, you'll be able to keep your test code better organized and produce useful error messages. The `Should.js` library extends `Object.prototype` with a non-enumerable getter that allows you to express how that object should behave. One of `Should.js'` powerful features is that every assertion returns a wrapped object, so assertions can be chained. This means that you can write readable expressions that pretty much describe the assertions associated with the tested object. For example, a chained assertion expression would be as follows:

```
user.should.be.an.Object.and.have.property('name', 'tj');
```

 Notice how each helper property returns a Should.js object, which can be chained using another helper property (be, an, have, and so on) or tested using assertion properties and methods (`Object`, `property()`). You can learn more about Should.js' features by reading the official documentation at `https://github.com/shouldjs/should.js`.

While Should.js does an excellent job testing objects, it will not help you with testing your HTTP endpoints. To do this, you will need to use a different kind of assertion library. This is where the minimal modularity of Mocha comes in handy.

Introducing SuperTest

SuperTest is another assertion library developed by TJ Holowaychuk, which differs from other assertion libraries by providing developers with an abstraction layer that makes HTTP assertions. This means that instead of testing objects, it will help you create assertion expressions that test HTTP endpoints. In your case, it will help you test your controller endpoints, thus covering the code that's exposed to the browser. To do so, it will make use of the Express application object and test the responses returned from your Express endpoints. An example SuperTest assertion expression is as follows:

```
request(app).get('/user')
  .set('Accept', 'application/json')
  .expect('Content-Type', /json/)
  .expect(200, done);
```

Notice how each method can be chained to another assertion expression. This will allow you to make several assertions on the same response using the `expect()` method. You can learn more about SuperTest's features by visiting the official documentation at `https://github.com/visionmedia/supertest`.

In the next section, you will learn how to leverage Mocha, Should.js, and SuperTest to test both your models and your controllers. Let's begin by installing these dependencies and properly configuring the test environment. The examples in this chapter will continue directly from those in previous chapters, so copy the final example from *Chapter 9, Adding Real-time Functionality Using Socket.io*, and let's take it from there.

Installing Mocha

Mocha is basically a Node.js module that provides command-line capabilities to run tests. The easiest way to use Mocha is to first install it as a global node module using npm. To do so, just issue the following command in your command-line tool:

```
$ npm install -g mocha
```

As usual, this will install the latest version of Mocha in your global `node_modules` folder. When the installation process is successfully finished, you'll be able to use the Mocha utility from your command line. Next, you'll need to install the Should.js and SuperTest assertion libraries in your project.

> You may experience some trouble installing global modules. This is usually a permission issue, so use sudo or super user when running the global install command.

Installing the Should.js and SuperTest modules

Before you can start writing your tests, you will need to install both Should.js and SuperTest using npm. To do so, change your project's package.json file as follows:

```json
{
  "name": "MEAN",
  "version": "0.0.10",
  "scripts": {
    "tsc": "tsc",
    "tsc:w": "tsc -w",
    "app": "node server",
    "start": "concurrently \"npm run tsc:w\" \"npm run app\" ",
    "postinstall": "typings install"
  },
  "dependencies": {
    "@angular/common": "2.1.1",
    "@angular/compiler": "2.1.1",
    "@angular/core": "2.1.1",
    "@angular/forms": "2.1.1",
    "@angular/http": "2.1.1",
    "@angular/platform-browser": "2.1.1",
    "@angular/platform-browser-dynamic": "2.1.1",
    "@angular/router": "3.1.1",
    "body-parser": "1.15.2",
    "core-js": "2.4.1",
    "compression": "1.6.0",
    "connect-flash": "0.1.1",
    "connect-mongo": "1.3.2",
    "cookie-parser": "1.4.3",
    "ejs": "2.5.2",
    "express": "4.14.0",
    "express-session": "1.14.1",
    "method-override": "2.3.6",
    "mongoose": "4.6.5",
    "morgan": "1.7.0",
    "passport": "0.3.2",
```

```
    "passport-facebook": "2.1.1",
    "passport-google-oauth": "1.0.0",
    "passport-local": "1.0.0",
    "passport-twitter": "1.0.4",
    "reflect-metadata": "0.1.8",
    "rxjs": "5.0.0-beta.12",
    "socket.io": "1.4.5",
    "systemjs": "0.19.39",
    "zone.js": "0.6.26"
  },
  "devDependencies": {
    "concurrently": "3.1.0",
    "should": "11.1.1",
    "supertest": "2.0.1",
    "traceur": "0.0.111",
    "typescript": "2.0.3",
    "typings": "1.4.0"
  }
}
```

To install your new dependencies, go to your application's root folder and issue the following command in your command-line tool:

```
$ npm install
```

This will install the specified versions of Should.js and SuperTest in your project's node modules folder. When the installation process is successfully finished, you will be able to use these modules in your tests. Next, you'll need to prepare your project for testing by creating a new environment configuration file and setting up your test environment.

Configuring your test environment

Since you're going to run tests that include database manipulation, it would be safer to use a different configuration file to run tests. Fortunately, your project is already configured to use different configuration files according to the NODE_ENV variable. While the application automatically uses the config/env/development.js file, when running in a test environment, we will make sure to set the NODE_ENV variable to test. All you need to do is create a new configuration file named test.js in the config/env folder. In this new file, paste the following code snippet:

```
module.exports = {
  db: 'mongodb://localhost/mean-book-test',
  sessionSecret: 'Your Application Session Secret',
```

```
    viewEngine: 'ejs',
    facebook: {
      clientID: 'APP_ID',
      clientSecret: 'APP_SECRET',
      callbackURL: 'http://localhost:3000/oauth/facebook/callback'
    },
    twitter:
    {
      clientID: 'APP_ID',
      clientSecret: 'APP_SECRET',
      callbackURL: 'http://localhost:3000/oauth/twitter/callback'
    },
    google: {
      clientID: 'APP_ID',
      clientSecret: 'APP_SECRET',
      callbackURL: 'http://localhost:3000/oauth/google/callback'
    }
};
```

As you can notice, we changed the db property to use a different MongoDB database. Other properties remain the same, but you can change them later to test different configurations of your application.

You'll now need to create a new folder for your test files. To do so, go to your app folder and create a new folder named tests. Once you're done setting up your environment, you can continue to the next section and write your first tests.

Writing your first Mocha test

Before you begin writing your tests, you will first need to identify and break your Express application's components into testable units. Since most of your application logic is already divided into models and controllers, the obvious way to go about this would be to test each model and controller individually. The next step would be to break this component into logical units of code and test each unit separately. For instance, take each method in your controller and write a set of tests for each method. You can also decide to test a couple of your controller's methods together when each method doesn't perform any significant operation by itself. Another example would be to take your Mongoose model and test each model method.

In BDD, every test begins by describing the test's purpose in natural language. This is done using the describe() method, which lets you define the test scenario's description and functionality. Describe blocks can be nested, which enables you to further elaborate on each test. Once you have your test's descriptive structure ready, you will be able to define a test specification using the it() method. Each it() block will be regarded as a single unit test by the test framework. Each test will also include a single assertion expression or multiple assertion expressions. The assertion expressions will basically function as Boolean test indicators for your test assumptions. When an assertion expression fails, it will usually provide the test framework with a traceable error object.

While this pretty much explains most of the tests you'll encounter, you'll also be able to use supportive methods that execute certain functionality in context with your tests. These supportive methods can be configured to run before or after a set of tests and even before or after each test is executed.

In the following examples, you'll learn to easily use each method to test the articles module that you created in *Chapter 8, Creating a MEAN CRUD Module*. For the sake of simplicity, we will only implement a basic test suite for each component. This test suite could and should be largely expanded to ultimately provide decent code coverage.

> Although TDD clearly states that tests should be written before you start coding features, the structure of this book forces us to write tests that examine existing code. If you wish to implement real TDD in your development process, you should be aware that development cycles should begin by first writing the appropriate tests.

Testing the Express model

In the model's test example, we'll write two tests that verify the model save method. To begin testing your Article Mongoose model, you will need to create a new file named article.server.model.tests.js in your app/tests folder. In your new file, paste the following lines of code:

```
const app = require('../../server.js');
const should = require('should');
const mongoose = require('mongoose');
const User = mongoose.model('User');
const Article = mongoose.model('Article');

let user, article;
```

```
describe('Article Model Unit Tests:', () => {
  beforeEach((done) => {
    user = new User({
      firstName: 'Full',
      lastName: 'Name',
      displayName: 'Full Name',
      email: 'test@test.com',
      username: 'username',
      password: 'password'
    });

    user.save(() => {
      article = new Article({
        title: 'Article Title',
        content: 'Article Content',
        user: user
      });

      done();
    });
  });

  describe('Testing the save method', () => {
    it('Should be able to save without problems', () => {
      article.save((err) => {
        should.not.exist(err);
      });
    });

    it('Should not be able to save an article without a title', () =>
{
      article.title = '';

      article.save((err) => {
        should.exist(err);
      });
    });
  });

  afterEach((done) => {
    Article.remove(() => {
      User.remove(() => {
        done();
      });
```

```
    });
  });
});
```

Let's start breaking down the test code. First, you required your module dependencies and defined your global variables. Then, you began your test using a `describe()` method, which informs the test tool that this test is going to examine the `Article` model. Inside the `describe` block, we began by creating new `user` and `article` objects using the `beforeEach()` method. The `beforeEach()` method is used to define a block of code that runs before each test is executed. You can also replace it with the `before()` method, which will only get executed once, before all the tests are executed. Notice how the `beforeEach()` method informs the test framework that it can continue with the test's execution by calling the `done()` callback. This will allow the database operations to be completed before actually executing the tests.

Next, you created a new `describe` block, indicating that you were about to test the model save method. In this block, you created two tests using the `it()` method. The first test used the `article` object to save a new article. Then, you used the `Should.js` assertion library to validate that no error occurred. The second test checked the `Article` model validation by assigning an invalid value to the `title` property. This time, the `Should.js` assertion library was used to validate that an error actually occurred when trying to save an invalid `article` object.

You finished your tests by cleaning up the `Article` and `User` collections using the `afterEach()` method. Like with the `beforeEach()` method, this code will run after each test is executed, and can also be replaced with an `after()` method. The `done()` method is also used here in the same manner.

Congratulations, you created your first unit test! As we stated earlier, you can continue expanding this test suite to cover more of the model code, which you probably will when dealing with more complicated objects. Next, we'll see how you can write more advanced unit tests when covering your controller's code.

Testing the Express controller

In the controller test example, we'll write two tests to check the controller's methods that retrieve articles. When setting out to write these tests, we have two options: either test the controller's methods directly or use the defined controller's Express routes in the tests. Although it is preferable to test each unit separately, we would choose to go with the second option since our routes' definitions are quite simple, so we can benefit from writing more inclusive tests.

To begin testing your articles controller, you will need to create a new file named `articles.server.controller.tests.js` in your `app/tests` folder. In your new file, paste the following code snippet:

```
const app = require('../../server');
const request = require('supertest');
const should = require('should');
const mongoose = require('mongoose');
const User = mongoose.model('User');
const Article = mongoose.model('Article');

let user, article;

describe('Articles Controller Unit Tests:', () => {
  beforeEach((done) => {
    user = new User({
      firstName: 'Full',
      lastName: 'Name',
      displayName: 'Full Name',
      email: 'test@test.com',
      username: 'username',
      password: 'password'
    });

    user.save(() => {
      article = new Article({
        title: 'Article Title',
        content: 'Article Content',
        user: user
      });

      article.save((err) => {
        done();
      });
    });
  });

  describe('Testing the GET methods', () => {
    it('Should be able to get the list of articles', (done) => {
      request(app).get('/api/articles/')
        .set('Accept', 'application/json')
        .expect('Content-Type', /json/)
        .expect(200)
        .end((err, res) => {
```

```
            res.body.should.be.an.Array().and.have.lengthOf(1);
            res.body[0].should.have.property('title', article.title);
            res.body[0].should.have.property('content',
                article.content);

            done();
        });
    });

    it('Should be able to get the specific article', (done) => {
      request(app).get('/api/articles/' + article.id)
        .set('Accept', 'application/json')
        .expect('Content-Type', /json/)
        .expect(200)
        .end((err, res) => {
          res.body.should.be.an.Object().and.have.property
              ('title',article.title);
          res.body.should.have.property('content', article.content);

          done();
        });
    });
  });

  afterEach((done) => {
    Article.remove().exec();
    User.remove().exec();

    done();
  });
});
```

Just as with your model test, first you required your module dependencies and defined your global variables. Then, you started your test using a describe() method, which informs the test tool that this test is going to examine the Articles controller. Inside the describe block, we began by creating new user and article objects using the beforeEach() method. This time, we saved the article before initiating the tests, and then continued with test execution by calling the done() callback.

Next, you created a new `describe` block indicating that you were about to test the controllers' GET methods. In this block, you created two tests using the `it()` method. The first test uses the `SuperTest` assertion library to issue an HTTP GET request at the endpoint that returns the list of articles. It then examines the HTTP response variables, including the `content-type` header and the HTTP response code. When it verifies the response is returned properly, it uses three `Should.js` assertion expressions to test the response body. The response body should be an array of articles that includes a single article which should be similar to the article you created in the `beforeEach()` method.

The second test uses the `SuperTest` assertion library to issue an HTTP GET request at the endpoint that returns a single article. It then examines the HTTP response variables, including the `content-type` header and the HTTP response code. Once it verifies that the response is returned properly, it uses three `Should.js` assertion expressions to test the response body. The response body should be a single `article` object and should be similar to the article you created in the `beforeEach()` method.

Just as before, you finished your tests by cleaning up the `Article` and `User` collections using the `afterEach()` method. Once you're done setting up the testing environment and creating your tests, all you have left to do is run them using Mocha's command-line tool.

Running your Mocha test

To run your Mocha test, you need to use Mocha's command-line utility, which you previously installed. To do so, use your command-line tool and navigate to your project's base folder. Then, issue the following command:

```
$ NODE_ENV=test mocha --reporter spec app/tests
```

Windows users should first execute the following command:

```
> set NODE_ENV=test
```

Then run Mocha using the following command:

```
> mocha --reporter spec app/tests
```

The preceding command will do a few things. First, it will set the NODE_ENV variable to `test`, forcing your MEAN application to use the test environment's configuration file. Then, it will execute the Mocha command-line utility with the `--reporter` flag, telling Mocha to use the `spec` reporter and the path to your tests folder. The test results should be reported in your command-line tool and will be similar to the following screenshot:

```
● ● ●                    B05071_10 — -bash — 80×24
[Amos@amoss-macbook-pro:~/Projects/MEANV2/B05071_10$ NODE_ENV=test mocha --report]
er spec app/tests
mongodb://localhost/mean-book-test
Server running at http://localhost:3000/


    Article Model Unit Tests:
      Testing the save method
        ✓ Should be able to save without problems
        ✓ Should not be able to save an article without a title

    Articles Controller Unit Tests:
      Testing the GET methods
        ✓ Should be able to get the list of articles (47ms)
        ✓ Should be able to get the specific article


    4 passing (140ms)

Amos@amoss-macbook-pro:~/Projects/MEANV2/B05071_10$ █
```

Mocha's test results

This concludes the test coverage of your Express application. You can use these methods to expand your test suite and dramatically improve application development. It is recommended that you set your test conventions from the beginning of your development process; otherwise, writing tests can become an overwhelming experience. Next, you'll learn to test your Angular components and write E2E tests.

Testing your Angular application

For years, testing frontend code was a complex task. Running tests across different browsers and platforms was complicated, and since most of the application code was unstructured, test tools mainly focused on UI E2E tests. However, the shift towards MVC frameworks allowed the community to create better test utilities, improving the way developers write both unit and E2E tests. In fact, the Angular team is so focused on testing that every feature developed by the team is designed with testability in mind.

Furthermore, platform fragmentation also created a new layer of tools called test runners, which allow developers to easily run their tests in different contexts and platforms. In this section, we'll focus on tools and frameworks associated with Angular applications, explaining how to best use them to write and run both unit and E2E tests. We'll start with the test framework that will serve us in both cases: the Jasmine test framework.

Although we can use Mocha or any other test framework, using Jasmine is currently the easiest and most common approach when testing Angular applications.

Introducing the Jasmine framework

Jasmine is an opinionated BDD framework developed by the Pivotal organization. Conveniently, Jasmine uses the same terminology as Mocha's BDD interface, including the describe(), it(), beforeEach(), and afterEach() methods. However, unlike Mocha, Jasmine comes prebundled with assertion capabilities, using the expect() method chained with assertion methods called **Matchers**. Matchers are basically functions that implement a Boolean comparison between an actual object and an expected value. For instance, a simple test using the toBe() matcher is as follows:

```
describe('Matchers Example', function() {
  it('Should present the toBe matcher example', function() {
    var a = 1;
    var b = a;

    expect(a).toBe(b);
    expect(a).not.toBe(null);
  });
});
```

The toBe() matcher uses the === operator to compare objects. Jasmine includes plenty of other matchers and even enables developers to add custom matchers. Jasmine also includes other robust features to allow more advanced test suites. In the next section, we'll focus on how to use Jasmine to easily test your Angular components.

You can learn more about Jasmine's features by visiting the official documentation at http://jasmine.github.io/2.5/introduction.html.

Angular unit tests

In the past, web developers who wanted to write unit tests to cover their frontend code had to struggle with determining their test scope and properly organizing their test suite. However, the inherent separation of concerns in Angular forces the developer to write isolated units of code, making the testing process much simpler. Developers can now quickly identify the units they need to test, so components, services, directives, and any other Angular entities can be tested as standalone units. Furthermore, the extensive use of dependency injection in Angular enables developers to switch contexts and easily cover their code with an extensive test suite. However, before you begin writing tests for your Angular application, you will first need to prepare your test environment, beginning with the Karma test runner.

Introducing Karma test runner

The Karma test runner is a utility developed by the Angular team that helps developers execute tests in different browsers. It does so by starting a web server that runs source code with test code on selected browsers, reporting the tests result back to the command-line utility. Karma offers real test results for real devices and browsers, flow control for IDEs and the command line, and framework-agnostic testability. It also provides developers with a set of plugins that enables them to run tests with the most popular test frameworks. The team also provides special plugins called browser launchers that enable Karma to run tests on selected browsers.

In our case, we will use the Jasmine test framework along with a PhantomJS browser launcher. However, testing real applications will require you to expand Karma's configuration to include more launchers and execute tests on the browsers you intend to support.

 PhantomJS is a headless WebKit browser often used in programmable scenarios where you don't need a visual output; that's why it works perfectly for testing purposes. You can learn more about PhantomJS by visiting the official documentation at `http://phantomjs.org/documentation/`.

Installing the Karma command-line tool

The easiest way to start using Karma is to globally install the command-line tool provided using npm. To do so, just issue the following command in your command-line tool:

```
$ npm install -g karma-cli
```

This will install the latest version of Karma's command-line utility in your global `node_modules` folder. When the installation process is successfully finished, you'll be able to use the Karma utility from your command line. Next, you'll need to install Karma's project dependencies.

 You may experience some trouble installing global modules. This is usually a permission issue, so use `sudo` or super user when running the global install command.

Installing Karma's dependencies

Before you can start writing your tests, you will need to install Karma's dependencies using `npm`. To do so, change your `package.json` file as follows:

```
{
  "name": "MEAN",
  "version": "0.0.10",
  "scripts": {
    "tsc": "tsc",
    "tsc:w": "tsc -w",
    "app": "node server",
    "start": "concurrently \"npm run tsc:w\" \"npm run app\" ",
    "postinstall": "typings install"
  },
  "dependencies": {
    "@angular/common": "2.1.1",
    "@angular/compiler": "2.1.1",
    "@angular/core": "2.1.1",
    "@angular/forms": "2.1.1",
    "@angular/http": "2.1.1",
    "@angular/platform-browser": "2.1.1",
    "@angular/platform-browser-dynamic": "2.1.1",
    "@angular/router": "3.1.1",
    "body-parser": "1.15.2",
    "core-js": "2.4.1",
    "compression": "1.6.0",
    "connect-flash": "0.1.1",
    "connect-mongo": "1.3.2",
    "cookie-parser": "1.4.3",
    "ejs": "2.5.2",
    "express": "4.14.0",
    "express-session": "1.14.1",
    "method-override": "2.3.6",
    "mongoose": "4.6.5",
```

```
    "morgan": "1.7.0",
    "passport": "0.3.2",
    "passport-facebook": "2.1.1",
    "passport-google-oauth": "1.0.0",
    "passport-local": "1.0.0",
    "passport-twitter": "1.0.4",
    "reflect-metadata": "0.1.8",
    "rxjs": "5.0.0-beta.12",
    "socket.io": "1.4.5",
    "systemjs": "0.19.39",
    "zone.js": "0.6.26"
  },
  "devDependencies": {
    "concurrently": "3.1.0",
    "jasmine": "2.5.2",
    "jasmine-core": "2.5.2",
    "karma": "1.3.0",
    "karma-jasmine": "1.0.2",
    "karma-phantomjs-launcher": "1.0.2",
    "should": "11.1.1",
    "supertest": "2.0.1",
    "traceur": "0.0.111",
    "typescript": "2.0.3",
    "typings": "1.4.0"
  }
}
```

As you can see, you added Karma and Jasmine core packages, Karma's Jasmine plugin, and Karma's PhantomJS launcher to your `devDependencies` property. To install your new dependencies, go to your application's `root` folder and issue the following command in your command-line tool:

```
$ npm install
```

This will install the specified version of Karma's core package, Karma's Jasmine plugin, and Karma's PhantomJS launcher in your project's `node_modules` folder. When the installation process is successfully finished, you will be able to use these modules to run your tests. Next, you'll need to configure Karma's execution by adding a Karma configuration file.

Configuring the Karma test runner

In order to control Karma's test execution, you will need to configure Karma using a special configuration file placed at the `root` folder of your application. When executed, Karma will automatically look for the default configuration file, named `karma.conf.js`, in the application's `root` folder. You can also indicate your configuration file's name using a command-line flag, but for simplicity reasons, we'll use the default filename. To start configuring Karma, create a new file in your application folder, and name it `karma.conf.js`. In your new file, paste the following code snippet:

```javascript
module.exports = function(config) {
  config.set({
    basePath: '',
    frameworks: ['jasmine'],
    files: [
      'node_modules/systemjs/dist/system.js',
      'node_modules/systemjs/dist/system-polyfills.js',
      'node_modules/core-js/client/shim.min.js',
      'node_modules/reflect-metadata/Reflect.js',
      'node_modules/zone.js/dist/zone.js',
      'node_modules/zone.js/dist/long-stack-trace-zone.js',
      'node_modules/zone.js/dist/proxy.js',
      'node_modules/zone.js/dist/sync-test.js',
      'node_modules/zone.js/dist/jasmine-patch.js',
      'node_modules/zone.js/dist/async-test.js',
      'node_modules/zone.js/dist/fake-async-test.js',

      { pattern: 'public/systemjs.config.js', served: true,
            included: false, watched: false },
      { pattern: 'public/app/**/*.*', served: true, included:
            false, watched: false },
      { pattern: 'node_modules/rxjs/**/*.js', served: true,
            included: false, watched: false },
      { pattern: 'node_modules/@angular/**/*.js', served:
            true, included: false, watched: false },

      'karma.shim.js',
    ],
    proxies: {
      '/lib/': '/base/node_modules/',
      '/app/': '/base/public/app/',
    },
    reporters: ['progress'],
    browsers: ['PhantomJS'],
```

```
    captureTimeout: 60000,
    singleRun: true
  });
};
```

As you can see, Karma's configuration file is used to set the way Karma executes tests. In this case, we used the following settings:

- `basePath`: This tells Karma to use an empty base path.

- `frameworks`: This tells Karma to use the Jasmine framework.

- `files`: This sets the list of files that Karma will include in its tests. Notice that you can use glob patterns to indicate file patterns. In this case, we included all of our library files and module files, excluding our test files. Moreover, we configured our application and library files to be served by the Karma server even though they're not being included directly in the page.

- `reporters`: This sets the way Karma reports its test results.

- `browsers`: This is a list of browsers Karma will test on. Note that we can only use the PhantomJS browser since we haven't installed any other launcher plugin.

- `captureTimeout`: This sets the timeout for Karma test execution.

- `singleRun`: This forces Karma to quit after it finishes the test execution.

These properties are project oriented, which means they will change according to your requirements. For instance, you'll probably include more browser launchers in real-world applications.

 You can learn more about Karma's configuration by visiting the official documentation at `https://karma-runner.github.io/1.0/config/configuration-file.html`.

We have two more things to do in order to finish with our Karma configuration. We'll begin by modifying the `System.js` configuration. To do so, go to your `public/systemjs.config.js` file and change it as follows:

```
(function(global) {
  var packages = {
    app: {
        main: './bootstrap.js',
        defaultExtension: 'js'
      }
  };
```

```
    var map = {
      '@angular': 'lib/@angular',
        'rxjs': 'lib/rxjs'
    };

    var ngPackageNames = [
      'common',
      'compiler',
      'core',
      'forms',
      'http',
      'router',
      'platform-browser',
      'platform-browser-dynamic',
    ];

    ngPackageNames.forEach(function(pkgName) {
      packages['@angular/' + pkgName] = { main: '/bundles/' +
        pkgName + '.umd.js', defaultExtension: 'js' };
      map['@angular/' + pkgName + '/testing'] = 'lib/@angular/'
        + pkgName + '/bundles/' + pkgName + '-testing.umd.js';
    });

    System.config({
      defaultJSExtensions: true,
      transpiler: null,
      packages: packages,
      map: map
    });
  })(this);
```

As you can see, we only told `System.js` to map our Angular testing modules to the right UMD module file. Next, we'll need to create our karma "shim" file that actually loads our tests. To do so, create a new file named `karma.shim.js` in the `root` folder of your application. Inside your new file, paste the following code:

```
__karma__.loaded = function () { };

System.import('/base/public/systemjs.config.js').then(loadTests);

function loadTests() {
  Promise.all([
    System.import('app/bootstrap.spec'),
    System.import('app/articles/articles.service.spec'),
    System.import('app/articles/list/list.component.spec'),
```

```
      System.import('app/app.routes.spec'),
      System.import('app/directive.spec'),
      System.import('app/pipe.spec')
    ]).then(__karma__.start, __karma__.error);
}
```

As you can see, our file basically stops Karma from running the tests automatically
on startup by overriding the loaded hook. Then, it loads the System.js configuration
file and imports our test files. Once it loads all the files, it tells Karma to run the tests
by calling its start hook. That's it! All we have left to do is to start writing our tests.

Writing Angular unit tests

Once you're done configuring your test environment, writing unit tests becomes an
easy task. While the general structure is the same, each entity test is a bit different
and involves subtle changes. In this section, you'll learn how to test the major
Angular entities. Let's begin with testing a component.

Testing components

Testing a component can vary in complexity. A simple component is quite easy to
test, while more complicated components can be a bit tricky. A good intermediate
example would be to test our articles list component, since it uses a service and it
renders a simple DOM for our articles. To test your component, go to your public/
app/articles/list folder and create a file named list.component.spec.ts. In
your new file, paste the following code:

```
import { Observable } from "rxjs/Rx";
import { Directive, Input }   from '@angular/core';
import { ComponentFixture, TestBed, async, fakeAsync } from
            '@angular/core/testing';
import { ArticlesService } from '../articles.service';
import { ListComponent } from './list.component';

class MockArticlesService {
  articles = [{
    _id: '12345678',
    title: 'An Article about MEAN',
    content: 'MEAN rocks!',
    created: new Date(),
    creator: {
      fullName: 'John Doe'
    }
  }];
```

```
    public list() {
      return Observable.of(this.articles);
    }
};

@Directive({
  selector: '[routerLink]',
  host: {
    '(click)': 'onClick()'
  }
})
export class RouterLinkStubDirective {
  @Input('routerLink') linkParams: any;
  navigatedTo: any = null;

  onClick() {
    this.navigatedTo = this.linkParams;
  }
}

describe('List component tests', () => {
  let componentFixture: ComponentFixture<ListComponent>;

  beforeEach(async(() => {
    TestBed.configureTestingModule({
      declarations: [ ListComponent, RouterLinkStubDirective ],
      providers:    [ {provide: ArticlesService, useClass:
                       MockArticlesService } ]
    }).compileComponents();
  }));


    beforeEach(fakeAsync(() => {
        componentFixture = TestBed.createComponent(ListComponent);
    }));

  it('Should render list', () => {
    componentFixture.detectChanges();

    const mockArticleService = new MockArticlesService();
    const listComponentElement = componentFixture.nativeElement;

    const articleElements =
        listComponentElement.querySelectorAll('li');
```

```
        const articleElement = articleElements[0];
        const articleTitleElement = articleElement.querySelector('a');
        const articleContentElement = articleElement.querySelector('p');

        const mockArticleList = mockArticleService.articles;
        const mockArticle = mockArticleList[0];
        const mockArticleTitle = mockArticle.title;
        const mockArticleContent = mockArticle.content;

        expect(articleElements.length)
            .toBe(mockArticleList.length);

        expect(articleTitleElement.innerHTML)
            .toBe(mockArticleTitle);

        expect(articleContentElement.innerHTML)
            .toBe(mockArticleContent);
    });
});
```

Let's go over this example. We begin with importing all the necessary modules for our test. Next, we create the MockArticlesService, which will replace our ArticlesService in order to provide the ListComponent with a list of articles. This is an important step, because as we write our unit tests, it's very important to isolate each unit as much as possible. In this case, we want to avoid any connection to the real ArticlesService, so we'll provide our component with a static data source. Then, we create a mock routerLink so that our component test can render our links.

Next, we create our test suite using the describe keyword, and we use Angular's TestBed object to configure our testing module. We provide the configureTestingModule method with the declarations and providers we need in our module and then use the TestBed object again to create a component fixture of our ListComponent. We then create our test using the it keyword and use the component fixture to get our ListComponent native element, so we'll be able to compare it with the data from the MockArticlesService using Jasmine's matchers. This is it! Next, we'll see how we test services, but before we can do so, we'll need to learn how to mock a backend data service.

Mocking backend data

While testing an Angular application, it is recommended that unit tests execute quickly and separately from the backend server. This is because we want the unit tests to be as isolated as possible and work in a synchronous manner. This means we need to control the dependency-injection process and provide mock components that emulate real components' operation. For instance, most of the components that communicate with the backend server usually use the `http` service or some sort of abstraction layer. Furthermore, the `Http` service sends requests to the server using the `XHRBackend` service. This means that by injecting a different backend service, we can send fake HTTP requests that won't hit a real server. As we previously stated, the Angular team is very committed to testing, so they've already created these tools for us in the form of the `MockBackend` class. The `MockBackend` class allows developers to define mock responses to HTTP requests. This class can be injected into any service that uses the `Http` service and be configured to supply HTTP requests with predefined data. Let's see how it can be used to test our `ArticlesService`.

Testing services

Testing services is a bit different from testing components. As we previously discussed, we'll need to use the `MockBackend` class in order to mock our service HTTP requests. Let's see how this can be applied with our `ArticlesService`. To create a sample test suite of our service, go to your `public/app/articles` folder and create a file named `articles.service.spec.ts`. In your new file, paste the following code:

```
import { async, inject, TestBed } from '@angular/core/testing';
import { MockBackend, MockConnection } from
        '@angular/http/testing';
import { HttpModule, Http, XHRBackend, Response, ResponseOptions }
from '@angular/http';
import { ArticlesService } from './articles.service';

let backend: MockBackend;
let service: ArticlesService;

const mockArticle = {
  title: 'An Article about MEAN',
  content: 'MEAN rocks!',
  creator: {
    fullName: 'John Doe'
  }
```

```
};

describe('Articles service tests', () => {
  beforeEach(async(() => {
    TestBed.configureTestingModule({
      imports: [ HttpModule ],
      providers: [
        ArticlesService,
        { provide: XHRBackend, useClass: MockBackend }
      ]
    })
    .compileComponents();
  }));

  beforeEach(inject([Http, XHRBackend], (_http: Http,
    _mockBackend: MockBackend) => {
    backend = _mockBackend;
    service = new ArticlesService(_http);
  }));

  it('Should create a single article', done => {
    const options = new ResponseOptions({ status: 200, body:
        mockArticle });
    const response = new Response(options);

    backend.connections.subscribe((connection: MockConnection)
        => connection.mockRespond(response));

    service.create(mockArticle).do(article => {
      expect(article).toBeDefined();

      expect(article.title).toEqual(mockArticle.title);
      expect(article.content).toEqual(mockArticle.content);

      done();
    }).toPromise();
  });
});
```

Let's go over this example. We begin with importing all the necessary modules for our test. Next, we create our test suite using the describe keyword and utilize Angular's TestBed object to configure our testing module. We provide the configureTestingModule method with the ArticlesService provider and the MockBackend as our XHRBackend provider. We then inject it along with the HTTP service and create an instance of our ArticlesService. In our actual test, we create a mock response and tell our MockBackend instance to respond with our mock response by subscribing to its connections. We finish our test by calling the create method of our ArticlesService and expect it to respond with our mock article instance properties. That's it! We've just tested one of the methods of our ArticlesService; to complete the test suite, you'll need to test the others as well. Next, we'll learn how to test our Angular routes definitions.

Testing routes

To test our routes, we will need to make sure our router can navigate to our application's URLs. In our case, we can test the routes created in our AppComponent. To do so, go to your public/app folder and create a file named app.routes.spec.ts. In your new file, paste the following code:

```
import { async, fakeAsync, TestBed } from '@angular/core/testing';
import { RouterTestingModule } from '@angular/router/testing';
import { SpyLocation } from '@angular/common/testing';
import { Location } from '@angular/common';
import { AppModule } from './app.module';
import { AppComponent } from './app.component';

let router: Router;
let location: SpyLocation;

describe('AppComponent Routing', () => {
  beforeEach(async(() => {
    TestBed.configureTestingModule({
      imports: [ AppModule, RouterTestingModule ]
    }).compileComponents();
  }));

  beforeEach(fakeAsync(() => {
    const injector = TestBed.createComponent(AppComponent)
        .debugElement.injector;
    location = injector.get(Location);
  }));

  it('Should navigate to home', fakeAsync(() => {
    location.go('/');
```

```
    expect(location.path()).toEqual('/');
  }));

  it('Should navigate to signin', fakeAsync(() => {
    location.go('/authentication/signin');
    expect(location.path()).toEqual('/authentication/signin');
  }));

  it('Should navigate to signup', fakeAsync(() => {
    location.go('/authentication/signup');
    expect(location.path()).toEqual('/authentication/signup');
  }));
});
```

As you can notice, testing routes is quite simple. We're just using Angular's `TestBed` object to create our testing module and import the `RouterTestingModule`. Next, we use our component injector to get the `location` instance. In our tests, we just use the `location.go` method and check whether the location path changed accordingly. Next, we'll learn how we can write unit tests for directives.

Testing directives

Testing directives in Angular 2 is basically testing the way structural and attribute directives affect the DOM. For instance, to test the `ngIf` directive, you can go to your `public/app` folder and create a file named `directive.spec.ts`. In your new file, paste the following code:

```
import { Component }  from '@angular/core';
import { ComponentFixture, TestBed } from '@angular/core/testing';
import { By } from '@angular/platform-browser';

@Component({
  template:
  `<ul>
    <li *ngIf="shouldShow" name="One">1</li>
    <li *ngIf="!shouldShow" name="Two">2</li>
  </ul>`
})
class TestComponent {
  shouldShow = true
}

describe('ngIf tests', () => {
  let componentFixture: ComponentFixture<TestComponent>;
```

```
beforeEach(() => {
  componentFixture = TestBed.configureTestingModule({
    declarations: [TestComponent]
  }).createComponent(TestComponent);
});

it('It should render the list properly', () => {
  componentFixture.detectChanges();

  let listItems = componentFixture.debugElement
    .queryAll(By.css('li'));
  expect(listItems.length).toBe(1);
  expect(listItems[0].attributes['name']).toBe('One');
});


it('It should rerender the list properly', () => {
  componentFixture.componentInstance.shouldShow = false;
  componentFixture.detectChanges();

  let listItems = componentFixture.debugElement
    .queryAll(By.css('li'));
  expect(listItems.length).toBe(1);
  expect(listItems[0].attributes['name']).toBe('Two');
});
});
```

Notice how we created a `TestComponent` for our directive and then used the `TestBed` utility to generate our component instance and test the way the `ngIf` directive changes the rendering of the DOM.

Testing pipes

As with directives, we haven't touched the subject of pipes enough. However, pipes are a very simple yet powerful component of Angular that help us easily transform data into readable format. The Angular pipes vary in functionality from simple case changing to date and internationalization, but most importantly, you can write your own pipes. Testing a pipe is very easy, since all you have to do is instantiate the `Pipe` class and provide it with input and expected output. For instance, to test Angular's `LowerCasePipe` class, you will need to go to your `public/app` folder and create a file named `pipe.spec.ts`. In your new file, paste the following code:

```
import { LowerCasePipe } from '@angular/common';

describe('LowerCasePipe tests', () => {
  let pipe = new LowerCasePipe();

  it('should capitalise', () => {
    expect(pipe.transform('MEAN')).toEqual('mean');
  });
});
```

As you can notice, we just imported the `LowerCasePipe` class and used its transform method to check its functionality.

Now that you have a few unit tests, let's see how you can execute it using Karma's command-line utility.

Running your Angular unit tests

To run your Angular tests, you will need to use the Karma's command-line utility you previously installed. Before you can do that, we'll need to finish our test setup. To do so, go to your `public/app` folder and create a file named `bootstrap.spec.ts`. In your new file, paste the following code:

```
import { TestBed } from '@angular/core/testing';
import { BrowserDynamicTestingModule,
    platformBrowserDynamicTesting } from '@angular/platform-
      browser-dynamic/testing';

TestBed.initTestEnvironment(
  BrowserDynamicTestingModule,
  platformBrowserDynamicTesting()
);
```

This will set the test environment for us with the proper platform modules. Now all you have left to do is to go to your project's base folder and then issue the following command:

```
$ npm run tsc
```

This will compile your TypeScript files, so you will now be able to run Karma using the following command:

```
$ NODE_ENV=test karma start
```

Windows users should first execute the following command:

```
> set NODE_ENV=test
```

Then, run your tests using the following command:

```
> karma start
```

The preceding command will do a few things. First, it will set the NODE_ENV variable to test, forcing your MEAN application to use the test environment configuration file. Then, it will execute the Karma command-line utility. The test results should be reported in your command-line tool, similar to the following screenshot:

```
●●●                    B05071_10 — -bash — 80×24
[Amos@amoss-macbook-pro:~/Projects/MEANV2/B05071_10$ NODE_ENV=test karma start    ]
16 11 2016 09:44:11.431:INFO [karma]: Karma v1.3.0 server started at http://loca
lhost:9876/
16 11 2016 09:44:11.434:INFO [launcher]: Launching browser PhantomJS with unlimi
ted concurrency
16 11 2016 09:44:11.443:INFO [launcher]: Starting browser PhantomJS
16 11 2016 09:44:12.388:INFO [PhantomJS 2.1.1 (Mac OS X 0.0.0)]: Connected on so
cket /#NWvNXH2GGkNKARZ5AAAA with id 67242722
PhantomJS 2.1.1 (Mac OS X 0.0.0): Executed 8 of 8 SUCCESS (0.587 secs / 0.749 se
cs)
Amos@amoss-macbook-pro:~/Projects/MEANV2/B05071_10$ █
```

Karma's test results

This concludes the unit-test coverage of your Angular application. It is recommended that you use these methods to expand your test suite and include more tests. In the next subsection, you'll learn about Angular E2E testing and how to write and run a cross-application E2E test.

Angular E2E tests

While unit tests serve as the first layer to keep our applications covered, it is sometimes necessary to write tests that involve several components together that react with a certain interface. The Angular team often refers to these tests as E2E tests.

To understand this better, let's say Bob is an excellent frontend developer who keeps his Angular code well tested. Alice is also an excellent developer, but she works on the backend code, making sure her Express controllers and models are all covered. In theory, this team of two does a superb job, but when they finish writing the login feature of their MEAN application, they suddenly discover it's failing. When they dig deeper, they find out that Bob's code is sending a certain JSON object, while Alice's backend controller is expecting a slightly different JSON object. The fact is that both of them did their job, but the code is still failing. You might say this is the team leader's fault, but we've all been there at some point or another, and while this is just a small example, modern applications tend to become very complex. This means that you cannot just trust manual testing or even unit tests. You will need to find a way to test features across the entire application, and this is why E2E tests are so important.

Introducing the Protractor test runner

To execute E2E tests, you will need some sort of tool that emulates user behavior. In the past, the Angular team advocated a tool called the **Angular scenario test runner**. However, they decided to abandon this tool and create a new test runner called **Protractor**. Protractor is a dedicated E2E test runner that simulates human interactions and runs tests using the Jasmine test framework. It is basically a Node.js tool that uses a neat library called **WebDriver**. WebDriver is an open source utility that allows programmable control over a web browser's behavior. As I stated, Protractor uses Jasmine by default, so tests will look very similar to the unit tests you wrote before, but Protractor also provides you with several global objects, as follows:

- `browser`: This is a `WebDriver` instance wrapper that allows you to communicate with the browser.
- `element`: This is a helper function to manipulate HTML elements.
- `by`: This is a collection of element locator functions. You can use it to find an element by a CSS selector, its ID, or even by the model property it's bound to.
- `protractor`: This is a `WebDriver` namespace wrapper containing a set of static classes and variables.

Using these utilities, you'll be able to perform browser operations inside your tests' specifications. For instance, the `browser.get()` method will load a page for you to perform tests on. It is important to remember that Protractor is a dedicated tool for Angular applications, so the `browser.get()` method will throw an error if the page it tries to load doesn't include the Angular library. You'll write your first E2E test in a moment, but first, let's install Protractor.

Protractor is kind of a young tool, so things are bound to change rapidly. It is recommended that you learn more about Protractor by visiting the official repository page at https://github.com/angular/protractor.

Installing the Protractor test runner

Protractor is a command-line tool, so you'll need to globally install it using npm. To do so, just issue the following command in your command-line tool:

```
$ npm install -g protractor
```

This will install the latest version of the Protractor command-line utilities in your global node_modules folder. When the installation process is successfully finished, you'll be able to use Protractor from your command line.

You may experience some trouble when installing global modules. This is usually a permission issue, so use sudo or super user when running the global install command.

Since Protractor will need a working WebDriver server, you will either need to use a Selenium server or install a standalone WebDriver server. You can download and install a standalone server by issuing the following command in your command-line tool:

```
$ webdriver-manager update
```

This will install the Selenium standalone server, which you'll later use to handle Protractor's tests. The next step would be to configure Protractor's execution options.

You can learn more about WebDriver by visiting the official project page at http://www.seleniumhq.org/.

Configuring the Protractor test runner

In order to control Protractor's test execution, you will need to create a Protractor configuration file in the root folder of your application. When executed, Protractor will automatically look for a configuration file named protractor.conf.js in your application's root folder. You can also indicate your configuration filename using a command-line flag, but for simplicity reasons, we'll use the default filename. So begin by creating a new file named protractor.conf.js in your application's root folder. In your new file, paste the following lines of code:

```
exports.config = {
  specs: ['public/tests/**/e2e/*.js'],
  useAllAngular2AppRoots: true
}
```

Our Protractor configuration file is very basic. The `specs` property basically tells Protractor where to find the test files, and the `useAllAngular2AppRoots` property tells Protractor to go over all Angular apps available in the page. This configuration is project oriented, which means that it will change according to your requirements.

 You can learn more about Protractor's configuration by going over the example configuration file at `https://github.com/angular/protractor/blob/master/lib/config.ts`.

Writing your first E2E test

Since E2E tests are quite complicated to write and read, we'll begin with a simple example. In our example, we'll test the **Create Article** page and try to create a new article. Since we didn't log in first, an error should occur and be presented to the user. To implement this test, go to your `public/tests` folder and create a new folder named `e2e`, inside this folder, create a new folder named `articles`. Inside the `articles` folder, create a new file named `articles.client.e2e.tests.js`. Finally, in your new file, paste the following code snippet:

```
describe('Articles E2E Tests:', function() {
  describe('New Article Page', function() {
    it('Should not be able to create a new article', function() {
      browser.get('http://localhost:3000/#!/articles/create');
      element(by.css('input[type=submit]')).click();
      element(by.id('error')).getText().then(function(errorText) {
        expect(errorText).toBe('User is not logged in');
      });
    });
  });
});
```

The general test structure should already be familiar to you; however, the test itself is quite different. We began by requesting the **Create Article** page using the `browser.get()` method. Then, we used the `element()` and `by.css()` methods to submit the form. Finally, we found the error message element using `by.id()` and validated the error text. While this is a simple example, it nicely illustrates the way E2E tests work. Next we'll use Protractor to run this test.

Running your Angular E2E tests

Running Protractor is a bit different from using Karma and Mocha. Protractor needs your application to run so that it can access it just like a real user does. So let's begin by running the application; navigate to your application's `root` folder and use your command-line tool to start the MEAN application, as follows:

```
$ NODE_ENV=test npm start
```

Windows users should first execute the following command:

```
> set NODE_ENV=test
```

Then, run your application using the following command:

```
> npm start
```

This will start your MEAN application using the test environment's configuration file. Now, open a new command-line window and navigate to your application's `root` folder. Then, start the Protractor test runner by issuing the following command:

```
$ protractor
```

Protractor should run your tests and report the results in your command-line window, as shown in the following screenshot:

```
[Amos@amoss-macbook-pro:~/Projects/MEANV2/B05071_10$ protractor
[16:37:00] I/local - Starting selenium standalone server...
[16:37:00] I/launcher - Running 1 instances of WebDriver
[16:37:00] I/local - Selenium standalone server started at http://192.168.1.20:5
5442/wd/hub
Started
.


1 spec, 0 failures
Finished in 1.691 seconds
[16:37:03] I/local - Shutting down selenium standalone server.
[16:37:03] I/launcher - 0 instance(s) of WebDriver still running
[16:37:03] I/launcher - chrome #01 passed
Amos@amoss-macbook-pro:~/Projects/MEANV2/B05071_10$
```

Protractor's test results

Congratulations! You now know how to cover your application code with E2E tests. It is recommended that you use these methods to expand your test suite and include extensive E2E tests.

Summary

In this chapter, you learned how to test your MEAN application. You learned about testing in general and the common TDD/BDD testing paradigms. You then used the Mocha test framework and created controller and model unit tests, where you utilized different assertion libraries. Then, we discussed the methods of testing Angular, where you learned the difference between unit and E2E testing. We then proceeded to unit test your Angular application using the Jasmine test framework and the Karma test runner. Then, you learned how to create and run E2E tests using Protractor. Once you've built and tested your real-time MEAN application, in the next chapter, you'll learn how to improve your development-cycle time using some popular automation tools.

11
Automating and Debugging MEAN Applications

In previous chapters, you learned how to build and test your real-time MEAN application. You learned how to connect all the MEAN components and how to use test frameworks to test your application. While you can continue developing your application using the same methods used in the previous chapters, you can also speed up development cycles using supportive tools and frameworks. These tools will provide you with a solid development environment through automation and abstraction. In this chapter, you'll learn how to use different community tools to expedite your MEAN application's development. We'll cover the following topics:

- Using NPM scripts
- Introducing Webpack
- Introducing ESLint
- Introducing Nodemon
- Debugging your Express application using V8 inspector
- Debugging your Angular application's internals using Angular Augury

Using NPM scripts

As you may have noticed, developing our application involves the operation of several tasks together. For instance, in order to run our application, we'll need to transpile our Angular files and then run our Express application. This pattern will repeat itself and even get more complicated. To solve this, developers prefer to automate some of the application functionality and use supportive tools to speed up their work. Some developers prefer using third-party tools, such as Grunt or Gulp, also known as task runners; however, we already use a tool that allows us to run scripts, a tool called NPM. To understand this better, take a look at your `package.json` file's `scripts` property:

```
...
"scripts": {
  "tsc": "tsc",
  "tsc:w": "tsc -w",
  "app": "node server",
  "start": "concurrently \"npm run tsc:w\" \"npm run app\" ",
  "postinstall": "typings install",
},
...
```

As you can see, you already have five scripts to manage your application developments. In the following sections, we'll learn how to add more scripts and how to use this NPM feature to help you automate your daily job. We'll begin with the Webpack module bundler.

Introducing Webpack

Webpack is a popular module bundler created by Tobias Koppers. It has taken over the world of JavaScipt and has become one of the most used tools in our ecosystem. As an alternative to other module bundlers, such as SystemJS (which we used up until now), it has a pretty straightforward motivation: to simplify code bundling, modularizing big applications, and code splitting. However, after a few years of active development, it can now do much more, including features such as asset bundling, preprocessing, and optimization. In our modest introduction, though, we'll learn how to simply replace SystemJS to bundle and load our Angular modules.

 It is highly recommended that you learn more about Webpack by visiting the official project page at `https://webpack.github.io/`.

Installing Webpack

Before we can start configuring our Webpack implementation, we will need to install Webpack's dependencies using npm. To do that, change your package.json file, as follows:

```json
{
  "name": "MEAN",
  "version": "0.0.11",
  "scripts": {
    "tsc": "tsc",
    "tsc:w": "tsc -w",
    "app": "node server",
    "start": "concurrently \"npm run webpack\" \"npm run app\" ",
    "postinstall": "typings install",
    "webpack": "webpack --watch"
  },
  "dependencies": {
    "@angular/common": "2.1.1",
    "@angular/compiler": "2.1.1",
    "@angular/core": "2.1.1",
    "@angular/forms": "2.1.1",
    "@angular/http": "2.1.1",
    "@angular/platform-browser": "2.1.1",
    "@angular/platform-browser-dynamic": "2.1.1",
    "@angular/router": "3.1.1",
    "body-parser": "1.15.2",
    "core-js": "2.4.1",
    "compression": "~1.6.0",
    "connect-flash": "0.1.1",
    "connect-mongo": "1.3.2",
    "cookie-parser": "1.4.3",
    "ejs": "2.5.2",
    "es6-promise": "4.0.5",
    "express": "4.14.0",
    "express-session": "1.14.1",
    "method-override": "2.3.6",
    "mongoose": "4.6.5",
    "morgan": "1.7.0",
    "passport": "0.3.2",
    "passport-facebook": "2.1.1",
    "passport-google-oauth": "1.0.0",
    "passport-local": "1.0.0",
    "passport-twitter": "1.0.4",
    "phantomjs-prebuilt": "2.1.13",
```

```
        "reflect-metadata": "0.1.8",
        "rxjs": "5.0.0-beta.12",
        "socket.io": "1.4.5",
        "systemjs": "0.19.39",
        "zone.js": "0.6.26"
    },
    "devDependencies": {
        "awesome-typescript-loader": "2.2.4",
        "concurrently": "3.1.0",
        "jasmine": "2.5.2",
        "jasmine-core": "2.5.2",
        "karma": "1.3.0",
        "karma-jasmine": "1.0.2",
        "karma-phantomjs-launcher": "1.0.2",
        "should": "11.1.1",
        "supertest": "2.0.1",
        "traceur": "0.0.111",
        "typescript": "2.0.3",
        "typings": "1.4.0",
        "webpack": "1.13.3"
    }
}
```

As you can see, you added Webpack and a TypeScript loader to your
`devDependencies` property. We also added a Webpack script to run Webpack in a
"Watch" mode so that every change to our file is automatically updated. We then
changed our NPM start script to use Webpack instead of transpiling our Angular
files using the TypeScript command-line tool. To install your new dependencies,
go to your application's root folder and issue the following command in your
command-line tool:

```
$ npm install
```

This will install the specified versions of Webpack and TypeScript loader in your
project's `node_modules` folder. When the installation process is successfully finished,
you will be able to use these modules to run Webpack and bundle your TypeScript
modules. Next, you'll learn how to configure Webpack.

Configuring Webpack

In order to control Webpack's execution, you will need to configure Webpack using a special configuration file placed in the root folder of your application. When executed, Webpack will automatically look for the default configuration file named `webpack.config.js` in the application's root folder. You can also indicate your configuration file name using a command-line flag, but for simplicity, we'll use the default filename. To start configuring Webpack, create a new file in your application root folder, and name it `webpack.config.js`. In your new file, paste the following code snippet:

```
const webpack = require('webpack');

module.exports = {
  entry: {
    'polyfills': './public/polyfills',
    'vendor': './public/vendor',
    'bootstrap': './public/bootstrap'
  },
  devtool: 'source-map',
  resolve: {
    extensions: ['', '.js', '.ts']
  },
  output: {
    path: 'public/build',
    filename: '[name].js',
  },
  module: {
    loaders: [
      {
        test: /\.ts$/,
        loaders: ['awesome-typescript-loader']
      }
    ]
  },
  plugins: [
    new webpack.optimize.CommonsChunkPlugin({
      name: ['bootstrap', 'vendor', 'polyfills']
    })
  ]
};
```

As you can see, Webpack's configuration file is used to set the way Webpack builds our modules. In this case, we used the following settings:

- `entry`: This tells Webpack what the entry point of our application is. Don't worry if you don't recognize these files; we'll create them in the next step. All you need to understand is that we bundle our application into three different files: our polyfills file, which will include all the polyfills-related modules, our vendor file, which will include all of our third-party modules—such as Angular core modules—and our application file, which will include our Angular application files.

- `devtool`: This tells Webpack which development tool to use; in this case, we want Webpack to create map files for transpiled application files.

- `resolve`: This tells Webpack what kind of module extensions to resolve; in this case, it will include module imports without extensions, TypeScript, and JavaScript files.

- `output`: This sets the way Webpack saves the output files. Here, we tell it we want to create the bundled files in a `public/build` folder with a JavaScript file extension.

- `module`: This is a list of modules Webpack will use. In our case, we tell Webpack to load all TypeScript files using the TypeScript loader we previously installed.

- `optimize`: This sets the way Webpack optimizes module bundling. In our case, we want Webpack to bundle every module once. This means that if Webpack finds a common module import in the Bootstrap file and the Vendor file, it will bundle it only once in the vendor file.

Note that these properties are project-oriented, which means that it will change according to your requirements. We'll continue by creating our missing files. First, go to your `public` folder and create a file named `polyfills.ts`. In this file, paste the following code:

```
import 'core-js/es6/symbol';
import 'core-js/es6/object';
import 'core-js/es6/function';
import 'core-js/es6/parse-int';
import 'core-js/es6/parse-float';
import 'core-js/es6/number';
import 'core-js/es6/math';
import 'core-js/es6/string';
import 'core-js/es6/date';
import 'core-js/es6/array';
import 'core-js/es6/regexp';
```

```
import 'core-js/es6/map';
import 'core-js/es6/set';
import 'core-js/es6/weak-map';
import 'core-js/es6/weak-set';
import 'core-js/es6/typed';
import 'core-js/es6/reflect';
import 'core-js/es7/reflect';
import 'zone.js/dist/zone';
import 'zone.js/dist/long-stack-trace-zone';
```

As you can see, we included all of our polyfills libraries. Next, we'll create a file named vendor.ts; in this file, paste the following code:

```
import '@angular/common';
import '@angular/compiler';
import '@angular/core';
import '@angular/forms';
import '@angular/http';
import '@angular/router';
import '@angular/platform-browser';
import '@angular/platform-browser-dynamic';
import 'rxjs';
```

As you can see, we included all of our core modules of the Angular and RXJS libraries. To finish up, we'll copy our previous bootstrap.ts file to the public folder. To do that, go to your public folder and create a file named bootstrap.ts. In this file, paste the following code:

```
import { platformBrowserDynamic } from '@angular/platform-browser-dynamic';
import { AppModule } from './app/app.module';

platformBrowserDynamic().bootstrapModule(AppModule);
```

As you can see, this is our application bootstrap file from previous chapters. All we have left to do is change our main application page. To do that, go to the app/views/index.ejs file and make the following changes:

```
<!DOCTYPE html>
<html>
<head>
  <title><%= title %></title>
  <base href="/">
</head>
<body>
  <mean-app>
```

```
    <h1>Loading...</h1>
  </mean-app>

  <script type="text/javascript">
    window.user = <%- user || 'null' %>;
  </script>

  <script src="/socket.io/socket.io.js"></script>

  <script src="build/polyfills.js"></script>
  <script src="build/vendor.js"></script>
  <script src="build/bootstrap.js"></script>
  </body>
  </html>
```

As you can see, we just replaced our older scripts with the new bundled script files. Once you are finished with these changes, your Webpack configuration should be ready for use! Use your command-line tool and navigate to the MEAN application's root folder. Then, run your application by typing the following command:

`$ npm start`

Once your application is running and Webpack finishes bundling your code, navigate to `http://localhost:3000/` and test your application. This is, of course, just a basic setup, so it is highly recommended that you continue learning about Webpack's other features.

Introducing ESLint

In software development, linting is the identification of suspicious code usage using dedicated tools. In a MEAN application, linting can help you avoid common mistakes and coding errors in your daily development cycles; moreover, it will allow you to set a unified code styling across your team. The most commonly used linting tool in our ecosystem is called ESLint. ESLint is a pluggable linting utility originally created by Nicholas C. Zakas in 2013. It allows us to lint our JavaScript code using a set of rules and preset configurations. We'll begin by installing the ESLint package in our application.

 It is highly recommended that you learn more about ESLint by visiting the official project page at `http://eslint.org/`.

Installing ESLint

Before we can start configuring our ESLint execution, we will need to install the ESLint package using npm. To do that, change your package.json file as follows:

```json
{
  "name": "MEAN",
  "version": "0.0.11",
  "scripts": {
    "tsc": "tsc",
    "tsc:w": "tsc -w",
    "app": "node server",
    "start": "concurrently \"npm run webpack\" \"npm run app\" ",
    "postinstall": "typings install",
    "webpack": "webpack --watch",
    "lint": "eslint --ext .js ./config ./app ./*.js"
  },
  "dependencies": {
    "@angular/common": "2.1.1",
    "@angular/compiler": "2.1.1",
    "@angular/core": "2.1.1",
    "@angular/forms": "2.1.1",
    "@angular/http": "2.1.1",
    "@angular/platform-browser": "2.1.1",
    "@angular/platform-browser-dynamic": "2.1.1",
    "@angular/router": "3.1.1",
    "body-parser": "1.15.2",
    "core-js": "2.4.1",
    "compression": "~1.6.0",
    "connect-flash": "0.1.1",
    "connect-mongo": "1.3.2",
    "cookie-parser": "1.4.3",
    "ejs": "2.5.2",
    "es6-promise": "4.0.5",
    "express": "4.14.0",
    "express-session": "1.14.1",
    "method-override": "2.3.6",
    "mongoose": "4.6.5",
    "morgan": "1.7.0",
    "passport": "0.3.2",
    "passport-facebook": "2.1.1",
    "passport-google-oauth": "1.0.0",
    "passport-local": "1.0.0",
    "passport-twitter": "1.0.4",
    "phantomjs-prebuilt": "2.1.13",
```

```
    "reflect-metadata": "0.1.8",
    "rxjs": "5.0.0-beta.12",
    "socket.io": "1.4.5",
    "systemjs": "0.19.39",
    "zone.js": "0.6.26"
},
"devDependencies": {
    "awesome-typescript-loader": "2.2.4",
    "concurrently": "3.1.0",
    "eslint": "3.10.2",
    "jasmine": "2.5.2",
    "jasmine-core": "2.5.2",
    "karma": "1.3.0",
    "karma-jasmine": "1.0.2",
    "karma-phantomjs-launcher": "1.0.2",
    "should": "11.1.1",
    "supertest": "2.0.1",
    "traceur": "0.0.111",
    "typescript": "2.0.3",
    "typings": "1.4.0",
    "webpack": "1.13.3"
    }
}
```

As you can see, you added, ESLint package to your `devDependencies` property. You also added a `lint` script to run ESLint and a lint JavaScript file placed in your `app` and `config` folders. To install your new dependencies, go to your application's root folder and issue the following command in your command-line tool:

$ npm install

This will install the specified version of the ESLint package in your project's `node_modules` folder. Next, you'll learn how to configure ESLint.

Configuring ESLint

In order to control ESLint's execution, you will need to configure it using a special configuration file placed in the root folder of your application. When executed, ESLint will automatically look for the default configuration file named `.eslintrc` in the application's root folder. Create a new file in your application's root folder and name it `.eslintrc`. In your new file, paste the following JSON object:

```
{
  "parserOptions": {
    "ecmaVersion": 6
  }
}
```

As you can see, this simple configuration basically tells ESLint that our code is written in ECMAScript 6. However, ESLint can do so much more; for instance, you can tell ESLint to validate our code indentation by changing the configuration as follows:

```
{
  "parserOptions": {
    "ecmaVersion": 6
  },
  "rules": {
    "indent": ["error", 2]
  }
}
```

This will tell ESLint to expect a two space indentation in our code files. Moreover, usually, you'll extend an existing configuration file using the extend property, as follows:

```
{
  "extends": "eslint:recommended",
  "parserOptions": {
    "ecmaVersion": 6
  }
}
```

This will extend ESLint's recommended rule set. However, these are just simple examples, so it is recommended that you continue learning about ESLint in order to find the best configuration for your project. To run your lint task, go to your command-line tool and execute the following command:

```
$ npm run lint
```

The linting results should be reported in your command-line tool and will be similar to what is shown in the following screenshot:

ESLint results

ESLint is a powerful tool. However, in this form, you would need to run the `lint` task manually. A better approach would be to automatically run the lint task whenever you modify a file.

Using Nodemon

Running your application using the Node's command-line tool may not seem like a redundant task. However, when continuously developing your application, you will soon notice that you stop and start your application server quite often. To help with this task, there is a common tool called Nodemon. Nodemon is a Node.js command-line tool that functions as a wrapper to the simple node command-line tool, but watches for changes in your application files. When Nodemon detects file changes, it automatically restarts the node server to update the application. To use Nodemon, you will need to modify your project's `package.json` file, as follows:

```
{
  "name": "MEAN",
  "version": "0.0.11",
  "scripts": {
    "tsc": "tsc",
    "tsc:w": "tsc -w",
    "app": "node server",
    "app:dev": "npm run lint && npm run app",
```

```
    "nodemon": "nodemon -w app -w config -w server.js --exec npm
      run app:dev",
    "start": "concurrently \"npm run webpack\" \"npm run node
      mon\",
    "postinstall": "typings install",
    "webpack": "webpack --watch",
    "lint": "eslint --ext .js ./config ./app ./*.js"
},
"dependencies": {
  "@angular/common": "2.1.1",
  "@angular/compiler": "2.1.1",
  "@angular/core": "2.1.1",
  "@angular/forms": "2.1.1",
  "@angular/http": "2.1.1",
  "@angular/platform-browser": "2.1.1",
  "@angular/platform-browser-dynamic": "2.1.1",
  "@angular/router": "3.1.1",
  "body-parser": "1.15.2",
  "core-js": "2.4.1",
  "compression": "~1.6.0",
  "connect-flash": "0.1.1",
  "connect-mongo": "1.3.2",
  "cookie-parser": "1.4.3",
  "ejs": "2.5.2",
  "es6-promise": "4.0.5",
  "express": "4.14.0",
  "express-session": "1.14.1",
  "method-override": "2.3.6",
  "mongoose": "4.6.5",
  "morgan": "1.7.0",
  "passport": "0.3.2",
  "passport-facebook": "2.1.1",
  "passport-google-oauth": "1.0.0",
  "passport-local": "1.0.0",
  "passport-twitter": "1.0.4",
  "phantomjs-prebuilt": "2.1.13",
  "reflect-metadata": "0.1.8",
  "rxjs": "5.0.0-beta.12",
  "socket.io": "1.4.5",
  "systemjs": "0.19.39",
  "zone.js": "0.6.26"
},
"devDependencies": {
  "awesome-typescript-loader": "2.2.4",
```

```
          "concurrently": "3.1.0",
          "eslint": "3.10.2",
          "jasmine": "2.5.2",
          "jasmine-core": "2.5.2",
          "karma": "1.3.0",
          "karma-jasmine": "1.0.2",
          "karma-phantomjs-launcher": "1.0.2",
          "nodemon": "1.11.0",
          "should": "11.1.1",
          "supertest": "2.0.1",
          "traceur": "0.0.111",
          "typescript": "2.0.3",
          "typings": "1.4.0",
          "webpack": "1.13.3"
      }
  }
```

As you can see, we added the Nodemon package to our development dependencies. We also added two new scripts and changed our `start` script. The first script we added is `app:dev`, which runs the `lint` and `app` scripts. Next, we created a `nodemon` script, which watches all of our server JavaScript files and runs the `app:dev` script whenever a file is modified. In our `start` script, we just execute our Webpack and Nodemon scripts concurrently. This is it! All you have left to do is install the Nodemon package by going to your application root folder and issuing the following command in your command-line tool:

```
$ npm install
```

Then, run your application using the regular `start` command:

```
$ npm start
```

This will start your application with the new setup. Try changing your Angular or Express application files; note that your application restarts if you change a server file and the way Webpack automatically compiles your code when you change an Angular file.

Debugging Express with V8 inspector

Debugging the Express part of your MEAN application can be a complicated task. Fortunately, there is a great tool that solves this issue called V8 inspector. V8 Inspector is a debugging tool that uses the Blink (a WebKit Fork) Developer Tools. In fact, developers using Google's Chrome browser are already familiar with it, in the form of the Chrome Developer Tools interface. The V8 inspector supports some pretty powerful debugging features:

- Source code file navigation
- Breakpoint manipulation
- Stepping over, stepping in, stepping out, and resuming execution
- Variable and property inspection
- Live code editing

To debug your application, you will need to access the V8 inspector interface using a compatible web browser. You will then be able to use it to debug your application code using the Chrome Developer Tools interface. To do that, all you have to do is add a debug script to your `package.json` file, as follows:

```
{
  "name": "MEAN",
  "version": "0.0.11",
  "scripts": {
    "tsc": "tsc",
    "tsc:w": "tsc -w",
    "app": "node server",
    "app:dev": "npm run lint && npm run app",
    "nodemon": "nodemon -w app -w config -w server.js --exec npm
      run app:dev",
    "start": "concurrently \"npm run webpack\" \"npm run
      nodemon\"",
    "debug": "node --inspect --debug-brk server.js",
    "postinstall": "typings install",
    "webpack": "webpack --watch",
    "lint": "eslint --ext .js ./config ./app ./*.js"
  },
  "dependencies": {
    "@angular/common": "2.1.1",
    "@angular/compiler": "2.1.1",
    "@angular/core": "2.1.1",
    "@angular/forms": "2.1.1",
    "@angular/http": "2.1.1",
    "@angular/platform-browser": "2.1.1",
    "@angular/platform-browser-dynamic": "2.1.1",
    "@angular/router": "3.1.1",
    "body-parser": "1.15.2",
    "core-js": "2.4.1",
    "compression": "~1.6.0",
    "connect-flash": "0.1.1",
    "connect-mongo": "1.3.2",
    "cookie-parser": "1.4.3",
```

```
    "ejs": "2.5.2",
    "es6-promise": "4.0.5",
    "express": "4.14.0",
    "express-session": "1.14.1",
    "method-override": "2.3.6",
    "mongoose": "4.6.5",
    "morgan": "1.7.0",
    "passport": "0.3.2",
    "passport-facebook": "2.1.1",
    "passport-google-oauth": "1.0.0",
    "passport-local": "1.0.0",
    "passport-twitter": "1.0.4",
    "phantomjs-prebuilt": "2.1.13",
    "reflect-metadata": "0.1.8",
    "rxjs": "5.0.0-beta.12",
    "socket.io": "1.4.5",
    "systemjs": "0.19.39",
    "zone.js": "0.6.26"
  },
  "devDependencies": {
    "awesome-typescript-loader": "2.2.4",
    "concurrently": "3.1.0",
    "eslint": "3.10.2",
    "jasmine": "2.5.2",
    "jasmine-core": "2.5.2",
    "karma": "1.3.0",
    "karma-jasmine": "1.0.2",
    "karma-phantomjs-launcher": "1.0.2",
    "nodemon": "1.11.0",
    "should": "11.1.1",
    "supertest": "2.0.1",
    "traceur": "0.0.111",
    "typescript": "2.0.3",
    "typings": "1.4.0",
    "webpack": "1.13.3"
  }
}
```

In your new script, all you did was run your application with two command-line flags. The `inspect` flag allows the attachment of the Chrome Developer Tools to our Node.js instance, and the `debug-brk` flag prevents Node.js from running your code before you attach the debugger. Next, we'll run our application using the new script and see how we can debug it.

Debugging your application

To use your new `debug` script, navigate to your application's root folder and issue the following command in your command-line tool:

```
$ npm run debug
```

This will run your application in a debug mode and wait for you to attach the Chrome Developer Tools debugger. The output in your command-line tool should be similar to what is shown in the following screenshot:

Running in Debug mode

As you can see, the `debug` script invites you to start debugging the application by visiting `chrome-devtools://...` using a compatible browser. Open this URL in Google Chrome, and you should see an interface similar to what is shown in the following screenshot:

Debugging with V8 inspector

As you can see, you'll get a list of your project files in the left-hand side panel, a file content viewer in the middle panel, and a debug dashboard in the right-hand side panel. This means that your `debug` script is running properly and is identifying your Express project. You can start debugging your project by setting some breakpoints and testing your application's behavior.

> Node inspection will only work on browsers that use the Blink engine, such as Google Chrome or Opera. Furthermore, this feature is still experimental. So, it is recommended that you stay updated on the official Node.js documentation.

Debugging Angular applications with Angular Augury

Debugging most of the Angular part of your MEAN application is usually done in the browser. However, debugging the internal operations of Angular can be a bit trickier. For this purpose, a joint team from Google and Rangle.io created a Chrome extension called Angular Augury. Angular Augury extends the Chrome Developer Tools with a new tab where you can debug different aspects of your Angular application. Installing Angular Augury is quite straightforward. All you have to do is visit the Chrome web store at `https://chrome.google.com/webstore/detail/augury/elgalmkoelokbchhkhacckoklkejnhcd` and install the Chrome extension.

 Angular Augury will work only on the Google Chrome browser.

Using Angular Augury

Once you're done installing Angular Augury, use Chrome to navigate to your application URL. Then, open the Chrome Developer Tools panel, and you should see an **Angular** tab. Click on it and a panel similar to what is shown in the following screenshot should open:

Angular Augury

The component tree

Our Angular application is built as a tree of components. Augury allows us to inspect these components in a hierarchical way; in order to understand this better, take a look at the following screenshot:

Augury Component Tree

As you can see, we're inspecting the `ViewComponent` from our articles module. Since our components router is based on a simple hierarchy you can notice that we also see `AppComponent` and `ArticlesComponent`. On the right side you can notice we have two tabs: **Properties** and **Injector Graph**. In the **Properties** tab you'll find the component state including the `article` and `user` properties and the component dependencies. The state is editable so it allows you to change your component state and see the impact on the rendering of `ViewComponent`. Furthermore, if we inspect `CreateComponent`, you'll be able to see how Augury works with forms:

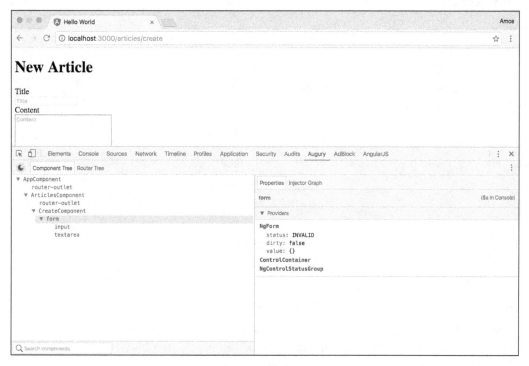

Augury with forms

As you can see, you can inspect your form state and understand its internal status. If you edit the value of your form inputs, you'll also be able to see it's state updated live on the right pane. If you click on the **Injector Graph** option, you'll be able to see how Angular's injector works and the current component's injected providers:

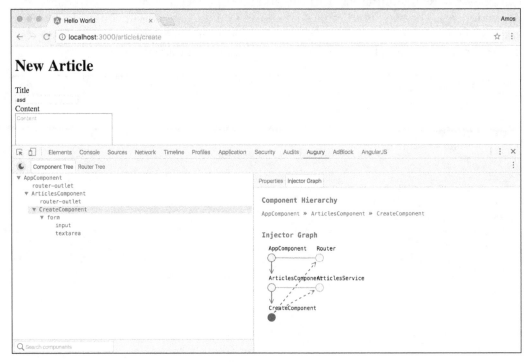

Augury Injector Graph

Note how the `Router` and `ArticlesService` providers are injected to `CreateComponent`. In bigger applications, this will give you a better understanding of your project state.

Router tree

To explore your Angular application routes, you can click on the **Router Tree** tab. Before you do that, you'll need to inject the router provider inside your application component as follows:

```
import { Component } from '@angular/core';
import { AuthenticationService } from './authentication/
authentication.service';
import { Router } from '@angular/router';

@Component({
```

```
  selector: 'mean-app',
  template: '<router-outlet></router-outlet>',
})
export class AppComponent {
  constructor(private _authenticationService:
    AuthenticationService,
  private router: Router) {}
}
```

Once you do that, you'll be able to see a panel similar to what is shown in the following screenshot:

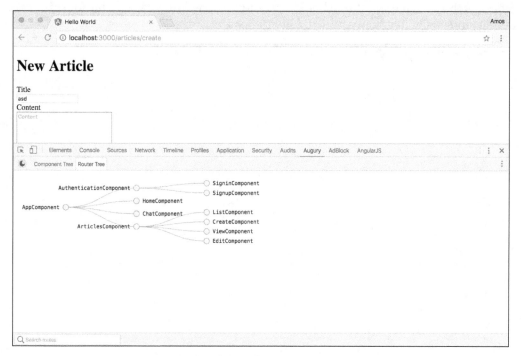

Augury Router tree

As you can see, the **Router Tree** tab allows you to understand your application routing scheme in an easy-to-understand graph.

Angular Augury is a simple yet powerful tool. Used right, it can save you a lot of time endlessly looking around and using console logging. Make sure you understand each tab and try to explore your application yourself.

Summary

In this chapter, you learned how to automate your MEAN application's development and how to debug the Express and Angular parts of your application. We started with a brief explanation of NPM scripts. We then discussed Webpack and its powerful features, and you learned how to restart and lint your application automatically. Then, you learned how to use the V8 inspector tool to debug your Express code. Towards the end of this chapter, you learned about the Angular Augury Chrome extension. You went through Angular Augury's features and found out how to debug your Angular internals.

Since it's the last chapter of this book, you should now know how to build, run, test, debug, and easily develop your MEAN application.

The next step is up to you.

Index

A

CPSIA information can be obtained
at www.ICGtesting.com
Printed in the USA
FFHW020841011218
49697777-54092FF